Charles Tylor

The Huguenots in the Seventeenth Century

Charles Tylor

The Huguenots in the Seventeenth Century

ISBN/EAN: 9783337293369

Printed in Europe, USA, Canada, Australia, Japan

Cover: Foto ©Lupo / pixelio.de

More available books at **www.hansebooks.com**

THE HUGUENOTS

IN THE SEVENTEENTH CENTURY.

LONDON:
WEST, NEWMAN AND CO., PRINTERS,
HATTON GARDEN, E.C

Facsimile of Clauses in the Act of Revocation.

CLAUSE IV.

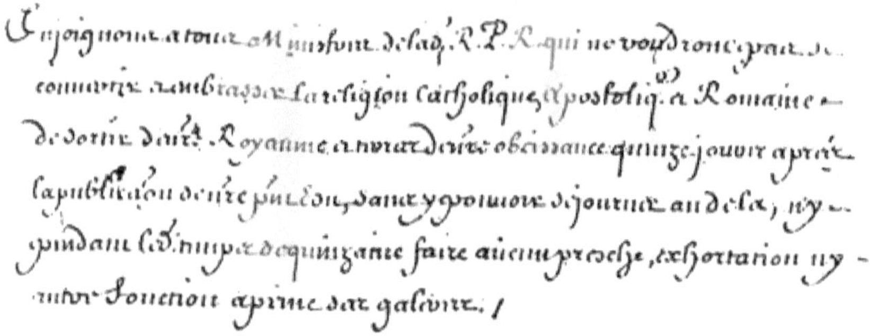

[handwritten French text]

Enjoignons à tous Ministres de ladite R. P. R. qui ne voudront pas se convertir et embrasser la Religion Catholique, Apostolique et Romaine, de sortir de notre Royaume et Terres de notre obéissance, quinze jours après la publication de notre présent Edit, sans y pouvoir séjourner au dela, ny pendant ledit tems de quinzaine faire aucun prêche, exhortation, ny autre fonction, à peine des Galères.

CLAUSE X.

[handwritten French text]

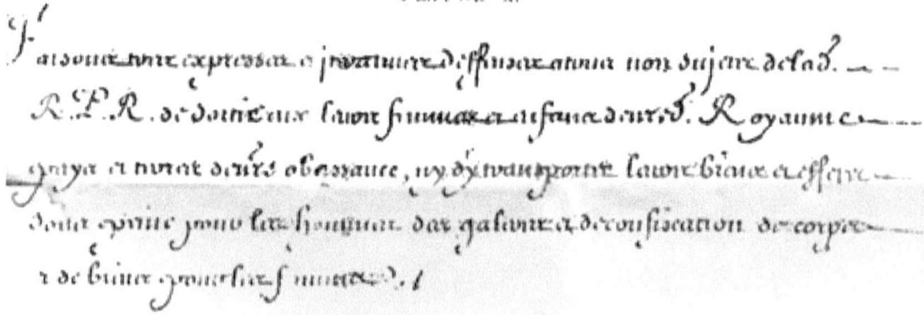

Faisons tres-expresses et iteratives défenses à tous nos sujets de ladite R. P. R. de sortir, eux, leurs femmes et enfans, de notre dit Royaume, Pays et Terres de notre obéissance, ny d'y transporter leurs biens et effets, sous peine pour les hommes des galères, et de confiscation de corps et de biens pour les femmes.

SIGNATURE.

Par le Roi,

Colbert (Marquis de Seignelay, eldest son of the great Colbert).

LOUIS.

Visa,
Le Tellier.

The Act was sealed with the Great Seal, in green wax, with a fillet of red and green silk.

Louis XIV. signing the Revocation of the Edict of Nantes.

THE HUGUENOTS

IN THE

SEVENTEENTH CENTURY,

INCLUDING THE

HISTORY OF THE EDICT OF NANTES,

From its Enactment in 1598 to its Revocation in 1685.

By CHARLES TYLOR,

JOINT AUTHOR OF BACKHOUSE AND TYLOR'S 'EARLY CHURCH HISTORY,' AND
'WITNESSES FOR CHRIST.'

LONDON:
SIMPKIN, MARSHALL, HAMILTON, KENT & CO., Limited.

1892.

PREFACE.

The "Revocation of the Edict of Nantes" is an historical phrase familiar to most readers. Comparatively few, however, would seem to have a distinct idea of what the Edict of Nantes was, or how it came to be revoked, or of the prolonged and terrible persecution with which its revocation was connected. In the present volume, after a brief account of the promulgation of the Edict by Henry IV., the steps are traced by which, through nearly a century, efforts were incessantly made to undo his work; and the narrative of the sufferings of the Huguenot Church is continued down to the year 1700.

It is a sad story, and would be utterly dark were it not illumined by heavenly light. It brings before us, in high relief, human depravity, human weakness, and the power of Divine Grace. We see, as in the persecution of the Early Church under Decius, whole communities giving way before the terrible storm; but we see the great majority, when the first shock was over, return to their allegiance; whilst a goodly number never yielded, but endured torments as cruel, and perhaps more prolonged, than any other company of martyrs whom the Church loves to honour. Their memory is sacred; their example animating; and the narrative of their sufferings and of the triumph of their faith awakens our warmest sympathy.

Most historians, whilst dilating on the events and character of the reign of Louis XIV.,—his administration, his court, his conquests, the halo of wit and learning which encircled his throne,—have little to say of the Huguenots. This is one of the many instances in which History has mistaken her true object. The persecution of the Huguenots is the one great event of Louis' reign, considered not only in regard to the magnitude of the crime, but also of the effects which resulted from it, both at the time and in every succeeding generation down to the present hour.

It is proposed to continue the history in a second volume, in which the Camisard war, with the causes which immediately led to it and the state of prostration which ensued, will be considered; together with the happy restoration of the French Protestant Church, mainly through the ministry of Antoine Court.

The Author desires to express his gratitude for the assistance he has received from a friend, to whose labour, sympathy, and judgment he has been largely indebted in the preparation of the work.

CONTENTS.

PART I.

FROM THE REFORMATION TO THE EDICT OF NANTES, 1598.

	PAGE
I. The Reformation and Rome	3
II. The League	4
III. Henry IV., 1589	6
IV. The Edict of Nantes, 1598	8

PART II.

FROM THE EDICT OF NANTES, 1598, TO ITS REVOCATION, 1685.

I. Du Plessis Mornay and the Bishop of Evreux, 1600	13
II. Louis XIII., 1610	15
III. The Desolation of Béarn.—Civil War	16
IV. Richelieu and La Rochelle	18
V. The New Era, 1629	19
VI. The Host.—Blasphemy.—The R. P. R.	19
VII. Cardinal Mazarin, 1642	22
VIII. Intolerance and Injustice	23
IX. Louis XIV., 1660	25
X. Psalm-singing	26
XI. The Exiles of La Rochelle	28
XII. The Relapsed	28
XIII. Le Grand Monarque	30
XIV. The Elector of Brandenburg	31
XV. Cramped and Fettered	32
XVI. The War with Holland, 1672—1678	35

		PAGE
XVII.	Marie Alacoque, 1675	35
XVIII.	Pélisson's Chest	37
XIX.	Bossuet and Jean Claude	39
XX.	National Decay	41
XXI.	Under the Harrow	44
XXII.	The Kidnapping of Children	48
XXIII.	Madame de Maintenon	50
XXIV.	The Dragonnade in Poitou, 1681	57
XXV.	Jean Migault.—Perils in the City	66
XXVI.	The House of the New Catholics	73
XXVII.	Fénelon, Superior of the New Catholics	77
XXVIII.	Claude Brousson	80
XXIX.	Demolition of the Temple of Montpellier, 1682	81
XXX.	The Temple of Montauban, 1683	85
XXXI.	Brousson's Project of Passive Resistance	87
XXXII.	Failure of the Project	89
XXXIII.	Causes of the Failure	95
XXXIV.	The Persecution in Saintonge, 1683—5	98
XXXV.	The Bell of La Rochelle	100
XXXVI.	The Imprisonment of Jacques Fontaine	101
XXXVII.	The Dragoons in Béarn, 1685	109
XXXVIII.	The Dragoons in Languedoc, 1685	111
XXXIX.	The Midnight Hour	117

PART III.

From the Revocation, 1685, to the End of the 17th Century.

I.	How to convert the New Converts	127
II.	Fénelon, Missionary in Saintonge, 1685—6	131
III.	The Shepherds Driven Away, 1685	139
IV.	The Reign of Terror	142
V.	Jean Tirel	147
VI.	Aërial Psalmody	148
VII.	The Fugitives	150
VIII.	The Perils of Jean Migault (concluded)	155
IX.	Escape of Daniel Brousson and Family	161
X.	The Sufferings and Shipwreck of M. Serres	176
XI.	The Escape of Nissole, Salendres and Vidal	178

PART I.

FROM THE REFORMATION TO THE EDICT OF NANTES, 1598.

FROM THE REFORMATION TO THE EDICT OF NANTES, 1598.

I.
THE REFORMATION AND ROME.

THE Reformation in France, as in Germany and England, was at the beginning a genuine religious movement. It was the awakening of the conscience from long ages of slumber to behold the true light of the Gospel and to comprehend the spiritual independence and personal responsibility of every human being.

By degrees, however, men began to take part in it from other motives. The long pent-up desire of the oppressed people for political freedom burst forth, whilst personal ambition urged many of the princes and nobles to make use of the Reformation as a stalking-horse to power. In this way the original community of the spiritually-minded men, intent on their own salvation and on the diffusion of the truth, were accompanied, like the Israelites of the Exodus, by a mixed multitude. The French, moreover, were the most military nation of Europe; every gentleman was trained to arms; and the Protestants no less than the Catholics, unprepared to accept Christ's commands in simple faith, made the fatal mistake of supposing that the Gospel is to be defended by the sword.

No sooner had the Reformation sprung into life than the papacy and the Catholic powers united to crush it.

Throughout the sixteenth and seventeenth centuries violent and incessant attempts were made to strangle the new-born "hydra." A Catholic league for the extermination of Protestantism was hatched at the Council of Trent (1545 to 1563), and afterwards matured under the Popes, the Jesuits, and Philip II. of Spain. First the blessed light was extinguished in Italy and Spain, and then the storm was directed against France and England. In 1572, 70,000 Protestants were butchered on St. Bartholomew's day; and in 1588 the great Armada was sent forth by Philip to chastise England and bring her back to the dominion of Rome.

II.

THE LEAGUE.

In 1584 the League became a powerful party in France, under the leadership of Henry Duke of Guise. Its immediate object was to prevent the Protestant King of Navarre from succeeding to the throne on the death of Henry III., whose life was regarded as precarious. Its ultimate purpose was to rid the nation of the Huguenots. Guise, moreover, aimed at sovereign power, flattering himself that he could wrest the government from the feeble hands of Henry III., who, by his folly and superstition, had incurred the contempt of the people.*

War broke out. There were three armies in the field, each independent of the others, the Royal, the League, and the

---

* The popular sentiment found vent in a lampoon, which was placarded in the streets of Paris:—"Henry, by the grace of his mother, inert King of France, Keeper of the Louvre, churchwarden of St. Germain l'Auxerrois, mountebank of the churches in Paris, plaiter of his wife's collars, hairdresser, warden of the four orders of Begging Friars, Conscript Father of the White Flagellants, and Protector of the Capuchins."

army of the Huguenots under Henry of Navarre. To recover his authority, the king, with his mother, Catherine de Medici, caused Guise to be assassinated at Blois, Dec. 23, 1588. No advantage was reaped from this cowardly crime; the Sorbonne revenged it by releasing Henry's subjects from their oath of allegiance; and the king, driven into a corner, saw no alternative but to make common cause with Henry of Navarre. The two kings united their forces and advanced on Paris. The papal world was stirred to its depths. The Pope excommunicated Henry III., and excited the people against him. On the 1st of August, 1589, a Dominican monk, Jacques Clément, under pretext of presenting a letter, obtained an audience of the king, and as Henry was unfolding the paper stabbed him with a poisoned knife. Henry died the next morning, after nominating Henry of Navarre as his successor.

The joy of the Parisians at the king's death knew no bounds; the assassin, who had been despatched by the royal attendants, was glorified in all the pulpits as the blessed son of St. Dominic and holy martyr of Jesus Christ, and his portrait placed on the altars with this inscription:—" St. Jacques Clément, pray for us." When the tidings reached Rome, the Pope held a consistory, at which, in a prepared discourse, he described Clément's act as " an enterprise so surprising and admirable that he was not afraid to compare it to the work of the Incarnation of the Word and the mystery of the Resurrection of the Saviour, spoken of by the prophet Habakkuk."*

It has been estimated that in this reign more than half of the nobility, more than half the towns, more than half the substantial inhabitants of the kingdom were Huguenots.

---

* De Thou, 'Histoire Universelle,' liv. xcvi., in vol. x. of the edition of 1734. What verses in Habakkuk the Pope had in his mind it is not easy to say.

The strength of the Catholics lay in the peasants, the priests, the Sorbonne, the city of Paris, the court, and the army.

III.

HENRY IV., 1589.

Henry of Navarre, although an object of detestation to the Romish party, was too powerful both in his lawful title and in the field to be set aside, and the Catholics consented to accept him as king on condition that he should not only maintain the Romish faith in France, but should himself enter the Romish Church. The position in which he was placed was one of extreme difficulty. The distracted state of the kingdom, apparent patriotic duty, inclination, all urged him to accept the terms; whilst his education, the claims of his party, and his religious convictions, although weakened by the love of pleasure, equally forbad such a course. The choice which he made is well known. He cast aside his friends and his Church, placed the crown on his head, and professed himself a Catholic.

When Queen Elizabeth, then the head of the Protestant cause in Europe, heard of his intention, she wrote to him:—"The natural impulse of all mankind at the fearful spectacle of a man in danger of drowning is to find some means of averting the misfortune. I tremble to see you plunging into a sea where the anchor cannot hold. If we abuse God's grace, all will be lost; but if we do our best to take heed to it, the issue must be good." The news that the step had been taken produced the following outburst:—"What grief, what groanings have I had in my soul at these tidings! My God! is it possible that any worldly honour can efface the terror of the Divine judgments? Can we look for a happy issue to so iniquitous an act? It is dangerous to do evil, in order to make good come out of it. Nevertheless, I shall not cease to give you the first place in my devotions, praying that the hands of Esau may not mar the blessing of Jacob." Henry replied in very courteous terms, pleading, in his excuse:—"I have only consulted the welfare and public necessity of my kingdom, from which I could not separate myself without giving too much offence to God."

Henry concealed his purpose from the Protestants as long as he could: at the very time when he was concluding his compact with the bishops, he told the ministers of Saumur that if they should happen to hear of his falling into some carnal excess they might believe it, because he was very weak on that side; but if a rumour should reach them that he had any thought of changing his religion, they were to give no credit to it.

Henry's conversion was speedily effected; the clergy were urgent; and after half a day's instruction the king declared himself satisfied with the Romish doctrine. But when the bishops would have followed up their advantage by requiring that he should abolish heresy in his dominions, he at once refused. Moreover, when they presented their formula, in which he was made to swear, one by one, to all the articles of the Romish faith, and in like manner to forswear the pretended heresies of the Reformed, he put the obnoxious document aside, and set his hand only to a general declaration, in which he accepted the Catholic doctrine as a whole.

It was on the 25th of July, 1593, that he made his public abjuration. As he entered the cathedral of St. Denis, which was hung with white drapery embroidered with the arms of France and Navarre, and where several prelates were assembled, the Archbishop of Bourges asked, "Who are you?" Henry replied, "I am the king." "What is your request?" "To be received into the pale of the Catholic, Apostolic, and Roman Church." "Do you desire it?" "I do desire it." Then, kneeling, he uttered the words:—"I protest and swear, in the presence of Almighty God, to live and die in the Catholic, Apostolic, and Roman religion, outside which there is no salvation, to protect and defend it against all its enemies at the hazard of my blood and life, renouncing all heresies contrary to this Catholic, Apostolic, and Roman Church." He then placed the same confession in writing in the hands of the archbishop, who held out his ring for him to kiss, and with a loud voice gave him absolution. At the same moment the Te Deum pealed forth in a note of triumph.

Henry's example was followed by a large number of the higher nobility, whose defection was a severe blow to the political importance of the Protestant party.

IV.
THE EDICT OF NANTES, 1598.

The Huguenots finding themselves abandoned assumed a resolute attitude. Their reiterated complaints, with the dangers to which the kingdom was at the time exposed from without, produced their effect, and led to the celebrated Edict of Nantes, April, 1598. By this Act, political rather than religious, the legal existence of the Protestant Church was recognised and its public worship ratified. As a religious measure the Edict was by far too tolerant for the age. Both Protestants and Catholics held it as a fundamental principle that there can be only one true Church and one right form of worship. In England, under Henry VIII., the only lawful religion was that of the king, who sent to the stake such as differed from him, whether Catholic or Protestant. If, under Mary, the Protestants were burned, not less under Elizabeth were the Catholic and Protestant dissenters proscribed. For Catholic France in such an age to accept as legitimate any other than the Romish faith, was a contradiction, an act of spiritual treason. If the Huguenots had obtained the ascendancy they would scarcely have afforded a full measure of liberty to the Catholics. Viewed in this light, the Edict was an extreme and unreasonable act of grace; examined by the light of our day, as a measure of toleration, it was utterly insufficient and despicable. The chief articles were :—

The free exercise of the Reformed worship in all places in which it was then practised.

Toleration of the Reformed worship at five leagues' distance from Paris, instead of ten as hitherto.*

The admission of the Reformed to offices in the State.

Their right to use National schools, hospitals, and charities.

The right to print Protestant books in certain cities.

The establishment of mixed courts of Catholic and Protestant judges, called Mi-party chambers, for the adjudication of cases between the two religions.

The licensing of four Protestant academies for science and theology.

The legalisation of the Reformed synods.

Lastly, the placing of certain fortified towns in the hands of the Protestants, as a guarantee for the performance of the Edict.

This last provision shows clearly that the compact was not so much a measure of toleration to subjects dissenting in religion, as a treaty of peace between two independent nations.

* This distance was still further reduced, a temple being built at the village of Charenton, two leagues S.E. of Paris, which grew into a rich town, and became the head-quarters of the Protestants in the capital. The temple was destroyed at the Revocation.

But the Edict was two-sided: the Catholics had their share in the benefit of its enactments. The Protestants were, henceforth, obliged to keep the Romish festivals and pay tithes. Property which had once belonged to the Catholic clergy was to be restored, and the Catholic worship re-established in all places where it had been abolished. By this last article the Mass was set up again in 250 cities and towns, and in 2000 country parishes. After the Edict the Catholic Church in France increased greatly in pomp and splendour, as well as in wealth and power.*

Notwithstanding these gains, however, the Edict, in its very nature, was utterly repugnant and hateful to the Romish party. Pope Clement VIII. called it "the most accursed ordinance ever made." It had been wrested from the Catholics only by dire necessity; and before Henry's signature to it was dry, the clergy, the Catholic nobility, and the Pope were all leagued together to effect its revocation, and, until that could be accomplished, to infringe and invalidate its provisions.

---

* The Edict, which consisted of ninety-two open and fifty-six secret, or explanatory, articles, had taken a year and three-quarters to prepare. It was drawn up by the Catholics—De Schomberg, Counsellor of the State; the President Jeannin; De Vic, Governor of Calais; and the illustrious historian, De Thou: in concert with the Protestant, Soffrein de Calignon. Henry himself discussed the articles with the Calvinist deputies assembled at Nantes.

		PAGE
XII.	The Sufferings and Shipwreck of M. Serres (Continued)	182
XIII.	Le Jeune	193
XIV.	The Bastille.—Jean Cardel	194
XV.	Chastened, but not Killed	196
XVI.	Fulcran Rey, the First Martyr of the Revocation	198
XVII.	Isaac Vidal	200
XVIII.	The Martyrdon of Teissier	202
XIX.	Emmanuel Dalgue	203
XX.	Orange and Dauphiné	204
XXI.	Blanche Gamond	207
XXII.	Jeanne Terrasson	219
XXIII.	The Chain	225
XXIV.	Bearing Another's Burden	226
XXV.	Louis de Marolles	227
XXVI.	Isaac Le Fèvre	231
XXVII.	The Last Days of Pierre Mauru	235
XXVIII.	Patience in Tribulation	238
XXIX.	Slow Martyrdom	241
XXX.	Fugitive Ladies	245
XXXI.	Escape of Mademoiselle Dubois	247
XXXII.	François Vivens	250
XXXIII.	Gabriel Astier	252
XXXIV.	The Youth Mazel	254
XXXV.	The Prophets, 1688	255
XXXVI.	The Return of the Shepherds	260
XXXVII.	The Adventures of Jean Roman	262
XXXVIII.	Paul Cardel.—The Isle of Ste. Marguerite	265
XXXIX.	Malzac and De Salve	270
XL.	Gardien Givry	275
XLI.	The Return of Vivens and Claude Brousson	278
XLII.	Brousson's Desert Ministry	283
XLIII.	Intrigues with Foreign Powers	286
XLIV.	Death of Vivens	288
XLV.	Deliverances	289
XLVI.	Claude Brousson's Second Desert Journey, 1693—4	292
XLVII.	Claude Brousson's Last Journey, 1697—8	298
XLVIII.	Trial and Martyrdom of Claude Brousson, 1698	302
	Conclusion	316

PLATES.

Louis XIV. signing the Act of Revocation . .	FRONTISPIECE
	TO FACE PAGE
Large Medal struck in Honour of the Revocation . . .	120
Two smaller Medals do. do.	120
The Ramparts of Aigues-Mortes	179
The Chain	225
The State Prison on the Isle of Ste. Marguerite . .	267
Portrait of Claude Brousson	293
Facsimile of Clauses from the Original Act of Revocation .	316

AUTHORITIES.

Histoire de l'Édit de Nantes. [By ELIE BENOIT.] 5 vols. 4to. Delft, 1693—1695.

> This work is the storehouse of facts and documents relating to the French Protestants and their persecution, from the promulgation of the Edict to its revocation.

An Account of the Persecution and Oppression of the Protestants in France. London, 1686. [Translated from the French of Jean Claude.]

> A tract of 18 pages.

Another tract, of the same year, containing three narratives of the cruelties practised on the Protestants at the Revocation.

Histoire Chronologique de l'Église Protestante de France jusqu'à la Revocation de l'Édit de Nantes. Par CHARLES DRION. 2 vols. Paris, 1855.

> A most useful work, got up in a superior style.

Histoire des Pasteurs du Désert. Par NAP. PEYRAT. 2 vols. Paris, 1842.

> Vigorous and picturesque; commended by Michelet; but the author puts his trust in the sword.

Éclaircissemens sur les causes de la Révocation de l'Édit de Nantes. Par RULHIÈRE, de l'Académie Française. Paris, 1819.

> An erudite work, in which the author endeavours to remove from Louis XIV. the odium of the Revocation.

Les Premiers Pasteurs du Désert. Par O. DOUEN. 2 vols. Paris, 1879.

L'Intolérance de Fénelon. Par O. DOUEN. Paris, 1872.

> These two works are of great value from the researches made by the author in the contemporary archives. In his judgment of Fénelon he is very severe.

Vie et Ministère de Claude Brousson. Par LEOPOLD NÈGLE. 1878.
   Contains important documents not before published.

The Evangelist of the Desert. By HENRY S. BAYNES. London, 1853.
   Full of curious and interesting material.

Album du Désert. Folio. Paris, 1888.

   A collection of facsimiles, autographs, prints, &c., illustrative of the history of the French Protestants during the persecution. We are indebted to this elaborate work for several of our plates, as well as for the Seal of the Desert Church, with its apt symbol and plaintive motto, which is stamped on the cover of this volume. The seal is lost, but the impression is still extant on some letters in the library of the Historical Society of French Protestantism.

Other works have been consulted, e.g. :—

SMEDLEY.   History of the Reformed Religion in France.
DE FÉLICE.   History of the Protestants of France.
MICHELET.   Histoire de France.
LAVALLÉE.   Correspondence Générale de Madame de Maintenon

   Together with many memoirs and autobiographies.

Some use has also been made of the 'Bulletin de la Société de l'Histoire du Protestantisme Français,' a voluminous miscellanea of much value, commencing with the year 1853. The correspondence (in French) between Queen Elizabeth and Henry IV. on his abjuration, partially quoted at page 6, first appeared in the 'Bulletin,' vol. vii., p. 260.

PART II.

FROM THE EDICT OF NANTES, 1598,
TO ITS REVOCATION, 1685.

FROM THE EDICT OF NANTES, 1598, TO ITS REVOCATION, 1685.

I.

DU PLESSIS MORNAY AND THE BISHOP OF EVREUX, 1600.

The first result of the new Edict was a war of words,—sometimes with the pen, sometimes in public disputations. Of these latter, the most famous was between the illustrious Du Plessis Mornay, for thirty years the familiar friend of Henry IV., and Du Perron, Bishop of Evreux. It took place at Fontainebleau in the year 1600. Henry played a disgraceful part on this occasion. He turned his back on his faithful comrade, and ostentatiously identified himself with the Catholics. When the bishops manifested some anxiety for the result, he reassured them: "Make yourselves easy; the business shall be so managed as to give the lie to the heretics." But the king himself was in reality far from confident; and the night before the deputation he was unable to sleep. His secretary, De Loménie, who lay in the room with him, said, "Your Majesty takes this matter very much to heart; the night before Courtois, Arques, and Ivry, three battles in which your all was at stake, you were much more tranquil."

Mornay, harassed and brow-beaten, fell sick on the second day of the conference, which caused the dispute to be broken off. Du Perron and the king claimed the victory. Henry was so elated that he wished to sup in the chamber where the conference took place, as if it were a field of battle; and he wrote to the Duc D'Epernon: "The diocese of Evreux has gained a victory over that of Saumur. The bearer will tell you I did wonders." But when Du Perron followed his example and boasted of his triumph, the king recovered his good sense, and in his sarcastic way said, "Let us acknowledge the truth; the good cause wanted a great deal of help." Moreover, he made some sort of reparation to the old friend whom he had so unworthily deserted, publicly declaring that he had never possessed an abler or a better servant. Du Plessis returned heart-broken to his government of Saumur. "Courage," said his wife; "it is God who has ordered it thus; still keep a good mind and heart for the performance of your duty."

The ill-treatment of their champion still further irritated the Protestants, who were at no pains to conciliate their opponents, or to conceal their hatred of popery. Their ministers had always preached that the Pope is Antichrist; and now, at a national synod held at Gap in 1603, this dogma was introduced as an article into their Confession of Faith:—"We believe and maintain that the Pope is really the Antichrist and Son of Perdition foretold in the Word of God; the harlot, clothed in scarlet, sitting on the seven hills; the great city having dominion over the kings of the earth." The new editions of the Liturgy, containing this article, were eagerly bought by the people. The Pope and the Catholics were stung to the quick; and the king threatened with condign punishment those who troubled the State with such "shocking and unseasonable propositions." The threat took effect; at the Synod of La Rochelle (1607) more moderate counsels prevailed, and the article was expunged.

In 1610, Henry's reign—which had conferred on the Protestants a measure of freedom and protection such as they had never before enjoyed—came to an untimely end. As the king was driving in his coach in Paris he was stabbed by Ravaillac, a gloomy fanatic, who, on being put to the torture, confessed he had done the deed, "because the king, in making war on the Pope, had made war on God, inasmuch as the Pope is God."

II.
LOUIS XIII., 1610.

Henry was succeeded by his son, Louis XIII., a boy of nine years, who had been educated in the strict observance of the Romish ordinances. In 1614, at the assembly of the States General, the nobility and clergy declared that sooner or later the young king must of necessity fulfil his coronation oath of allegiance to the papacy, and must rid the land of the heretics. This declaration received a fitting comment from his Jesuit confessor. "Royal promises," said this astute theologian, referring to the Edict of Nantes, "are either matters of conscience or matters of State. Those made to the Huguenots are not promises of conscience, for they are contrary to the precepts of the Church; and if they are promises of State, they ought to be referred to the Privy Council, which is of opinion they are not binding."

These were not empty words; they were followed by decree after decree, diminishing the liberties of the Protestants and nullifying the measures of the Edict. The alarm of the Protestants was great, and was further increased by the double marriage between the royal families of France and Spain. In this union of grandchildren of Philip II. they saw "the spectre of that persecuting monarch and of their own Charles IX., of sanguinary memory, rise from their graves." Events outran their worst fears. The hatred which the papal party bore to the Huguenots, and their determination to extirpate "the cursed religion," burst forth like a flame. The principality of Lower Navarre and Béarn, which had been brought to the French crown by Henry IV., was in 1617 incorporated with the monarchy. Three-fourths of the population of these provinces, some say nine-tenths, belonged to the Reformed communion. Nevertheless, a royal order was issued to restore to the priests all the estates, which since 1569 had been enjoyed by the Protestants for the maintenance of their temples, places of worship, schools, hospitals, and poor. To insure the performance of this order, the young king marched into the principality at the head of an army.

III.

THE DESOLATION OF BÉARN.—CIVIL WAR.

The royal progress was marked everywhere with violence; and when the army arrived at Pau the soldiers broke into the temples, tore in pieces the service-books, and battered down the walls. They robbed and beat the peasants who came to the market, taking them all for Huguenots, and forced the Reformed citizens to make the sign of the cross and to fall on their knees when the Host passed by. Women who appeared in the streets were hooted and insulted, and made to promise that their unborn infants should be baptized into the Romish Church; and children were carried off from their parents. In the country districts the soldiers who were quartered on the people drove away the ministers, outraged the women, beat the husbands, and compelled everyone to go to Mass. It was the prelude to that fearful tragedy acted sixty years later, known as the Dragonnades.

The Huguenots throughout France were maddened by these enormities, and flew to arms. A war ensued, which was carried on with great bitterness on both sides. One of the king's first exploits was to obtain fraudulent possession of Saumur. To console De Mornay, who had been governor of the castle from the time of Henry III., a Marshal's bâton and 100,000 crowns were offered to him.* He indignantly rejected the offer, saying, "I cannot sell the liberty and security of others." He retired to his own house, where he soon afterwards died, full of peace, Nov. 11, 1623. On his death-bed he confessed that he had received much from God, but had profited little by it. Some one answering that he had used his talent faithfully, he exclaimed, "It is nothing of mine; do not say me; it is God."

The king took city after city; but when he arrived at Montauban he encountered a most obstinate and heroic resistance. All the inhabitants, even women and children, took part in the defence; and the thirteen Huguenot preachers, relieving one another every two hours, harangued the defenders at the breach. One of them, Chamier, fell whilst shouting, "Woe to thee, Babylon, Babylon!" After a siege of between two and three months, the king grew weary, and made a treaty of peace with his insurgent subjects, A.D. 1622. But the treaty did not bring peace. The Reformed party, disgusted with royalty, began to entertain republican projects. Their leaders also, the Dukes of Rohan and Soubise, were personally discontented; and in 1624 the war was renewed in a guerilla fashion.

* A crown was value three livres; a livre, like the franc which has replaced it, twenty sous, tenpence English.

IV.

RICHELIEU AND LA ROCHELLE.

The same year Richelieu became chief minister of the Crown, and at once infused new vigour into the royal counsels. He saw that if the monarchy was to be saved, the Huguenot party must be crushed. They had lost their strong places in the north and centre, and now regarded La Rochelle, one of the most flourishing and enterprising ports in the kingdom, as the rampart of their liberty. This city possessed an ancient constitution, which made it a republic within the kingdom, an Imperium in Imperio, and to its reduction Richelieu directed all his energies. The twelve-months' heroic defence; the hope of help from England, always delayed, or always inadequate; the extremities of famine endured by the besieged;—all these are well-known matters of history. The city was taken, August 28, 1628, and with it fell the political power of the Huguenot party. The news of the capture caused great rejoicing at Rome: Pope Urban VIII. wrote to the king:—"Great Prince! God is seated on your right hand; may He ever aid and maintain the vigour of your spear."

But although Richelieu had annihilated the Huguenots as a political party, it did not harmonize with his far-seeing policy to extinguish their religious existence; and when the next year (July, 1629) they finally submitted, he issued, in the king's name, an Edict of Grace, by which the Reformed were nominally re-established in all their religious liberties.

A few years previous, Cardinal Bentivoglio, the Pope's legate, who made extensive enquiry into the constitution of the French Protestants, reckoned the number of their churches at 700, and their population at upwards of a million, out of fifteen millions, at which he rated the whole kingdom.

This epoch, politically speaking, was the nadir of the Protestant cause throughout Europe. The Palatinate had been over-run by the Catholic armies, and North Germany, with the exception of some sea-port towns, lay at the feet of Tilly and Wallenstein.

V.

THE NEW ERA, 1629.

Richelieu's Edict of Grace was the commencement of a new era to the French Protestants. Stripped of political power, and by degrees excluded from government employment and from nearly all civil offices, they thenceforth devoted themselves to commerce and industry; and it was largely to them that France owed the period of prosperity which she enjoyed in the middle part of this century.

Richelieu's policy led him to protect the Huguenots from their inveterate enemies, the clergy, but it would have taken a greater than Richelieu to have put a stop to the downward movement. The revocation of the Edict of Nantes was a foregone conclusion, and every year brought the consummation nearer. A few of the Edicts and Orders in Council by which the process was carried on may be here referred to.

VI.

THE HOST.—BLASPHEMY.—THE R. P. R.

In 1634 it was ordered that when the bell gave notice of the passing of the Host the Protestants should withdraw from the streets, or else do reverence, the men by uncovering, the women by kneeling. The ill-will of the populace, however, made withdrawal no easy matter;

and if a Huguenot attempted to take shelter in the house of a Romanist, he was almost sure to find the door closed against him. Even when he made haste to conform he was not unfrequently jeered and hooted. Very many yielded, silencing their conscience with the sophistical argument that it was not the Host to which they paid reverence, but to the priest who carried it and to the company who followed. The Protestant National Synod of 1645 strongly condemned both the practice and the equivocation, and declared that no course was open but prompt withdrawal.

In 1636, at the periodical assembly of the French clergy,* the Bishop of Orleans, in the customary address to the king, accused the Protestants of profanity and blasphemy. The complaint was in retaliation for the outspoken language of two Reformed ministers, Drélincourt and Daillé, respecting the Virgin and the Mass. Many new houses, and even orders, of monks had been founded with the avowed purpose of drawing the Huguenots into the Romish Church; and now commissions were granted for the same object to secular priests and lay persons, with the promise of rewards proportioned to the number and importance of the converts. Mercers, shoemakers, cutlers, left their shops and went forth to puzzle and entrap the unwary Huguenots with casuistical questions, such as: "Do you believe that Charlemagne and St. Louis and our king are all damned?" It was high treason to answer, Yes; and the answer, No, was taken as an admission of salvation within the Romish Church. Drélincourt, in a series of familiar tracts, furnished the people with short

---

* The "General Assembly of the Clergy of France" dates from 1579. It consisted of sixty-four representatives, *viz.*, two bishops and two priests from each ecclesiastical province, who met every ten years, with an intermediate session for auditing the accounts of the receiver-general.

answers to these and similar fallacies. The clergy were irritated, and, as has been said above, appealed to the king, who responded by issuing an edict for the punishment of blasphemy, whether against God, the Virgin, or the saints; the penalty being, for the first four convictions, progressive fines; for the fifth, the pillory; for the sixth, to have the upper lip slit; for the seventh, to lose the lower lip; for the eighth, to have the tongue cut out.

The charges made against the Reformed under this statute were never of blasphemy against God, but always against the Virgin and the saints, and were nothing more than the Reformed doctrines expressed in terms obnoxious to the Romanists.

In 1665, Pierre Viger, of Montevillier in Normandy, was condemned to perform public penance in front of the church, wearing on his forehead the words, "Blasphemer against the honour, purity, and virginity of the holy Virgin." He was besides fined 100 livres, and obliged to set apart the sum of 500 livres for a perpetual Mass in honour of the Virgin. A repetition of the offence was to be punished with death.

In 1681, Antoine Vanier performed public penance on the market-day at the principal gate of the town, stripped to his shirt, with bare head and feet, and holding in his hand a lighted taper of two pounds weight. In this attitude he was made to declare that having wickedly and maliciously uttered blasphemies against the holy sacrament and the saints, and spoken contemptuously of the Catholic, Apostolic, and Roman religion, he repented of the same, and entreated pardon of God, the king and justice. He was besides banished for five years under pain of the halter, and amerced in 200 livres, ten of which were to be expended on a picture of the crucifixion, to be placed in the most conspicuous part of the court.

In 1640, the parliament of Pau forbade the Reformed to

call their religion by any other name than that of the *Religion Prétendue Réformée*, familiarly known by the initials R. P. R. This local decree was made general by Order in Council, January, 1657, renewed in February, 1663, where the reason for the enactment is thus given:—"The ministers of the R. P. R. cannot assume the title of ministers of the Word of God, seeing that the Word of God is true, holy, and pure; whilst that which is taught and preached by the ministers of the R. P. R. is false, profane, and corrupt."

VII.
CARDINAL MAZARIN, 1642.

Richelieu died in 1642, and Mazarin took the helm of the State. The next year Louis XIII. died, leaving a son only five years old, who succeeded him as Louis XIV. It was the policy of Mazarin, still more than of Richelieu, to let the Huguenots alone. "I have," he said, "no complaint to make of the little flock; if they browse in an unwholesome pasture, at least they do not stray." The little flock were not ungrateful. Throughout the struggle of the Fronde, 1648 to 1653, they adhered faithfully to the king and Mazarin; and in reward for their fidelity the Cardinal, May 21, 1652, issued a Declaration, confirming the Edict of Nantes, and revoking the Orders by which it had been infracted.

The condition of the Huguenots, indeed, in the middle of this century was not yet that of a proscribed people. In many places the intercourse between them and the Catholics was still on terms almost of equality, sometimes of friendship; and where this was not the case, their numbers and wealth often enabled them to hold the ground against their adversaries. The following anecdote will show how bold they could be where they formed the bulk of the population. One Sunday, Jacques Fontaine, pastor of the united churches of Vaux and Royan, near the mouth of the Gironde, had just given out his text, when he perceived some Capuchins and Jesuits enter the temple (so the Protestants called their churches). He paused, and, addressing his own people, said :—" The text I have read to you is suitable for those who, by the grace of God, are well instructed in pure religion ; but I see persons before me whom I believe to be still in a state of superstition and ignorance. I, therefore, feel it my duty on this occasion to leave the ninety and nine and go after the lost sheep, if haply I may bring them back to the fold." Thus saying, he turned over the leaves of his Bible, took a controversial text, and delivered an extempore discourse with so much force and perspicuity, that the Fathers on going out declared they had never heard error so well defended.

VIII.
INTOLERANCE AND INJUSTICE.

Mazarin's gratitude to the Huguenots was not shared by the nation in general, high or low, clergy or laity. The Protestant marshal, Turenne, during the war of the Fronde, had saved the lives of the young king and of his mother, Anne of Austria; yet the latter, on her death-bed in 1666, exacted from her son an oath to abolish Protestantism in France. If, it was argued, the Protestants are strong enough to save the State, they are able also to overthrow it, and there will be no safety to the kingdom so long as they are suffered to exist. The Declaration of 1652 was especially intolerable to the clergy. At the King's Coronation, June 8th, 1654, the Bishop of Montauban delivered an harangue, in which he styled the Romish Church the only daughter of God, and maintained that kings are in duty bound to employ all the authority they derive from Him in nipping error whilst in the bud, or destroying it when full blown. And, at the Assembly of the Clergy in 1656, the Archbishop of Sens declared that the indulgent Declaration of 1652 had been issued unknown to the king, and in the absence of his first minister. He designated the temples of the Reformed as " synagogues of Satan, erected on the patrimony of the Son of God"; and reminded the king of the example of St. Ambrose, who preferred to suffer every extremity rather than yield up a single church to the Arian heresy; and of the law of Theodosius, forbidding heretics to hold their meetings in the cities. These appeals were not in vain. The same month an Order was issued, virtually annulling the Declaration of 1652; and the parliament of Paris, which had left that Declaration unnoticed, hastened to register the new Order. From this time forward the government sank into the condition of a puppet in the hands of the clergy.

In 1659 the Protestants, vexed and shorn on every hand, memorialized the king. But Cromwell, whose name had been an ægis to the Reformed Churches abroad, was now dead, and instead of listening to their complaints, Louis only added to their grievances. In 1660 the National Synod, which had been held for a hundred years, was abolished, the royal commissioner declaring that the Protestants had become much too insolent, and must now be content with their provincial synods. Even these were left to them in little more than name, for by another Order, following close on the former, they were forbidden to be held except in the presence of a royal commissioner.

The following occurrence will show the hatred and contempt with which the Huguenots were regarded in the more Catholic provinces. A cup was stolen from a parish church in Brittany. A Huguenot gentleman was arrested on suspicion, tortured (but without wringing from him any confession), broken alive on the wheel, and his body burned. A short time afterwards the real thieves confessed the crime. The widow of the murdered man applied for a judicial certification of her husband's innocence; it was refused.

IX.
LOUIS XIV., 1660.

In 1660 (the year in which our Charles II. recovered his throne), Louis married the Infanta of Spain. One of the articles of the treaty by which these two great-grand-children of that gloomy bigot Philip II. were united, was a mutual engagement for the suppression of heresy. Mazarin died the same year, and from this date the actual reign of Louis XIV., who was then twenty-two, may be said to have commenced. When his ministers asked to whom they should thenceforth address themselves, he repled, "To me." If, however, we may believe another story, he had already, some years before, given indication of his intention, not only to reign, but to govern with the absolute majesty of the Roman emperors. When only seventeen, the parliament of Paris remonstrating with him on an arbitrary Order in Council which put a stop to their deliberations, and pleading that these were for the benefit of the State, he is said to have answered, "I am the State" (L'état c'est moi). If any monarch ever believed himself to be king by divine right it was Louis. "He was," says Michelet, "both in his own eyes and those of the nation, nothing less than a miracle. He was nourished up in the Romish religion at an immense distance from humanity, and he was possessed with the belief that God was in him. The adoration he received did not turn his head, simply because he received it as his due. Mazarin had kept him in profound ignorance of State affairs, and this ignorance remained with him more or less during his whole reign. In his instructions to his son he counsels him 'to confide in God, to know little, and to be resolute.'" But Louis believed himself to be, not the State only, but the Church. To the Archbishop of Rheims, who asked with whom he was in future to transact the business of the clergy, he replied, as he had replied to his Minister of State, "With me." Louis did not perceive, that with all this affectation of supreme authority, he was only a tool in the hands of the Jesuits. "The proudest of men, the most absolute of monarchs, he knew not," remarks S. Priest, "that he was all the while wearing the Jesuit yoke, which he imposed also on his people, his court, and his family."

What rule he laid down for his conduct towards his Protestant subjects we learn from his own pen. In his Memoirs, written for the Dauphin in 1670, he says:— "From 1661 I formed the plan of my conduct towards my subjects of the R. P. R. I thought the best means of bringing them back was not to press them with new rigour, but to observe what my predecessors had granted them, only restricting the same within the narrowest limit warranted by justice and benevolence." The limit he here sets for himself was narrow enough; but it was wide when compared with his actual conduct.

X.

PSALM-SINGING.

One of the first acts of the new government was to forbid the singing of Psalms in private houses so as to be heard outside, December, 1661. Cut off from the rights of citizens, scorned by the priests of a Church which they deemed apostate, and shunned by their neighbours, often their inferiors in morals and intelligence, the Huguenots were driven to their own hearths, where they could relieve their burdened spirits and find heavenly consolation by chanting the Psalms of David in the noble verse of Marot and Beza.*

The Curé of Ville-Goudon, a suburb of Castres, heard some women singing in their own house. He entered the house and ordered them to desist. As they took no notice of his interference, but continued their singing, he laid an information against them. The case came before the Mi-party chamber. The judges were divided; the Catholics holding that the women ought to pay the penalty, 500 livres; the Protestants, that the prohibition was in itself unjust, and that, if the fine was to be levied at all, it must be paid by the curé, for it was a trespass for any other than an officer of justice to make an inquisitorial entrance into a private house. The curé carried the cause before the king in Council, where the ruling of the Catholic judges was confirmed, and the fine directed to be paid by the women and to be handed over to the local hospital.

The next year the prohibition was extended to the singing of Psalms in shops and streets. In regard to these irritating measures, however, the clergy were not entirely of one mind. The name of one honourable dissentient has come down to us. Bishop Godeau had the courage to say, that far from being offended by the sacred melodies of the Protestants, he deplored the absence of such amongst

---

* This metrical translation of more than a century before, the joint work of the first French poet of the age and of one of its greatest divines, was popular far beyond the Reformed Church. The music was equal to the poetry, and although the Catholics objected to it as too lively, everybody, Catholic and Protestant, as soon as the version appeared, was heard singing the words and humming the airs.

his own people. "Whilst," said he, "the Huguenot artisan in his workshop and the labourer in the field sing the praises of God, the Catholics are mute, or employ their voices only to troll out disreputable ballads."

XI.

THE EXILES OF LA ROCHELLE.

The cruel temper of the court at this time is shown in the treatment of La Rochelle. This city, on its surrender in 1628, was subjected to humiliating conditions, one of which affected the citizenship of new settlers of the Reformed faith. It was now resolved, November, 1661, to enforce these restrictions to the utmost letter of the law. The measures taken, indeed, went beyond the law, the net being enlarged to enclose other classes of persons. Under one plea or another, with little or no warning, in an inclement season, 300 families were suddenly driven out of the city and their property wasted. Aged men and women, who could not walk without assistance, were thrust out of their houses, and infants in their cradles were laid in the streets. Many of the sick and feeble died before they could leave the city; others lived only until they reached a place of refuge and then expired.

XII.

THE RELAPSED.

The blow thus dealt on La Rochelle was especially designed as a warning to the Relapsed. Nothing exasperated the court and the clergy so much as the return of Catholic converts to their original faith. In 1663 the penalty of banishment was adjudged to such offenders, the minister who received them back being condemned to be mulcted of his whole property, and the temple where the ceremony was performed to be razed to the ground.

A Protestant nobleman, named Duchail, wooed a Catholic lady, and to win her hand renounced his own faith. His infidelity sat heavy on his conscience, and he determined to make a public recantation. The rigorous laws against the Relapsed, however, induced him to defer the act from time to time, until the year 1673, when a severe illness brought him to the point. He did not recover. During the remainder of his days he was postered by the monks and priests. Death even did not deliver him. Having been too ill to be put on his trial during his lifetime, his body was dragged to the court, condemned, and only saved from being cast to the dogs by his mother-in-law, a Catholic, undertaking that it should not be buried in any cemetery, Protestant or Catholic. The minister who had received his confession was sent to prison. Duchail's wife, who had learnt the Reformed doctrine from her husband, and had inculcated it in her children, stood bravely by him, notwithstanding that a company of archers was quartered upon her. After his death, to retain possession of the children, she weakly promised to embrace the Romish faith and bring them up in the same. She broke her promise, made a secret abjuration, and went to La Rochelle to communicate. This becoming known, the Jesuits took away her children; her mother by her will left her penniless; and, betrayed by a servant, she was seized and cast into prison and her goods confiscated. Her friends contrived to obtain her release, and in 1681 she passed over into England with five of her children.

At the same time another engine of coercion was set in motion against the Protestants. The genius of Colbert had given a new impetus to the French marine, and the king was in want of forçats (galley-slaves) to man the fleet. It was accordingly ordered that "sturdy beggars, infractors of the salt-laws, and malefactors over fifteen years of age," should be drafted to the ports to which the galleys belonged; and to these were added (1662), "Huguenots who kept on their hats when the Host passed by."

XIII.
LE GRAND MONARQUE.

In this year France would seem to have risen at a bound to an extraordinary degree of greatness. Two years of peace had brought back plenty; the birth of the Dauphin had established the throne. The council was composed of ministers who saw that it was easier to make their fortune by servility and the orderly working of their departments, than by the intrigues to which they had been accustomed. Le Tellier and Colbert divided between them the king's confidence; the latter by his sagacity and tried fidelity; the former by his financial skill, by which the revenues of the Crown were prodigiously increased, and ample means supplied to gratify the ambition and luxurious magnificence of the monarch. The French, naturally loyal, learned now to count their servitude an honour, even though all ranks and orders of the people were humbled to the dust. The parliaments were made dependent on the royal will; the provinces trembled at a word from an intendant; the royal orders were enforced with a summary vigour which left no time to remonstrate. The nation, in fine, found its prince so great, that it took his tyrannical rule as a thing of course, and obeyed his will without a murmur.

In 1670 the king took up his abode at Versailles, in the magnificent palace built for him by his minister, Louvois.

"Paris, parliamentary, devout, satirical, fertile in cabals, had become insupportable to him. The very dress of the citizens was offensive; they still wore the costume of Louis XIII., which had passed over to Puritan England, and which was a standing rebuke to the costume of the court, embellished with a hundred colours, tricked out with ribbons and lace, surmounted with a plumed hat, and grotesque with a lion's mane. At Versailles Louis lived like a solitary god, seen of men only on those days when he launched his thunderbolts."

XIV.

THE ELECTOR OF BRANDENBURG.

It must not be supposed that the Protestant nations were indifferent to the wrongs of the Huguenots. In 1665, the Elector of Brandenburg (the Great Elector) wrote a letter to the king, interceding for his oppressed subjects. The king's answer was such as might have been expected: royal veracity and royal gratitude are not proverbial, least of all were they to be looked for from Louis. "Brother, I would not have discoursed the matter of which you have written to me with any other prince; but the esteem I entertain for you induces me to say that some disaffected persons have spread abroad seditious pamphlets, as though the acts and edicts passed in favour of my subjects of the Pretended Reformed Religion by the kings, my predecessors, and confirmed by myself, were not kept; which would have been contrary to my intentions: for I take care that they are maintained in all the privileges which have been granted to them. To this I am engaged, both by my royal word and in gratitude for their loyalty during the late troubles, in which they took up arms for my service, and successfully opposed the evil designs of a rebel faction."

XV.
CRAMPED AND FETTERED.

At the Assembly of the Clergy, in 1665–1666, the Bishop of Uzès boasted that the Church had won triumphs in province after province, and that the Reformed Religion, "that monster of heresy," was already in the throes of death. In effect, during the past four years, the Protestant worship had been suppressed in 227 places, notably in Poitou, the temples in most cases being demolished. In 1666, in order to drive the nail home, the Decrees and Orders in Council were collected and codified in a General Declaration, from which it is manifest that the Protestants were by this time fettered in every relation of life,—in the city and the State, in shop and market, in worship and Church discipline, in the school, and at the domestic hearth.

Restrictions in trade commenced with the guilds, not with the government; the women leading the way. So early as 1645, the *Lingères* (women who dealt in ready-made clothes) in Paris decided that no Protestant sempstress should be admitted to contaminate their immaculate corporation. In 1665, the *Repasseuses* (ironers) adopted a similar resolution; and when a Protestant woman, being refused admission into their guild, appealed to the parliament, the counter-plea that their society having been instituted by St. Louis, they could on no account admit heretics, was held to be a good and sufficient reason. In 1669, Protestant embroiderers were forbidden to take Catholic apprentices; and in 1672 the parliament of Rouen excluded the Reformed from the trade of wool-combing.

The printing of Protestant books without the royal sanction was now prohibited. Protestant schools were always a thorn in the eyes of the clergy; from this time none were to be permitted, except in places in which the Protestant worship was allowed, and nothing was to be taught in them but reading, writing, and arithmetic. The academies for the children of the nobility were closed, the object being to oblige the parents to send their sons to Catholic colleges. The Protestants were compelled to observe the fête-days of the Church, and were not allowed to sell meat on fast-days. No minister was permitted to take Catholic boarders, or more than two Protestant. Professors were forbidden to style themselves doctors of divinity, and preachers to take any other title than ministers of the R. P. R. They were forbidden also to preach, or to wear the cassock or gown with sleeves, except in their own temples. When they went to the prison to comfort members of their own flock, they were to see them in private, and to speak only in a low voice. We have already spoken of the interdiction of Psalm-singing. It was now enacted that on days of public rejoicing, and at the execution of Protestant criminals, there should be no Psalm-singing, either by ministers or others; and that when the Host should be carried before a temple during service, the singing should cease. The disturbance to the Catholic worship from the bells of the temples was a frequent source of complaint. Many a temple was pulled down merely because it stood too near to the church, so that the carillons were spoilt by its bells.

These and many other infringements of their liberties, with frequent and high-handed acts of local violence, spread dismay through the Protestant community. Deputies sent up from the churches threw themselves at the king's feet. "In God's name, Sire," said their spokesman, Dubosc, "hearken to our groans. Have pity on so many of your poor subjects, who live only by their tears." The king's answer was, "I will think of it" (*J'y penserai*). The result of the royal cogitations appeared in a fresh blow to the Edict of Nantes, namely, the suppression of two of the five Mi-party chambers (regarded by the Protestants as the pillars of their existence), Paris and Rouen. (The other three, Toulouse, Bordeaux, and Grenoble were abolished in 1679.) What Tyndal said of the people of England in his time might be applied to the Huguenots, but in a far worse sense, viz., that they were "shorn, shaven, polled, scraped, pared." The last process which he enumerates, that of "flaying," was yet to come.

Now commenced that great tide of emigration which lasted for many years, and by which France was deprived of the best and most industrious of her children, and England and the other Protestant countries were enriched at her expense in the arts, commerce, and moral worth. The loss was felt especially on the western coast, where the removal of the marine population was so serious a blow to the defence, as well as to the commerce of the country, that the king, in 1669, closed the ports, and forbad any of his subjects to leave the kingdom without his special permission.

We may call to mind that the Huguenots in France at this period had fellow-sufferers in England and Scotland. In 1662, the Act of Uniformity was passed, by which dissenters from the State Church were grievously harassed, and in consequence of which 2000 Presbyterian and other ministers resigned their benefices. In 1666, the Covenanters of the West of Scotland, driven to desperation by Episcopal tyranny, took up arms, and were defeated by Dalziel at Rullion Green. The prisoners and the abettors of the insurrection were treated with merciless severity.

XVI.
THE WAR WITH HOLLAND, 1672—1678.

The king hated the Dutch because they were republicans and plebeians, and more than all because they were Protestants. The old traditions of the League were strong in him; he believed himself divinely called to fulfil its great object, viz., the complete extinction of the Protestant religion in Europe. When, in 1672, he declared war against Holland, and himself accompanied the immense army which was poured like a flood into that devoted country, he exclaimed, "This is a religious war!" In truth, the barbarity with which the French carried on the war entitled it to such a name. Louis's general, Marshal Luxembourg, gave his troops free-handed licence to plunder, ravish, and destroy, a licence of which, during seventeen months, in the province of Utrecht, they availed themselves to such purpose that the miserable inhabitants believed the end of the world was come. With equal fury the great Turenne overran Westphalia in 1673, and the Palatinate in 1675, giving up those fair and populous countries to the soldiery to pillage, burn, sack, and consume. The Prince Palatine, from his castle at Heidelberg, beheld at one time thirty-two towns and villages in flames. The war, which lasted six years, was concluded by the Treaty of Nimeguen, August 10, 1678.

XVII.
MARIE ALACOQUE, 1675.

During the war the government pressure on the Protestants was somewhat relaxed; but at the same time the popular hatred was embittered by the occurrence of one of those "miracles" which, from age to age, like a flood, have carried away the Catholic mind.

The Visitandists were nuns who watched for the coming of the Bridegroom, and who called themselves Daughters of the Heart of Jesus. One day, in 1675, a nun of Paray-le-Monial, named Marie Alacoque, received the expected visit, and was permitted to kiss the wounds of the Saviour's bleeding heart. She was twenty-seven years of age when this celestial grace was vouchsafed to her. In a transport of joy she told what had happened to her abbess, a crafty woman, who conceived the daring idea of a contract of marriage between the Saviour and Marie. The abbess signed for the Saviour, the nun wrote her name in her own blood. Thenceforth she received monthly visits from the Bridegroom. The Jesuits declared : " This is the worship of the true Bleeding Heart, of the flesh and blood of Jesus." "A new materialistic phase came over the Catholic world. A mystical jargon, produced by the ambiguity of the material heart and the moral, found its way everywhere. In twenty-five or thirty years there sprang up 428 convents of the Sacred Heart. The word itself became a war-cry against Protestantism."

Paray-le-Monial is a small town in the south-west corner of Burgundy (Sâone et Loire), and is one of the cleanest and neatest in France. The writer was there in 1886. The Chapel of the Visitation is a plain building, erected on the spot where Marie Alacoque is said to have received the Saviour's visits. Opposite to it are shops filled with numberless trinkets of every description for the devotees of the Bleeding Heart. Before the chapel doors stood women offering for sale wax tapers, which they seemed to think it strange we did not provide ourselves with before entering the shrine. Daylight is excluded from the chapel, which is illumined by small lamps, of a beautiful crimson colour, suspended from the roof; but the light is so dim that it took some little time to determine whether any other persons were present. There might be a score or so, scattered over as many forms on the two sides of the aisle. Against the walls are set long lines of banners, emblazoned with the Sacred Heart, a symbol which was everywhere to be seen. At the upper end was an altar, at which stood a priest, intoning the service in a deep mellow voice; and, at intervals, from behind a screen, came the responses, soft and slow, sometimes scarcely audible, the cadences gently winding their seductive way into the charmed ear.

When we left the town and went on to Macon we travelled with two decent country-women, who informed us they were going to Lourdes. This is a town in the Pyrenees, near Bagnères-de-Bigorre, sacred to the Virgin, and which, in our day, from the supposed miraculous virtue of its waters, has eclipsed Paray as a place of pilgrimage. Its name is familiar to English readers in connection with Henri Lasserre, the intrepid and picturesque translator of the Gospels into French, who is still waiting at the gates of the Vatican until the Pope shall be honest enough to redeem his promise and authorize the circulation of the version. These good women seemed to indulge the hope of finding at the new shrine a more plentiful supply of spiritual advantages than the older sanctuary could offer; and with this object they had undertaken a journey half the entire length of France. They carried with them bread and wine to sustain them by the way.

XVIII.
PÉLISSON'S CHEST.

As already observed, it was not expedient during the war with Holland to proceed to extremities against the Protestants; it was therefore resolved to try for a while milder but not less infamous means. Bribery on a small scale had been practised for many years; it was now proposed to apply it in a wholesale way.

Accordingly, the revenues of two rich abbeys, Citeaux and St. Germain des Près, together with a third of the vacant bishoprics, were set apart for this object. The sacred chest was committed to a new convert named Pélisson, who had been a prisoner in the Bastille four years, and had purchased his release by changing his religion.* Pélisson dispensed the money to the bishops, who distributed it through their agents. The price of conversion varied according to the social position of the convert and the difficulties of the work. "The tariff," remarks Peyrat, "was not high, each soul costing on an average six livres, a little less than the price of a pig." The bishops sent back long lists of conversions, but not sufficient to satisfy Pélisson. "Send, send," he wrote continually; "the money is here,— five, ten, fifteen, twenty thousand livres"; and every three months he laid before Louis a schedule of the scandalous bargains. "The golden doctrine of M. Pélisson," said the courtiers, "is more convincing than the arguments of the Bishop of Meaux" (Bossuet). The Protestants called the chest Pandora's box; Pélisson himself compared it to the barrel and cruse of the widow of Sarepta which never failed. Money bribes were only for the lower class; the rich and the noble were angled for with a different bait. For the substantial burgess there was an office or a pension; for the nobility, orders of merit and the royal smile; for the Protestant ministers, Bossuet's scheme of reunion with the Catholic Church, which, however, when examined, was found to mean little else than complete submission. The converts sometimes found it necessary to take security

* On his death-bed Pélisson refused the ministry of the priest and died professing the religion which he had abjured, and which he had bribed so many to forsake.

for their bargain, otherwise they ran the risk of getting nothing. An officer pleading his change of religion as a reason for his advancement, the Minister of State congratulated him on his happy reunion with the Church, but told him drily that royal favours were not for those who had been, but for those who were to be, converted. Although Pélisson's success appeared to be so great, it was less in reality than on paper. Not only were the quarterly returns exaggerated, but many of the ignorant people who signed their abjuration with a cross were quite unconscious of what they had done.

XIX.

BOSSUET AND JEAN CLAUDE, 1678.

In 1668 Bossuet published his famous *Exposition de la Foi Catholique*, a work which raised up many antagonists and gave him many conquests, the most illustrious of which was that of Marshal Turenne. It had long been a prime object with the court to win over to the Romish faith the greatest general of his age. Mazarin had offered him one of his nieces with a rich dowry; Louis XIV. attempted to bribe him with the governorship of Dauphiné and the sword of the Constable of France. From all such glittering offers he turned magnanimously away. But the controversial writings of the Jansenist Arnauld against the Protestants, and still more Bossuet's eloquent *Exposition*, staggered him; and in 1668 he was privately admitted into the Catholic Church. As soon as the event was known, the papal world was in triumph. The king would have heaped honours upon him if he would have suffered it; and the Pope offered to make him a cardinal. "Mon Dieu," replied the veteran marshal, "what should I do with that little cap and long tail?"

Turenne's defection was a severe blow to his party; he had been preceded by his brother, the Duke de Bouillon, and he was followed by his nephews, the Dukes of Duras and de Lorges, and by many others. Now, it was said, that Turenne, so just, so wise, so weightily judicious, is gone, no one can remain without covering himself with ridicule. Nevertheless, not a few of the nobility, some even of high rank, still clung to the Protestant cause.

One of the new converts, Turenne's niece, Mademoiselle Duras, prompted, says Peyrat, by feminine vanity rather than piety, aspired to signalize her conversion by a public disputation between Bossuet and the Protestant theologian, Jean Claude. The contest took place in Paris, March 1st, 1678, in presence of a select company, Catholic and Protestant. The question at issue (which was chosen by Bossuet and the lady) was the same as that which was debated between Cyprian and Novatian in the third century, and between Augustine and the Donatists in the fourth, *viz.*, What is the Church? The duel, which lasted five hours, was fought with singular vigour and dexterity, and, which is better, with uninterrupted courtesy and good temper. Bossuet took his stand on the infallibility of the Church as an incontestible axiom. Claude proposed that this fundamental dogma should itself be the subject of their examination. Bossuet refused, saying:—"We are both agreed that a true Church exists; that the Holy Spirit dwells in it, and that in the revelation of the truth He makes use of two external means, the Church and Scripture." It is impossible here to follow out the discussion. In the course of his argument Claude seems to have made an unguarded admission, of which his watchful adversary was not slow to take advantage. "Enough, Sir," exclaimed Bossuet, "there is then in your religion a point at which the Christian does not know whether the Gospel is truth or fable." At these words the company rose.

Each of the combatants paid a high tribute to the skill and character of his adversary. Bossuet says of Claude: "I had to do with a man who listened patiently, spoke with perspicuity and force, and knew how to push home a difficulty. He defended his cause with all possible skill, and so ingeniously that I feared for the hearers." Claude's appreciation of Bossuet was equally profound. "I shall always retain for him, not only the respect due to his rank, but the esteem and admiration claimed by his great gifts and talents. I recognize in him a quick and penetrating spirit, a clear conception, a correct and easy expression, and a lofty integrity. He painted his principles in the strongest colours and maintained them with all possible force." Each party drew up a report of the disputation, and when Louis XIV. forbad Claude's to be printed, Bossuet interceded for him and obtained the royal permission.

At this time the Scottish Covenanters again broke out into open revolt. Archbishop Sharpe was murdered May 3rd, 1679, and a month later, the royal troops under Claverhouse were defeated at Drumclog, a disaster which that commander, three weeks afterwards, avenged with merciless ferocity at the famous battle of Bothwell Bridge.

XX.

NATIONAL DECAY.

The extraordinary prosperity of the country of which we spoke awhile ago lasted but a short season. Possibly it may have been as much in show as in reality; but Louis's reckless and costly wars, and the prodigality with which the court was maintained, were enough to beggar any nation. When the campaigns were over and the winter set in, the continual marching of troops was a grievous burden upon the provinces. The victories of the sovereign were the misery of the people. Whilst the king was winning laurels they were sinking into poverty and servitude. The court was the most brilliant and luxurious in Europe; the ever-growing expenditure required to maintain the royal state and the royal mistresses and their families, forced Colbert continually to impose new taxes, which, as the clergy and nobility were, to a large degree, exempt, pressed more and more heavily on the industrial classes. Similar taxes in some other countries would have produced a revolt. The terrible salt tax was raised through farmers-general, who paid the king two millions of livres a year, and spent as much more upon revenue officers; the consequence being that whereas the manufacturer on the marshes near Aigues-Mortes sold the salt to the farmer-general at five sous the measure, the latter sold it again at sixteen livres. In some places the peasants could not eat their soup because they could not afford to buy salt to put into it.

A picture of the poverty of the country at this time has been left us by the English philosopher, John Locke, who spent two or three years in France on account of his health:—" Montpellier, May 1, 1676. The rent of lands in France has fallen one-half in these few years by reason of the poverty of the people; merchants and handicraftsmen pay [in taxes] near half their gains. Noble-land pays nothing in Languedoc, in whose hands soever it may be; in some other parts lands in the hands of the nobles pay nothing." At another time, travelling down the western side of the kingdom, he found many houses in the smaller towns fallen to decay, notwithstanding the country was entirely cultivated. The gentlemen's seats, which were numerous, also bore marks of decay. At Niort (August, 1678) the people complained bitterly of the quartering of troops. A poor bookseller's wife told the

English traveller that during the previous winter, 1200 soldiers had been quartered in the town, of whom she and her husband had two for their share. For these they had to provide three meals of meat a day, besides a collation in the afternoon, all of which it was their interest to give, and a fifth meal too, if it was demanded, rather than displease their terrible guests. These two soldiers, during the two and a-half months they were in the house, cost their hosts 120 livres.

As time went on things grew worse. Colbert had forced the country to an unnatural pitch of development, and its fall was rapid and hopeless. "The three fiscal terrors," says Michelet, who quotes a contemporary writer, Pesant de Boisguillebert, "the taxes, the excise, and the customs, were so many flaming swords. See there, marching through the villages, those wretched peasant-collectors who gather the taxes and are answerable for the amount. They go in bands for fear of being knocked down. But they can squeeze nothing out of nothing; the deficit falls on themselves. The royal officer seizes their oxen; if these are not sufficient, he takes the cattle of the whole village; after that he comes down upon the head-collectors themselves, who are cast into prison. The excise is a little worse. The clerks become dealers, and wage a relentless war against such of the merchants as buy their wine from the grower and not from them. Communication is everywhere hindered. Goods imported from Japan only quadruple their value, whilst produce which passes from one province of France to another sells for twenty-four times its original price. Wine bought at Orleans for a sou fetches 24 at Rouen. Thus the revenue clerk is six times more to be dreaded than the pirate or the tempest. France is uprooting her vines; the people drink only water." As the taxes of the excise destroyed internal industry, so the customs ruined foreign commerce. In this way the nation, and even Colbert, became the slaves of financiers, farmers-general, contractors, who were more powerful than the king himself. As has been intimated, the money thus wrung from the oppressed people was lavished on the basest objects. The duty on tobacco was given to Madame de Montespan to pay her debts at the gambling-table. "It was now," adds Michelet, "that the French people, over-worked and half starved, earned from the rest of Europe the epithet of *maigre*, and became familiarly known to their neighbours across the Channel by the name of Monsieur Frog."

XXI.
UNDER THE HARROW.

The temporary lull occasioned by the war with Holland was followed by a storm of increased violence. Liberty in trade and profession was now reduced within the narrowest limits. In 1680 Protestant women were forbidden to act as *sage-femmes*, and the next year Catholics serving in that office were authorized to receive Protestant infants into the Romish Church by sprinkling, whenever they believed such infants were not likely to live. At the same time the magistrates were directed to visit sick Protestants and to enquire in which religion they wished to die. The parliament of Rouen, in registering this edict, ordered physicians attending on sick Protestants to inform the magistrates whenever they considered death as impending. The magistrates abused their charge, and instead of putting the simple question to the dying persons, inveigled them by captious and embarrassing interrogations. Often the wife or the children were excluded from the room, and when the sick man became light-headed or unable to articulate, a procès-verbal to suit the case was prepared, the room being guarded by Catholics so that the family should not enter. The priests often forced themselves into the sick chamber and usurped the functions of the magistrates. But as they were less respected than these, they got many rebuffs, and in retaliation filed informations against those who opposed them.

January 26, 1681, the wife of Costils Brisset, a merchant, being ill, fell into a lethargy. The curé of the parish and his vicar,* in spite of the courteous opposition of the husband, made their way to the bedside and admonished the sick woman to think of eternity. Unable to obtain any answer they left the house, but in the evening returned with a magistrate, who, taking it for granted that entrance would be denied him, ordered the shop-door to be broken open. The husband, to prevent such an outrage, admitted them by a side door. Hereupon the magistrate ordered the husband and daughters to quit the house, and when the former asked the reason of so strange a proceeding, the judge drew up a charge against him of resisting the law. The next day the judge returned with some officers and other Catholics, made his way into the sickroom, and put the husband and daughters outside. A Catholic doctor declaring that the patient had revived for a short time and had called on the Virgin and St. Anne, the judge pronounced her a Catholic, and placed a guard of Catholic women over her. But the woman coming to herself denied that she had made any such confession, so that the vicar, who was prepared to administer extreme unction, was obliged to desist. Enraged at his failure, he exclaimed against the daughters, and raised a tumult which lasted till midnight. An information was laid against the family, who forwarded a counter-complaint to

---

* In France the parish-priest is called *curé*; and his curate, *vicaire*.

Paris. The sick woman dying, the Catholics remained in possession of her body and the matter ended.

The Reformed were forbidden to receive sick persons into their houses, and were ordered to send them to the hospitals. Protestant schools were still further restricted, and the masters prohibited from taking boarders. When they complained, they were told that no edict had ever granted them this permission. On an intendant returning this pitiful reply, the complainant rejoined that many liberties had been granted them of which, under various pretexts, they had been deprived, and that if they were also to be deprived of such as were not to be found in the edicts, it would only be necessary to forbid them to buy bread of the baker, corn in the market and meat of the butcher, and they would all die of hunger. "At these words," adds Bénoit, who was present, "I saw the intendant blush and turn away in silence."

The Protestant academies, so long renowned for learning and piety, Châtillon, Sedan, Die, Saumur, Montauban, were suppressed, Sedan being given to the Jesuits. Tradesmen and sailors of the Reformed religion were now forbidden to establish themselves abroad. Protestants were excluded from the offices of notary, usher and the like; and judges and advocates were forbidden to take Protestant clerks; and a little later all Protestants employed in the royal palaces were dismissed. Lastly, in 1685, just before the Revocation, they were forbidden to act as apothecaries, surgeons or physicians, printers or bookbinders, doctors of law or advocates.

Worship was restricted to temples with the presence of the minister, under pain of corporal punishment; and the parliament of Rouen forbad "Catholic school-boys, footmen and others, incapable of arguing on religion, from attending the preaching of Protestants." The magistrates' seats, fleur-de-lys, and royal arms, with which the temples had been ornamented, were at the same time removed. Ministers were forbidden to reside more than three years in one place, or within six leagues of any place where the Protestant worship had been interdicted. Attendance at marriages and baptisms was limited to twelve persons, who were forbidden to walk in procession. The registers were taken away and placed in the hands of the civil authorities. The provincial synods were suppressed. The last was held at Lisy, in the diocese of Meaux, in 1683. Allix, the pastor of Charenton, who presided, could not refrain from lamenting what seemed to him the approaching end of Protestantism. The royal commissioner brutally interrupted him: "If you continue thus to censure the king's commands, I will, with my own hands, throw you down from the pulpit."

There was still another edict by which a large number of Protestant families were reduced to beggary. Notwithstanding national prejudice and even direct enactments, Colbert, who knew that the king could not be so well served as by his subjects of the Reformed religion, had appointed them to many offices in the department of finance. Now, however, the tide became too strong even for this experienced and faithful minister, who for some time past had been falling into disgrace; and by a stroke of the pen Protestants were removed from all such offices. Colbert did not long survive the overthrow of his enlightened policy. His opponents in the cabinet procured his removal in 1683, shortly after which he fell sick. During his illness the king sent him a letter. "I do not wish," said the dying minister, "to hear any more of the king; let him only suffer me to die in peace"; and then, the approach of death dissipating the illusions of time, he exclaimed with bitterness, almost in the words of Wolsey, "Had I done for God what I have done for this man, I should have been saved ten times over, but now I know not what will become of me." So unpopular had this able and brave minister become that the people, if they had been suffered, would have torn his body to pieces.

XXII.
THE KIDNAPPING OF CHILDREN.

But we have not yet related the worst. If there was one measure rather than another which carried dismay into the homes and bosoms of Protestants, it was the law providing for the conversion of their children. In every part of the country boys and girls were systematically kidnapped. Although the age of conversion was fixed at fourteen for boys and twelve for girls, it was no uncommon occurrence for infants of a more tender age to be carried off to a convent, from whence, even if a magistrate's order was obtained for their restitution, the difficulties of recovery were almost insuperable. If these children in their prison-house did not yield to coaxing and promises, other measures were resorted to, sometimes of a cruel and revolting character.

In 1663, complaints were sent up from all quarters against the conduct of the clergy in this matter, especially in the province of Normandy, where the parliament had reduced the legal age of conversion to eight and seven years respectively. These complaints happened to reach the king's ear just when he was mortally offended with the Pope; and, in 1668, an Order in Council was issued, forbidding the removal of young children from their parents, and directing that such as were confined in convents should be restored. But the clergy were too sensible of the importance of gaining the children before parental influence had established itself, to give up the point. Jansenists and Jesuits alike rose against the Order;

and the spokesman of the clergy, the coadjutor of Arles, after the usual salutation of flattery of the monarch and the usual malediction of heresy, demanded the repeal of the obnoxious Order, declaring the limitation of age to be a matter in which it was the duty of the clergy to disobey his majesty. It was not, however, until 1681, that the Order was rescinded. The royal edict by which this was done, after setting forth " the great success of the spiritual inducements and reasonable methods which the king had employed to aid the divine motions in the hearts of his subjects of the R. P. R.," declared children of seven years to be capable of choice in the all-important matter of their salvation.

From this time the abduction of young children went forward more openly, and on a more extensive scale. "Words are wanting," says Benoit, "to describe the terror caused to the Protestants by this edict. Every pious father, and still more the mothers, tender and sensitive, felt as though they were stabbed to the heart, expecting every day to see their children torn from their arms. Who can imagine the feelings of a mother at seeing her daughters decoyed and carried off, to be enslaved by men and women whom she despised, and drilled into a religion which she abhorred? The Huguenot family lived in a state of perpetual alarm: the caresses and gifts of Catholic friends were looked upon as so many snares; and Catholic servants were regarded as the spies of the converters. The children were dazzled by the glitter of the State-worship, the lighted tapres, the images, the vestments. Any childish eagerness they manifested to see the Catholic spectacles was laid hold of as a divine call, the seed of piety. Too often the fears of the parents were realised. A Catholic neighbour, a nurse, still more an enemy, or a debtor who had been pressed to settle an account, gave information that a child had made the sign of the cross, or had cried because it was not allowed to enter the church where the altar was lighted up, or, seeing the Host pass by, had called it 'Le bon Dieu.' Such testimony was received with seriousness by the judges; and without affidavit or examination the children were handed over to the nuns. Courts of justice, too, acted on the maxim that in conversion from the Protestant to the Romish Church, right motives were always present and good faith observed; whereas in passing from the Catholic faith to the Reformed, fraud was always to be presumed."

So profound a grief was caused by the new law that the Protestant churches ordered a general fast, and Jean Claude petitioned the king against the intolerant edict. "Children of seven years," he said, "are incapable of a choice, which is the highest effort of the human mind;" and he declared that "the Reformed would suffer all kinds of ill, even death itself, rather than be separated from their children at so tender an age." Louis refused to see the pastor of Charenton; and the petition, which was presented through the deputy-general, Ruvigny, remained unnoticed.

XXIII.
MADAME DE MAINTENON.

About the year 1676, there entered on the stage a personage of very remarkable character. In France, more than in any other country, the secret springs of government have been worked by women; and of all those who, behind the throne, have wielded a power greater than that of the throne, the greatest has been Madame de Maintenon.

Françoise D'Aubigné was the grand-daughter of Theodore Agrippa D'Aubigné, the celebrated Protestant historian and friend of Henry IV., and was born in

1635. Her mother was a Catholic; and her father made little resistance to her being baptized in the Romish Church. Nevertheless, the Protestant ideas, which were the heirloom of her family, remained with her until her seventeenth year, when through the influence of an adroit instructress in an Ursuline convent in Paris, she embraced the Romish faith. Shortly afterwards she married the cynic poet, Scarron, who died in 1660. Ten years later she consented to take charge of a royal infant, the child of Louis XIV. and his mistress, Madame de Montespan, which was conveyed to her lodgings with the utmost secrecy; and afterwards all their children in succession were committed to her care. Louis himself paid her frequent visits, removed her in 1674 to the palace, and, on the fall of Madame de Montespan, created her Marchioness de Maintenon.

The king found the society of the new favourite indispensable to him. She was possessed of extraordinary qualities of disposition and intellect, which were set off by uncommon personal beauty. Her resources were endless, her discretion rare, and her conversation charming. The king found it more agreeable and soothing than anything else in the world. "She has," says Madame de Caylus, "taken the king into quite a new country, the region of friendship and conversation, without dissimulation and without restraint." To some extent she softened Louis's rugged nature. The queen, yielding to the loose code of morals which prevailed at the court, encouraged the intimacy. "The king," she said, "has never been so kind to me as since he listens to her. It is to her influence that I owe his affection."

In the midst of his debaucheries and of his schemes for aggrandising France and winning fresh laurels for himself, Louis seems to have discovered that the pomp and pleasures of the world were empty, and that something better was needed to satisfy his soul. Madame de Maintenon undertook to supply the void. She wrote to the ladies of St. Cyr: "When I began to see that it would not perhaps be impossible to contribute to the king's salvation, I began also to be convinced that God had conducted me to the court for that purpose, and to this end I limited all my views." It might be too much to say that in thus taking upon her to direct the king's conscience she was acting the hypocrite, but her love of power, the equivocal position she herself occupied, and the atmosphere in which she lived, forbid us to believe that her religious teaching was anything better than sentimental and sterile. What her attitude was in regard to the grand project of expunging Calvinism from France has been sharply contested between Protestant and Catholic historians. The former regard her as equally guilty with Le Tellier, Louvois, La Chaise, and the bishops; the latter deny the charge in toto. Until of later years the current of public opinion ran strong against her: on the death of Louis XIV. a reaction from the adulation which the nation had lavished on him had set in; the transactions of his reign were subjected to severe criticism; and Madame de Maintenon was fixed upon as the secret spring from which so many evils had flowed. Especially was she reproached with being one of the chief instigators of the Revocation of the Edict of Nantes. The publication of her 'Letters' in 1752-1756, and of the 'Memoirs of the Duke de St. Simon' soon after the Revolution, served to intensify this feeling.

Now, however, the pendulum began to swing back again. St. Simon, it was notorious, habitually dipped his pen in gall; and if his facts were true, his portraits were too often distorted. Still less would the 'Letters' bear scrutiny. Their history is curious. They were in the possession of Louis Racine, son of the poet, and were by him entrusted to La Beaumelle, a literary knight-errant and a Protestant. La Beaumelle seized the occasion of rendering odious the persecution under Louis XIV., and especially the name of Madame de Maintenon, whom, like many others, he regarded as a prime instigator of it. In accordance with a practice not uncommon at that day, he had the meanness to "cook" the 'Letters,' altering, combining, enlarging, and even fabricating some which had no claim to existence beyond a phrase or a sentence. The fraud was more than suspected during La Beaumelle's lifetime; but it was not until some five and twenty years ago that it was fully exposed. This was due to the discovery of the copy which had belonged to Louis Racine, to which notes, indicating the authenticity or otherwise of the several 'Letters,' were appended in his own hand. Comparison with manuscript copies of the 'Letters' in family collections confirmed the accuracy of his annotations, and the certainty of La Beaumelle's fraud. Under these circumstances we have refrained from using the correspondence, unless when supported by other evidence than that of La Beaumelle's collection. If, therefore, the reader should miss some well-known sayings of the lady, he will understand the cause of the omission.

But even if it cannot be shown that Madame de Maintenon joined in urging the king on in the fatal course of persecution, neither is it proved that she used her vast influence to restrain him. Ambition was her ruling passion, and to have opposed the Jesuits and the clergy on this point would have been the ruin of all her schemes. Once only is she said to have lifted a finger on behalf of the afflicted Protestants, her brethren after the flesh. At the Revocation, when the last and most violent turn was being given to the screw, she is said to have made some remonstrance against the severity with which the Calvinists were treated. The king's reply was: "I fear the indulgence you would ask proceeds only from a lingering affection for your old religion." "The king," observes Voltaire, "in the midst of his banquets, his conquests, and his mistresses, had no time to waste on the trifling details of such horrors."

If, again, Madame de Maintenon did not actually instigate or promote the tyrannical decrees of the government, she at least busied herself with personal conversions. In her zeal to bring her Protestant relatives into the Church, she was not at all scrupulous as to the means she employed: seeing fraud and violence in operation all around her, she freely made use of the same. "She was," says Madame de Caylus, "supported in this object by all the weight of the royal authority." She had a near relative, M. de Villette, who had distinguished himself in the naval war with the Dutch, to whom she held out hopes of promotion if he would consent to renounce his religion. Finding him impracticable, she sent him on a distant service, and during his absence contrived, under a false pretence, to get possession of his little daughter. The child (afterwards Madame de Caylus) related the story when she was grown up: "At first I wept much, but the next day I found the royal Mass so charming that I consented to become a Catholic, on condition that I might hear it every day, and that I should not be whipped." When the father returned to France his grief and anger were extreme, and he gave vent to his emotion in a letter to Madame de Maintenon. She replied, April 15, 1681: "Judge yourself, if, having used force to gain possession of your daughter, I am now going to be so foolish as to restore her. Rather give me the others for friendship's sake; for, if God preserve the king's life, in twenty years' time there will not be a Huguenot left."

In the case of another cousin, M. de St. Hermine, who withstood all her attempts to convert him, she proceeded so far as to shut him up in the Bastille; and when intercession was made to her to release him, she wrote in reply: "His wife has not communicated; it is her husband who hinders her; I cannot endure such mock conversions. It does not suit me to set M. de St. Hermine at liberty." As to her Catholic relations, she was willing that they should take advantage of the calamities of the Huguenots. (We shall soon come to the events which laid Poitou open to the harpies). Sept. 27, 1681, she wrote to her brother: "You cannot do better than buy an estate in Poitou or in the environs of Coignac; they will soon be given away, in consequence of the flight of the Huguenots."

In 1683 the queen died, and at the end of 1685, or in January, 1686, Madame de Maintenon became the wife of Louis XIV. The marriage was performed with the utmost secrecy. It took place at night, in a private apartment of Fontainebleau, the officiating priest being the curé of the parish. The new wife ardently desired that her rank should be acknowledged; but the union was hateful to the ministers, and the king himself had no wish to make it public. It remained a secret of State until after his death. She had now reached the highest step to which, as a subject, she could aspire; but rank and power did not bring happiness. She looked back with regret to the days of her youth, when, as she said, "Although I was poor I was contented and happy; I was a stranger to chagrin and ennui; I was *free*." Watching one day the gold-fish in the royal gardens, swimming uneasily round and round in the marble basin, she sighed:—"They are like me; they pine for their mud."

Contemporary writers give us an insight into the royal cabinet, both when the king and the marchioness were alone, and when the minister was present. In June, 1680, Madame de Sévigné writes: "I hear that the conversations of his majesty with Madame de Maintenon grow and flourish; that they last from six o'clock till ten.

His daughter-in-law, who sometimes pays them a short visit, finds them each in a great chair, and when her visit is over they resume the thread of their discourse. The lady is no longer approached except with fear and respect, and the ministers pay the same court to her as other persons do to them." The scene in the royal chamber is thus drawn by St. Simon:—" The king and Madame de Maintenon occupied each an arm-chair with a table before them at the two chimney-corners; she, on the side where the bed stood, the king, his chair backed against the wall, on the side of the ante-chamber door, with two stools before his table, one for the minister who came to transact business, the other for the minister's bag. Madame de Maintenon read or worked tapestry, hearing all that passed, for the king and the minister conversed aloud. She seldom offered a word, more rarely one of any moment; but the king often asked her opinion, when she replied in measured terms. Seldom or never did she appear moved by anything, still less interested for anyone; nevertheless the minister let nothing fall which came from her lips. If the king inclined to her opinion, the minister stopped there and went no further. If the king inclined to a different opinion, the minister tried to embarrass him, when the king would hesitate and ask Madame de Maintenon how the matter seemed to her. She would smile, profess her incapacity, utter sometimes one sentiment, sometimes another, then return to the minister's opinion, and in the end determine matters in such a way that three-fourths of all favours and promotions, and again three-fourths of the remaining fourth of all that was done by the ministers, was disposed of by her."

XXIV.
THE DRAGONNADE IN POITOU, 1681.

The Peace of Nimeguen, as has been already said, left Louis free to devote himself to the conversion of his Protestant subjects. Three years after the treaty was concluded, the Dragonnades were put in motion. This was not altogether a new invention. Something like it had been employed against the Protestant inhabitants of Béarn in the early part of the century; and in 1661 the city of Montauban was harried in this way four months. It was at the suggestion of Marillac, intendant of Poitou, that this terrible engine of arbitrary power was now invoked to quicken the conversion of that province. This was more than four years before the revocation of the Edict of Nantes, which act indeed, as we have all along seen, was not a single blow, but the culmination of a long series of measures for the extirpation of heresy. Louvois was delighted with the suggestion, and wrote back, March, 1681:—" His majesty has learnt with great joy how large a number of Huguenots continue to be converted in your department. It is his will that in the billeting of the army the greater number of horse-soldiers should be assigned to the Protestants. If in the assessment they are rated at ten, you must give them twenty." Marillac lost no time in letting loose on the Protestants all the troops at his disposal; the soldiers rushed on their prey like a pack of furious wolves. Such a comparison is no exaggeration, as will be evident when we consider the character of the French soldier at this time.

The army had not long returned from Holland and the Rhine, where, as we have seen, they had been flushed with slaughter and surfeited with licence. Thus steeled in his nature and brutalized in his habits, the dragoon was the fittest tool in the world to be used by absolute power for the coercion of men's consciences. "Between him and the Huguenot household on which he was quartered there was no sympathy. He hated their religion; he could not understand their seriousness and gravity; and he was determined to overcome what he took to be their pride and obstinacy. To them, on the other hand, he was the incarnation of horrors. The children fled from him; the husband remained gloomy; the wife and daughters, shocked by the noise, coarse behaviour and obscene songs, and choked by the fumes of tobacco, could with difficulty conceal their disgust. He used them as his slaves; he treated them far worse than brute animals. The wife showed her horror of popery more than the husband; she was the pillar of the family."

The quartering of the soldiers in Poitou was effected in a loose and arbitrary manner, in some cases not even a billet being sent with them, only a verbal order. The intendant had a sergeant, whom he directed to go from house to house, bidding the dragoons live sumptuously; and he charged the officers to cane such as spared the Huguenots, and to send their names to him. Nothing was good enough for these fellows; they wasted the provisions and threw them away; they washed their horses' feet in the wine; and when they could not obtain what they wanted, they broke up and set fire to the furniture. Many Huguenots were beaten and dragged to prison, where, as the judges would order them no rations, the jailers refused to provide them with food, and they would have starved but for the charity of the towns-people. The priests urged on the soldiers:—" Courage, gentlemen, it is the king's will that these Huguenot dogs should be harried." "I pursue the Huguenots," wrote the curé of Soubise, "and they dare not utter a syllable;

you take them by the bill like a snipe, and if they say a single word, you pack them off to Rochefort." The soldiers did the work of the priests. At Niort they stuck crucifixes into the muzzles of their guns and thrust them into the faces or chests of such as refused to kiss them.

The women were not spared; they seem indeed to have come in for the heavier share of suffering. A mother, with an infant at her breast, whose offence was that she had said that she would never go to Mass, was beaten, thrown down, and dragged by the neck, her tormentors paying no regard to the cries of the child. The husband of a young wife, endeavouring to shield her, was bound to the bed, and his wife insulted in his presence. Her cries brought her mother, on whom the wretches fell with such violence, that, supposing they had killed her, they took to their heels. It should here be said that, as if in mockery, it was forbidden to the soldiers to take life. Accordingly the offenders in this case were brought before the intendant; he only laughed at the affair.

Some dragoons, unable to induce a young woman to recant, made a fire of faggots and threatened to throw her upon it. Her cries brought her father and brother; the soldiers took all three and cast them on the flames; their clothes were burnt and their bodies scorched. Fire, indeed, seems to have been a favourite pastime. One poor fellow was held near a furnace until his sabots caught, when the fear of being slowly burnt to death wrung from him a promise to go to Mass. But as soon as he was released he retracted. Being taken back to the fire, he again gave way; and this cruel game was repeated until the sufferer could hold out no longer.

A householder named Pierre Bonneau had a captain and trumpeter quartered upon him, with their valets and three horses. On their departure they were succeeded by twenty-three dragoons, who, to find out where he kept his money, made him stand before a large fire until he confessed. These in turn were replaced by twelve others, who dragged the poor man by the hair to the grate, where they scorched him for twelve hours.

Such acts exceeded even the measure of compulsion recognized by the governor, the Duke de Vreville, who, when a deputation from the Protestants waited on him and asked what he was pleased to call violence, answered:—" When soldiers burn the feet of their hosts, I call it violence." The duke's actions did not belie his words. Notwithstanding he professed to have brought a royal message that the king desired the conversion of the Huguenots should be effected without constraint or violence, he sent his guards to the town of Foussai, where they used such forcible arguments that in five days 300 of the Reformed made abjuration.

At Vouillé the curé dragged a Huguenot into his house, forced him down on his knees, and making him place his hands on a book, declared him to be a Catholic. It was in vain the Huguenot protested and carried his complaint before the intendant; all the answer he received was that the testimony of his opponents was more worthy of belief than his.

The soldiers meeting Protestant labourers on the road or at the plough, drove them into the churches, pricking them like oxen with their own goads, and when this was not enough, riding over them.

A complaint being made to the intendant that a child of eight years had been taken from the shop of his father, a locksmith, and bribed by the offer of a farthing to promise to become a Catholic, the intendant replied that he had himself examined the child, who had assigned a good reason for his change of religion, *viz.*, that what he saw and heard at church was much better than what he saw and heard at the preaching. The child's mother persisting in her refusal to part with him, was sent to prison.

The reader may have heard of a singularly ingenious and diabolical method of torment invented at this time to subdue the Huguenot spirit. We mean depriving the victims of sleep. When other means of conversion failed, they were told that they would not be allowed to sleep any more until they abjured. Relays of soldiers were provided, who relieved one another, and who, says Benoit, "by drums, cries, oaths, and violently breaking up the furniture, compelled the poor wretches to keep awake. If this was not enough, they pinched, pricked and jostled them, and even hung them up by cords." "The strongest men amongst the dragoons," says another witness, "took hold of them and walked them incessantly up and down, or tickled and tossed them to and fro, for hours and days together. When the sufferers grew so weary and faint as no longer to be able to stand, they laid them on a bed and continued to tickle them as before." "There were," adds Benoit, "men who resisted this kind of torture twenty-four days; others sank at the end of three or four." Many, however, yielded at once, or after a brief trial; and many became imbecile or raving mad.

Besides these violent means, others were employed to break the spirit of the Protestants. The assessment at which the Catholics were rated for the king and the municipality' was reduced, and the New Converts wholly exempted, whilst the taxes were doubled on the Protestants. Collectors who refused to lend themselves to this injustice were removed or imprisoned.

The authorities were but too zealously supported by the Catholic inhabitants. When a temple was pulled down, the people piled up the doors, windows, chairs and benches, and crowning the stack with the Bible, set fire to it, dancing round with savage joy. They ploughed up the cemeteries and swept the bones into the river.*

Petitions to the king were drawn up in every place, but neither sergeant nor judge could be found to make a procès-verbal. At length two Protestant noblemen succeeded in obtaining an audience of Louvois at Fontainebleau. The minister received them at first in a jaunty manner, as though what they had to complain of was a trifle; but when they showed him the gravity of the case, and offered their heads as a guarantee of the truth of their statements, he became more serious. They told him that although they could not recognize as judges the governor or the intendant, yet to prove their confidence in the justice of their cause, they would accept the Bishop of Poitiers and the king's lieutenant of the province. They related a flagrant instance of cruelty which had just happened, and which appeared to make some impression on the minister, for he promised to speak to the king on their behalf. A few days afterwards, however, when the deputies returned to Fontainebleau to hear his answer, he received them with effrontery, and said:—"Gentlemen, I blush for shame at having reported your complaint to the king, because his majesty assures me the statements you have made are a pure invention." The noblemen withdrew in silence, and the next morning were served with a royal order to depart from the town. The fact is Louvois had kept the king in entire ignorance of what was being perpetrated in his name. Being minister of war, he had the control of the marching and quartering of the troops,

---

* In the like spirit were the abbeys and churches destroyed at the Revolution. At the demolition of the splendid abbey of Cluny, when the last massive buttress had been battered down, the people made a pile in the public square, of the paintings, statues of wood and carved work, and setting fire to it celebrated their triumph by dancing round with yells and shouting.

and the orders he sent down emanated only from himself.
It is difficult to conceive how such a state of secrecy could
be maintained, for the court was full of lords, military
officers, and ecclesiastics, who well knew what was going
on, and amongst whom the actions and success of the
booted missionaries in Poitou were a common topic of
conversation, at table, on the promenades, in the galleries,
and even in the ante-chamber. Nevertheless, they appear
never to have been allowed to penetrate within the royal
sanctum. To mislead the king, troops were sent into
Dauphiné and some other provinces, where they were kept
under strict discipline, and he was made to believe that the
same order was maintained in Poitou.

To prevent further deputations to the court, Marillac
now directed his violence against the Protestant nobility,
sending dragoons to their mansions to practise pillage and
debauchery. Many nobles and others prepared to quit the
kingdom, upwards of 400 of whom were arrested: some
of them were imprisoned at La Rochelle, where they were
so starved and ill-treated that the Catholics were moved
to tears and brought them food. But Marillac had over-
acted his part. The court had been assured that only the
indigent and worthless would flee; and when it was found
that the country was being drained of its strength, orders
were sent down to release the prisoners and send home the
fugitives. No fewer, it is said, than 3000 families quitted
France in the course of this year, amongst whom were a
large number of sailors of the western ports, reckoned the
best seamen in the kingdom. This was a loss which could
not be borne in silence; and Marillac, accordingly, was
recalled from his intendancy, and fell into disgrace. He
might be seen hanging about the court, with his head
down and his hat over his eyes, shunned by all except the
Jesuits. Four years later, however, when the rest of the
kingdom was treated like Poitou, this unscrupulous prefect

became again a necessary man, and was appointed intendant of Rouen.

The storm of persecution lasted from March to the end of September. It was not confined to Poitou, but extended into the adjoining provinces of Aunis and Saintuoge, where the intendant of La Rochelle and the governor of Brouage rivalled Marillac in violence and cruelty.

The outrages which have been related, with many others for which we have not space, produced a profound sensation in Protestant countries. England, Denmark, Prussia, and Holland held out a hand to the emigrants, offering them a safe asylum, with many civil immunities. In England, the Archbishop of Canterbury and the Bishop of London were specially commissioned to provide for their spiritual and material wants. Sir George Wheler, who had travelled through France for the purpose of collecting reliable evidence, drew up a statement of the grievances of the Protestants, a copy of which he presented to every member of parliament. Along with other Englishmen, he saw that the extirpation of heresy in France was only the prelude to a second Armada, a new crusade for the extinction of the Protestant religion in Europe.

The Romish Church boasted that during this year, 1681, in Poitou and the adjacent provinces, 33,000 converts had been gained from Calvinism. How many of these recanted is not stated, nor how many became a prey to remorse. Some took to their bed in anguish of spirit; some put an end to their own existence. "You might see them," says Benoit, "fall down in the road, tear their hair, beat their breasts, and cry for mercy. When two of these wretched beings met at the foot of an image or in some act of Catholic devotion, they joined in sobs and bitter lamentations. Husbands might be heard reproaching their wives, and wives their husbands, as the authors of their common misery. And," he adds, "as soon as the persecution relaxed there were scarcely any who did not return to their ministers and protest against the violence by which they had been compelled to abjure."

The hour of retribution for the enormities perpetrated in Poitou, and for the numberless acts of wanton cruelty which had preceded and which followed in other provinces, came at last. It was a saying of the heathen philosopher, Plutarch, " The mill of the gods grinds slow "; and more than a century elapsed before the day of reckoning came. The religious fanaticism of the Revocation, and the social fanaticism of the Revolution, were a counterpart of each other; they differed only in name. La Vendée and Nantes border on Poitou; and in 1793, Carrier, a greater monster even than Marillac, was sent down from Paris to establish the Reign of Terror in that quarter. Supported by the sans-culottes of the city, he set to work on Vendéans, royalists, and moderate republicans, first with the guillotine, then with musketry and artillery, and then, as these means were not rapid enough for him, he instituted the infamous noyades. He had the victims bound hand and foot, and forced on board barges with loose bottoms, called valve-boats (*caisseaux à soupape*), from which they were dropped into the Loire; and at last, as time was still lost in preparing the *soupapes*, men, women, and children were embarked on larger craft, driven over the sides of the vessel at the point of the bayonet, and shot down as they struggled in the water. This was accompanied with revolting barbarities. Fifteen thousand persons, of all ages, perished by the guillotine, the fusillades, and the noyades, or by cold and hunger, or the diseases engendered in the crowded prisons. These horrors lasted nearly four months. As in the seventeenth century, Louis XIV. and the Jesuits were ready to outrage all rights and perpetrate all enormities to render France Catholic; so in the eighteenth century, Carrier said, on entering Nantes, "We will turn all France into a cemetery rather than fail to regenerate it in our own way."

The internal state of this devoted province, during the dragonnade which we have been describing, will be best understood from the personal narrative of one who played a conspicuous part in the heroic resistance.

XXV.
JEAN MIGAULT.—PERILS IN THE CITY.

Jean Migault was reader in the church of Moullé in Poitou, a few leagues from Niort; he was also public notary of the town, and he kept a small school. The decree which deprived the Protestants of their employments took away both his office and his pupils, and compelled him, with his wife and eleven children, to remove to Mougon, another small town in the neighbourhood, where the consistory offered him a slender pittance as reader and secretary. The curé of this place tried to deter him from settling there, telling him it would be at his peril if he came into his parish. Migault and his wife had for a long time anxiously watched the gathering of the dense clouds which now burst on every side. With a heavy heart he saw his Protestant neighbours, one after another, give way before the storm, many at the mere rumour of the approach of the dragoons. Such, indeed, was the panic fear caused by this terrible cavalry, that it is said a single soldier riding into a town with some scraps of paper in his hand was sufficient to induce the first families in the place to abjure.

There seems to have been a regular mode of procedure when a regiment entered a town. They began by demanding for a superior officer fifteen francs a day; for a lieutenant, nine; for a private soldier, three. If these demands were not promptly complied with, they seized and sold the furniture, the cattle, and the implements of trade. In these sales regard was seldom paid to the real value of the articles; they took whatever price was offered; if one thing did not bring enough money, they sold more to make up the deficiency. Thus cruelly spoiled, those who would not apostatize were compelled to seek refuge in flight, which they were obliged to do under cover of darkness, and then had no resource but to wander in the woods without food and almost without clothing. There, mothers might be seen with their little ones, separated from their husbands, driven wild by terror and distress, and still flying when no longer pursued.

Jean Migault and his wife, foreseeing the danger, sent away their children, and in trembling trust in divine help awaited the issue. On the 22nd of August, 1681, as the Protestants of Mougon were dispersing from their worship, they were alarmed by the appearance of a troop of cavalry, commanded by an officer notorious for his cruelty, who, advancing at a gallop, posted his men in the temple-yard. Scarcely had the Migaults reached their house than a quarter-master rode up, and without alighting asked in an imperious tone whether they intended to turn Catholics. They assured him nothing should ever induce them to change their religion. He was presently succeeded by the commanding officer, who sternly demanded what sum they would give him per day during his stay in the place, giving them to understand that the more they gave him the fewer would be the soldiers quartered on them. They told him they had no money at all to give him. Regardless of this assurance he proceeded to search the house. As soon as he had departed two soldiers presented themselves with their billets. Having stabled their horses they called for dinner, ordering as much as would have sufficed for twenty men. Whilst the food was being prepared two more arrived, and soon afterwards five others, who, pretending the hay was bad, abused their host with oaths and blasphemies. Then they all began to order luxuries, which it was impossible to obtain in that little town. Migault telling them that if they wanted such articles they must send to Niort, they gave him leave to go out and seek for a messenger.

Being thus momentarily free, Jean went immediately next door, which was occupied by two Catholic ladies, the devoted friends of himself and his family, and between whose house and his own there was a secret communication. Whilst he was enquiring of these ladies for some one to send to Niort, six soldiers rode up to the door and asked for Migault's house. The ladies pointed it out to them, and then returning to their poor friend urged him to fly, as his only chance of safety, for they knew the curé would leave no means untried to accomplish his destruction. They promised to take care of his wife, and even assured him that before the end of the day they would find means to withdraw her also from danger. Thus saying, one of them led him by a back street into a garden belonging to them, enclosed within high walls, where she left him, locking the door after her. Here he remained several hours, a prey to a thousand fears on account of his wife. He fancied he even heard her calling upon him to rescue her, gently reproaching him for having abandoned her at the time when she most needed his support.

In truth, Madame Migault's sufferings were greater even than her husband's imagination had painted them. She was in a delicate state of body, not having recovered her strength since the birth of her infant, her twelfth child. But nothing could move the soldiers to pity. As soon as they suspected that Migault had given them the slip, they began to wreak their vengeance on his wife. Weak as she was, and exhausted with cooking for and attending on them, upon their calling for more wine she had dragged herself to the cellar to fetch it. One of the soldiers now went in search of her, and, violently striking her, brought her back into the dining-room; then, telling her that in her weak state she ought to keep as warm as possible, he set her in the chimney-corner, whilst his comrades heaped up the fire, feeding it with the articles of furniture which were in the room. This they did until the heat became so great as to oblige them to relieve one another every few minutes. "But this admirable woman," says her husband, "knowing in whom she had believed, did not for an instant lose her tranquillity, but committed to her Saviour all that could disquiet or torment her." At length, overcome by her sufferings, she fainted, and became insensible.

The good Catholic ladies had not been unmindful of their promise. They had let themselves into the house, and witnessed her torments, which they had made every effort to avert and to mitigate. Throwing themselves at the feet of the officer, they besought him to release her, but in vain; the officer was as obdurate as his men. But God had provided a deliverer. A few days before, the curé had been called away, and his place supplied by his vicar. This good and merciful man was with a company of friends when he was informed of what was going on in Migault's house. He hastened to the place, and succeeded in rescuing the wife from the hands of her persecutors, but not until he had engaged to restore her to them if he could not, by argument, induce her to embrace the Catholic religion. Her charitable neighbours, who heard the engagement, were resolved to leave the vicar no opportunity of fulfilling it. They took their poor friend, more dead than alive, into another room, and, when he would have followed, told him that in the state in which she was it was absolutely necessary to leave her alone with them for a short time of repose. Without losing a moment they hurried her through the secret door into their own dwelling, and carrying her up into the garret hid her under a heap of linen. Then returning to Migault's house they presented themselves calmly before the vicar, who demanded, "Where is my prisoner?" "She is safe from the hands of these monsters." "Ah, well," he replied, "may the Almighty grant to her and her husband His merciful protection;" and without staying to speak again to the soldiers he left the house. It would be difficult to describe the rage of the dragoons when they found their victim had escaped. They examined every corner of the house, and then proceeded next door, where they searched the very garret in which Madame Migault was hidden, all but the heap of linen under which she lay.

The ladies hastened to let Migault know of his wife's safety, and directing him to take the least frequented road to the neighbouring forest, promised to bring her to him at nightfall. This they did; and the two fugitives found refuge in a friendly château on the way to Niort. But they could not close their eyes the whole night; every sound seemed to them the trampling of steeds, and every voice like the threats of soldiers seeking their destruction. Unable to feel secure so near to Mougon, they proceeded two leagues further to the house of another friend, where after some days, hearing that the dragoons had left the town, Migault's courageous wife ventured back to their desolate home; and after a while, finding all quiet, they again took up their abode there, collected their children, and began life afresh, sad, yet rejoicing.

Only two weeks, however, had gone by when they heard that the troops had returned again to the adjoining parish of Thorigné. It was chiefly inhabited by Protestants, who had stood their ground during the former tempest; and the curé, as great a bigot as the priest of Mougon, now instigated the soldiers to fresh acts of violence in order to break the spirit of the people. Very few, however, apostatized, and the forest was again crowded with fugitives.

This alarming news determined Jean Migault at once to seek safety in flight; and on the last day of October he went into the country to borrow a horse on which to carry three of the younger children. Meanwhile, the curé of Mougon, being determined to destroy the Migaults and the other two Protestant families in his parish, who still stood out, sent to the commander of the troops in Thorigné to make a sudden march into the place.

Whilst Madame Migault was waiting her husband's return, she saw the soldiers enter at both the gates. Snatching up two of the three children she made her way through the private door into the adjoining house, where she found the good ladies as ready as ever to shelter her. They hid her and her two children in a corn-loft. The soldiers, led by the curé, searched both dwellings, but without success. For some hours Madame Migault remained concealed in the loft, anxiously revolving the fate of her husband, and listening to the distant cries of the little boy she had left, which reached her through the party-wall, calling on her for help. By and bye his cries ceased. She afterwards learned that when he had for some time endured the harsh treatment of the soldiers, he contrived to slip out into the garden, where he was observed by a poor woman, who had the compassion to take him home. Madame Migault's mother, who also was in the house when the dragoons appeared, found refuge in a neighbouring dwelling, where she gathered up four others of the children, who were wandering in the streets.

The soldiers sold the beds and such clothing as they did not want, and with the help of a carpenter, sent by the curé, destroyed all that remained of the furniture, broke down the cupboards, and demolished the doors and windows, leaving the house a complete wreck. Madame Migault, through the wall, heard the work of destruction as it went on.

In the course of the night, all being silent, she ventured to quit her hiding-place, and to betake herself to the good woman who was nursing her youngest child, then only twelve weeks old. She found the infant in a dying state. Unable to remain beside it, she took a last kiss, and hurried on to the Protestant minister, hoping to hear tidings of her husband. It was late in the evening before Migault returned with the horse, and as he drew near his home he was met by an acquaintance who informed him that the soldiers were searching for him. Dismounting, he proceeded on foot, and, favoured by the darkness, stole unobserved into the nurse's house. From her he learned that his wife had gone to the minister; in his turn, taking a last kiss of his dying child, he hastened to join her.

Some kind friends found for them their two eldest children and the little boy; and with this portion of their family they set out for the château of Grand Breuil. The mother was mounted on the horse, carrying the youngest child in her arms; two others were in panniers slung across the animal's back; the two eldest walked with their father. The owner of the château was a Protestant lady, Madame de la Bessière. She was absent, but as soon as she heard that Migault's family had taken refuge in her house she sent them the keys, and insisted on their using her corn and wine, and burning her wood. Here they had the supreme satisfaction of seeing all their children with the grandmother, again brought together in safety.

Towards the end of the year the persecution slackened, and Jean Migault was free to leave the château and settle at another small town, Mauzé, where he resumed his school; "and where," he adds, "it pleased heaven to give us the love of the inhabitants."

XXVI.
THE HOUSE OF THE NEW CATHOLICS.

Meanwhile more secret and specious methods for bringing back the lost children to the Mother Church were always in active operation. As already said, religious houses for the conversion of the Protestants were founded at an early period of the century. In the houses intended for women, the following rules were laid down:—" Wives may be received without the consent of their husbands, children without that of their fathers, servants without that of their masters." "If the pupils commit a fault they are to be gently admonished; if the fault is repeated they are to be reproved with charity; if they persist in disobedience, the lady superior is to impose suitable penances; if they are incorrigible their safety is to be provided for." In the *Règlemens de Visite* is the following article:—" If it should happen that any insane persons should be found among the *New Catholics*, we strictly forbid the sisters to have any intercourse with such, except by express command of the lady superior."

It seems to have been no uncommon circumstance that the treatment to which the inmates were subjected should lead to insanity. Mademoiselle Des Forges, daughter of the king's *maitre d'hôtel*, was taken to the House of the New Catholics in Paris. The harshness with which she was treated, the forced abstinence, the sleepless nights, which she endured at the hands of the sisters, soon deprived her of reason. After she became insane they made her sign a paper of abjuration, and she was dismissed from the convent. Hardly had she returned to her family, than she threw herself from the window of the third storey, and falling on the pavement was killed.

The House of the New Catholics in Paris (in the quarter of the Palais Royal) was the model institution for the kingdom. It had a dependence at Charenton, five miles distant. The two houses were under the direction of a lady superior and ten young ladies volunteers, most of them of noble families. It was endowed by Louis himself, who took a personal interest in keeping it supplied with inmates. The researches which have been made of late years in the archives of the government have brought to light strange revelations of the way in which the house was replenished.

April 24, 1685, the Marquis de Seignelay, secretary of state, writes to the lieutenant of police :—" His majesty commands you to place in the *New Catholics* the infant children of the woman Rousseau. As to her children who are older, his majesty leaves it to you to take such means to convert them as you shall think proper." October 24th of the same year :—" His majesty commands you to send to Charenton, take Madeleine Risine, and place her in the *New Catholics*." Again, January 24, 1686 :—" The king is aware that the wife of Trouillon, apothecary of Paris, is one of the most stubborn Huguenot women in his dominions, and as her conversion might be followed by that of her husband, his majesty commands you to arrest her and take her to the *New Catholics*."

The king did not lose sight of these unhappy women after he had shut them up; he manifested a personal interest in the progress of their individual conversion. January 27, 1686, the secretary of state wrote to La Mère Garnier, the lady superior :—" The king being informed that Madame Le Cocq receives all sorts of people to the hindrance of her conversion, his majesty desires you to inform her that it is his will that she should see no one, and requests you will take care that this is attended to." Again, February 12th of the same year:— "It is the king's will that none of the women or girls of the R. P. R. should receive any visits or even letters unless read by you beforehand." Five days later the secretary of state wrote again:— "His majesty being informed that some of the women refuse the instruction given them, commands you to warn them that such conduct is displeasing to his majesty and will compel him to take measures which will not be agreeable to them." These private mandates being insufficient, the king, on the 8th of April, issued a public ordinance:— "His majesty, wishing to enable women of the R. P. R. to be reunited to the Catholic, Apostolic and Roman religion, has given orders for receiving many of them into the House of the New Catholics in Paris, in which house his majesty is informed they are sufficiently instructed in the duties of the said religion. But finding there are some who refuse to hearken to the said instruction, and who still remain in a guilty obstinacy, his majesty commands the lady superior of the said house to warn such, and all others who shall be received into the house, that if within a fortnight they do not become reunited to the Church, they are to be reported, so that his majesty may see what is proper to be done with them."

In 1686 the houses in Paris and Charenton contained together 224 pupils. Of these at least twenty-five made their abjuration under the hands of Fénelon, who was for many years superior of the convent. Sixty others proved refractory, forty-four appearing to have set themselves to weary out their persecutors. Sixteen of the sixty were removed to other convents, and nineteen consigned to fortresses; ten were expelled the kingdom. A lady named Paul, discharged from the house in May, 1686, was brought back in July. A second time discharged, no better converted than at first, she was again brought back (May, 1690); and as Fénelon refused to receive her the third time, she was sent to the castle of Loches, with its dungeons one below the other, "the cradle of the Plantagenets," where, at the end of three years of prison discipline, she once more signed her abjuration.

Some of the pupils were wealthy, kept waiting-maids, and paid large sums for their entertainment. Such ladies were in request. La Mère Garnier writes to the secretary of state, praying him to send from the provincial convents some great ladies and noble damsels whose conversion was tardy, in order that she might expedite it. Such as were thought to be able, but did not keep up their payments, were reported to the court, and their names sent to the police, with notes such as these:— " Make her pay"; " Mademoiselle Moriset will pay when she receives her money from the canon of St. Germain-l'Auxerrois, who owes her between four and five thousand livres; get the money from the canon." The poor were unwelcome. In 1686 only one-tenth of the whole number were received without payment. One of the laconic notes remitted to the police runs thus:—" Has nothing to pay with; send her elsewhere." Two Turkish children of the ages of six and seven, who were admitted into the *New Catholics*, May, 1685, being without means of payment, the police, in February, 1687, received this memorandum: —" Send them to the General Hospital," a jail-infirmary, described by Michelet as "that vast lazar-house of 7000 souls, a gulf of diseases, vice, and licensed crime,—the Gomorrah of the dying."

XXVII.
FÉNELON, SUPERIOR OF THE *NEW CATHOLICS*.

Fénelon, so well known as Archbishop of Cambray, was in 1678 appointed superior of the House of the New Catholics. He was twenty-seven years of age. His gifts and character seemed to point him out as singularly fitted for such a post. To an intellect of the highest order he joined an uncommon suavity of manners and a deep experience in spiritual things. As soon as he entered the house he constituted himself the father, counsellor and friend, both of the sisters and of their pupils. To the latter he gave rules and catechisms, listened patiently to their doubts and objections, and consoled their troubled spirits. His rule was in striking contrast to the rough and harsh treatment which the Protestant women in many similar institutions received from their teachers and directors. In the list of the inmates of the house, in December, 1686, the following note stands opposite some of the names:—"These have been very harshly treated in the country; their spirits are exasperated; they need to be quieted."

Whether, in being removed to the *New Catholics*, lacerated hearts were always in the way to be healed will appear very doubtful to those who have read the last chapter; and, except by his own personal conduct, Fénelon seems to have done little to mitigate the cruelty inseparable from such an institution. With all his natural amiability and his rich spiritual experience, he suffered himself, alas! to become a tool for accomplishing the purposes of the government. He possessed an inflexible will, and he regarded all toleration of heresy as a deadly sin. Instead of being in advance of his age, as has been usually supposed, he was in reality as bigoted as the Jesuits, or the bishops. He thus gives his opinion of the Reformation :—" What do we see on all sides? An unbridled curiosity, a presumption which nothing can daunt, an incertitude which shakes the foundations of Christianity; a tolerance which, under the cloak of peace, falls into incurable irreligion." Again, when he thinks of the infant daughters of Protestant parents, it is with the poignant lament that " children so tender, so innocent, should suck in poison with their mother's milk "; and it is only through unquestioning confidence in the divine judgment, that he can endure to see in " the parents God has chosen for them, the very cause of their ruin." These were the principles on which he acted. In his approval of compulsion in the conversion of heretics, as being laudable, obligatory, indispensable, he does not come behind Augustine, whose treatment of the Donatists did so much to commit the Roman Church to that course of persecution in which she has ever since persisted. " Nothing," says Fénelon, " could be more cruel than a lax compassion which should tolerate contagion in the flock." " We must," he adds, quoting Augustine, " employ a medicinal rigour, a terrible gentleness, and a severe charity. The vigilance of the shepherds must destroy the wolves wherever they are found." He held fast these maxims to the end. Not long before he died he wrote :— " Observe, the Church never makes schism; innovators desire to dwell in her communion, and she cuts them off; the separation comes from them, not from her; they excommunicate themselves. It is their stubborn, incurable unteachableness that separates them."* A supposed instance of his advocacy of better principles is often

---

* He applied these principles, not to the Protestants only, but to all whom he believed to be in error. He carried his intolerance of Lady Guion to the extremest limit.

referred to, *viz.*, the charge to the Pretender, known by his adherents as James III. In writing to James, he is made to say:—" No human power can force the impenetrable intrenchments of the liberty of the heart. Violence can only make hypocrites. When kings meddle with religion, they reduce it to slavery." But M. Douen has shown that the treatise in which these words are found, *viz.*, the Supplement to *The Examination of Conscience on the Duties of Loyalty*, was not written by Fénelon, but is from the pen of a biographer.

Whilst then Fénelon's gifts and experience marked him out as singularly adapted for his delicate mission, it must not be overlooked that in accepting such an office he had made himself part of a vicious and iniquitous system, which no honest man could support with impunity. If those over whom he exercised the magic of his intellectual superiority and his spiritual gifts had only been free to hear or to refuse as they listed, or to withdraw from his influence, the case would have been different. But behind the sweet instruction and genuine sympathy of the teacher there stood the barred door of the convent, the sharp penances, the harsh usage, and behind all these the dungeon, the General Hospital, exile. Those who are acquainted with Fénelon's writings, who have had their spirits soothed and settled by his experience, and carried upwards on the wings of his devotion, will be startled thus to find that he was a persecutor. But history is full of such contradictions, and men are to be judged by the age in which they lived. The men who are before their age are few; and it would have been more wonderful for an ecclesiastic under Louis XIV. to have held the principles of the nineteenth century, than for Fénelon, with all his piety, to have shown any toleration for heretics. Odious as the character of a persecutor is to us at this day, we must remember that the Archbishop of Cambray had for companions some of the brightest ornaments of the Church: Augustine, St. Bernard, Calvin, Sir Thomas More.

XXVIII.
CLAUDE BROUSSON.

From Paris the scene changes to Languedoc.

Claude Brousson was born at Nimes, in 1647. His parents, Protestants, committed his education to a tutor, who inspired him with generous sentiments, and set before him the Scripture worthies as examples for his imitation.

He chose the profession of an advocate, which he practised with integrity and in a liberal spirit, taking no fees from his poorer clients. At the same time he diligently attended to his religious duties as an elder in the Church. He entered the Mi-party chamber of Castres, which was transferred in 1670 to Castelnaudary,* and in 1679 was incorporated with the parliament at Toulouse, or, in other words, suppressed.† Brousson followed the retreating chamber, to plead before the parliament the cause of his oppressed brethren. The position of a Protestant advocate at this time was not enviable. A contemporary says:—" I was in Languedoc when the chamber of Castelnaudary was suppressed and the Huguenot advocates were ordered to go to Toulouse. They were in a consternation not to be described, declaring the king had sent them to slaughter. Two of

---

* The motive was obvious. In Castres the Reformed were in a majority; in Castelnaudary their worship had been interdicted.

† The French parliaments, of which there were ten, were not legislative bodies, but superior tribunals. That of Toulouse consisted of four courts of judicature. One of these, the grand chamber, to which the Protestant causes were now transferred, was composed of a first and four other presidents, twenty-four episcopal and other ecclesiastical dignitaries, and nineteen lay counsellors.

them, in fact, coming one day out of the palace where the parliament was held, were hanged up in the palace court without trial or any form of law."

The efforts of the clergy were at this time especially directed against the Protestant temples, of which, from 1679 to 1683, one hundred were condemned by the parliament of Toulouse alone. In this unequal struggle the Protestants had no outward help to depend upon but the eloquence of their advocates. Of these Brousson was the ablest and the most intrepid; his boldness astonished even his clients.

XXIX.

DEMOLITION OF THE TEMPLE OF MONTPELLIER, 1682.

Montpellier was one of the strongholds of Calvinism, and in 1682 it was resolved that the temple in that city should be demolished. A pretext was easily found.

Paulet, a Protestant minister, had abjured and had been rewarded with a pension, but his wife and his daughter Isabeau remained faithful to their profession. The daughter, a child of ten or eleven, was in consequence carried away to a convent at Teirargues, where means were used for her conversion. Being found intractable she was at the end of twelve months restored to her mother. Five years afterwards another attempt was made to overcome her resolution, but with no better success. This girl was selected as a convenient lever for the overthrow of the temple. The father confessor of the nuns at Teirargues, who had twice changed his religion, forged two documents, the one setting forth that when Isabeau was in his convent she had consented to return to the Church, the other a formal abjuration of Protestantism, both purporting to be signed by her own hand. These were accompanied by an allegation that a Protestant pastor had admitted her to communion after being advised of her conversion. An information was filed against the pastor and the young lady; they were tried, convicted, and sentenced to a severe penalty.

The bishops were eager to proceed at once from the condemnation of the offenders to the destruction of the temple. But the parliament reserved this crowning act for an august event which was about to take place, *viz.*, the assembly of the States of Languedoc.

The Duke of Maine, an illegitimate son of Louis XIV., had been appointed governor of the province, but as he was a child, the Duke de Noailles, the lieutenant-general, was sent to open the states in his stead, with an especial charge to use diligence in the suppression of the Protestant religion. To mark the occasion, the entry of the duke into the city was celebrated with unusual pomp. One of the first acts of the states was to confirm the sentence of the parliament on Isabeau and the pastor, and to decree the destruction of the temple, with the prohibition of Protestant worship within the city. The Protestants appealed against this iniquitous decree, four of the ministers and several elders waiting upon De Noailles to obtain permission to continue their religious services until they should have submitted their cause to the king in council. The request was refused; upon which two of them remonstrated on the illegality of the proceedings, in which those most nearly interested had not been cited or heard in their defence, and indignantly asked whether his excellency was aware that there were eight hundred thousand Protestant families in the kingdom?* The only reply the duke deigned to give to this question was to turn to the officer of his guards with the

---

* This estimate is much too large.

words: "Whilst we wait to see what will become of these eight hundred thousand Protestant families, you will please conduct these two gentlemen to the citadel." One of the duke's attendants, either from pity or shame for his master's honour, interceded for them, and the order was changed into confinement to their own houses; but the four ministers were sent to prison.

The same day the duke and the intendant wrote to Versailles for a royal mandate for the execution of their decree. The Protestant consistory prepared a counter-petition, which they sent to the king by M. Planchet, a gentleman of Montpellier. The duke's courier arrived first, and when Planchet presented himself, and announced his errand, he was at once marched off to the Bastille. The royal mandate was as imperative as the most zealous prelate could desire, requiring the demolition of the temple within twenty-four hours, with a private message from the king to the duke: "And you will give me pleasure if you can accomplish it in two." On receiving the mandate, De Noailles sent for the consistory, and enquired whether their messenger had returned from Versailles and what orders he had brought. On their replying that he had not yet returned, the duke produced his own order and asked them whether they would themselves undertake the work of demolition and so save the materials. Stupefied with so insulting a question, they could scarcely stammer out that they desired to be spared the indignity. "In that case," said the duke, "I shall be happy to do it for you"; and he immediately gave orders to the city consuls* to despatch fifty or sixty masons to the temple.

As soon as the duke was informed that the men had arrived, he set forth, followed by his suite and a body-

---

* The municipal officers were so called in some towns of France.

guard. Alighting from his horse he entered the building, and addressing himself to the masons who occupied the aisles, gave the command: "Courage, my friends, fear nothing; put your hands to the work and labour hard. Vive le roi!" At this signal they rushed to the pulpit and dragged it down before him. He then went out and re-mounted his horse, but waited to see the roof dismantled and to give orders to place sentinels round the building to prevent accidents from the falling materials. When the demolition was complete, a calvary was erected on the site. The states returned thanks to the king for his grace in signing the mandate, and received for answer: "I can say that I only await from heaven a recompense for my zeal for the good of religion."

The great object of the prosecution being gained, it remained to justify the proceedings. False witnesses were brought forward to swear to Isabeau's handwriting; but she proved that at the time when it was pretended she had signed the two documents, she had not learned to write, and asking for a pen she wrote under each of them: "I affirm that the above signature is not written by my hand." On the pretended evidence, however, the parliament declared the young woman guilty of the crime of relapse, and condemned her to the *amende honorable* (public penance), and banishment from the kingdom. But her steadfastness had alarmed her judges, and they feared that once out of their power she might publish a narrative of her trial which would cover them with shame. They therefore obtained from the king an order to convert her sentence into perpetual imprisonment, that is to say, to substitute, contrary to all rules of justice, the heavier for the lighter penalty. Seeing that the poor girl staggered at the prospect of a life imprisonment in a loathsome dungeon, the priests followed up their advantage by lavishing caresses upon her with offers of money and of an advantageous marriage. Her resolution gave way; she abjured, and at their instance signed a petition to the king, in which she confessed all she had hitherto denied and prayed for pardon. Hereupon the demolition of the temple in Montpellier was declared to be according to law.

XXX.
THE TEMPLE OF MONTAUBAN, 1683.

The temple at Montpellier being demolished, it was resolved to proceed against the temple which still remained in Montauban. The Reformed Church of that city had been one of the most flourishing in the kingdom. Its Protestant inhabitants had shed their blood for their sovereign. But already their college had been transferred to the Jesuits, and the principal temple pulled down. The charges on which the proceedings were founded were false and of the most frivolous description; nevertheless, the ministers and other officers were carried off to Toulouse, where the trial was to take place before the parliament.

All the bishops and a multitude of priests were present, and the court was crowded. Brousson made a singularly skilful and eloquent defence, invalidating both the grounds of the prosecution and the character of the witnesses. Extraordinary as was his skill, his intrepidity was even greater. He finished his harangue with a masterly apology for the Reformation. The procurator-general, interrupting him, asked if he thought he was in a temple. "Yes, sir," he replied, "in the temple of Justice, where it is always permitted to speak the truth"; and he proceeded to demonstrate with the same freedom and cogency of argument, the purity and spirituality of the Protestant faith and the loyalty of its professors, the beauty of his countenance no doubt adding grace to his words. The court was agitated; the bishops whispered together in evident confusion. A Catholic advocate rose and exclaimed: " It is in vain that we seek to close the temples of the Huguenots whilst their doctrines are permitted to be preached in open parliament." The procurator-general, in his reply to Brousson, tauntingly said : " It must be acknowledged these are fine ideas, but the Pretended Reformed do not carry them into practice." When the trial was over he advanced towards Brousson, offering his hand and saying: " I do not despair of yet seeing you a good Catholic." " You see, sir," replied Brousson, " how I am beginning to be so." A Jesuit, who sat behind Brousson during his speech, was deeply impressed, and said to him in an earnest tone: " You have greatly edified me; yes, sir, I have been greatly edified." And when the crowd issued from the palace, Roman Catholics were overheard saying to each other: " We never thought their religion was such as we have heard to-day."

Brousson's eloquence, however, could not save the temple. It was pulled down June, 1683, public worship within the city interdicted, and the ministers forbidden to exercise their vocation for all time to come. His defence had the effect, however, of mitigating the penalties usually inflicted.

Brousson held instructions for the defence of fourteen temples against which proceedings had been taken. It had been customary to bring forward such cases one by one, in order not to alarm the Protestants. Brousson persuaded the deputies of the fourteen churches to demand that their causes should all be brought forward at one time, which being done, he demurred to the jurisdiction of the parliament in such matters, and appealed to the king. The prosecution was dismayed at this stroke of policy, and deliberated whether to arrest the audacious advocate, or to buy him over with the offer of a seat in the parliament. But Brousson was equally proof against bribes or threats, and the matter was suffered to drop, the fourteen temples being allowed to stand until the Edict of Revocation was promulgated.

XXXI.
BROUSSON'S PROJECT OF PASSIVE RESISTANCE, 1683.

For some months past the churches of Languedoc and the neighbouring provinces, seeing the net drawn closer and closer round them, and that nothing but ultimate ruin was to be looked for, had resolved to strike a blow for liberty and life. They had for many years borne the weight of oppression with such unresisting submission that Huguenot patience had passed into a proverb. But the destruction of their temples, the banishment of their ministers, the intrusion of a Catholic commissioner into their synods, and innumerable other vexations, were too grievous any longer to be borne. Accordingly, in January, 1683, a secret conference was convened, consisting of deputies from Poitou, Languedoc, the Vivarais, Dauphiné, and the Cevennes; and the better to elude suspicion, they met in the very Catholic city of Toulouse itself, and in the house of Brousson.

A Project or Declaration was drawn up, consisting of eighteen articles, the purport of which was peaceable resistance to the royal authority in matters of religion. Brousson, who was the soul of the enterprise, set forth the grounds on which it was undertaken in the following words, written many years afterwards:—" I did not doubt that his majesty's wrath would at first blaze forth against those who resisted his will; but I was convinced that as soon as ten or twenty persons had suffered death and sealed their profession with their blood, the king would judge it improper to push the matter further for fear of producing a wide breach in his kingdom." It was resolved in the articles of the Project that on a given day public worship should be resumed in all the interdicted temples, or, where these had been demolished, in their immediate neighbourhood, and that new temples should be built where it should be judged proper. In the services, the Psalms were to be chanted on bended knee. A form of service was prescribed for those churches which had been deprived of their pastors, and the pastors who remained were charged not to leave the kingdom without permission of the Church. The day fixed for this bold demonstration was June 27th, and a general fast, with prayer, was ordered in anticipation. These resolutions were sent round to all the churches. At the same time a memorial was forwarded to the government, which, besides the usual *apology*, or reasons for dissent from the Romish doctrine, contained a loyal and humble protestation of love and respect for the king, and prayed that he would recall the declarations and edicts which had taken away from the Reformed both their civil rights and the free exercise of their religion. "What," they asked, "is our situation? If we show the least resistance, we are treated as rebels; if we obey, the king is deceived into the supposition that we are converted."

Brousson, who saw that his presence at Toulouse could no longer be of service to his people, but that he might be of use to them at Nimes, removed thither in June, just before the demonstration took place.

XXXII.
FAILURE OF THE PROJECT.

The Protestants were greatly divided on this adventurous step. The more timid or moderate party, who were also the more numerous, when they received the Declaration, exclaimed: "It is too bold; such language could scarcely be uttered if we had two hundred strong places in our hands; we shall be treated as rebels, and exterminated." The more confident and eager, on the contrary, who were known as "the Zealots," condemned the Declaration as too timid and moderate. "Half measures in rebellion," said they, "are fatal: to arms, to arms!" The effect of these divisions was to retard by some weeks the execution of the Project; and when the time came there was no concert, some churches meeting on one day, some on another, and many not at all.

In some places the meetings went off peacefully. At St. Hippolyte, 3000 persons assembled in a field, unarmed. The preacher took for his text the appropriate words, "Render to Cæsar the things that are Cæsar's, and to God the things that are God's," which he expounded so judiciously that the curé himself had nothing to object against the sermon.

In other provinces, as Dauphiné and the Vivarais, the meetings took place with a very different result. The Catholics, alarmed, declared that the Huguenots were in insurrection, and that the old wars of religion were returning, and they flew to arms. The Protestants were but too ready to accept the challenge, and made preparations for defence. D'Aguesseau, intendant of Languedoc, hastened into the Vivarais, and entreated the people to remain quiet, and to abstain from public worship in the forbidden places. His character and arguments prevailed for a time; but Louvois reproached him for his clemency to "those scoundrels;" and in the end he, too, was driven to adopt severe measures.

In Dauphiné no methods of conciliation were tried; the infamous St. Ruth was despatched with three regiments of horse to put down the meetings. At the village of Bourdeaux, near Die, the pastor was preaching in the temple on Sunday, when he was told the troops were approaching. He immediately left the pulpit and placed himself at the head of his people, who, in anticipation of an attack, had provided themselves with arms. They divided into two companies, which took different roads. The preacher, with a hundred and fifty men, was met by St. Ruth, whom he hotly attacked. He was driven back, but entrenched himself behind the low wall of a vineyard, where he held the royal troops at bay for two hours. Most of the Protestants were slain; but the warlike pastor and a score of followers effected their retreat to some farmbuildings, where they again made a courageous stand. The dragoons surrounded the barn and set fire to it; all the Huguenots perished, singing Psalms. The other division of the insurgents was easily overcome. St. Ruth took sanguinary vengeance, compelling one of the peasants to be the executioner of his comrades, and torturing and putting to death such of the leaders as he could lay hands on. The court was alarmed at the news of the disturbance, and published an amnesty, from which, however, so many were excluded that it was little more than a mockery, and the executions went forward.

A young advocate was broken on the wheel in front of his father's house. A citizen of Saillans, who had been present at a meeting, was tortured and hanged. Two young men of Dieu-le-fit, for the crime of being seen with guns beside a fountain, were put to death. A nobleman, of Montelimar, was promised a pension if he would recant.

Being proof against this temptation, terror was resorted to, and he was thrice brought out for execution; but faith sustained him through all, and, like the rest, he suffered death with Christian fortitude.

The effect of D'Aguesseau's influence on the inhabitants of the Vivarais was dissipated by the arrival of fugitives from Dauphiné, and the mountaineers armed themselves. The Duke de Noailles hastened up, defeated the insurgents, and hanged the prisoners on the trees. Isaac Homel, minister of the village of Soyon, being proscribed, took to flight, accompanied by another preacher, who, like himself, had been distinguished by his opposition to popery. The latter was arrested, but unable to endure the refining fire, purchased his life by abjuring and by betraying Homel. Homel had not only warmly supported the Project, but had counselled the taking up of arms, and preached at interdicted places and armed meetings. In his enthusiasm he looked for a speedy interposition of the divine hand, which should be stretched forth and miraculously deliver the Church out of her afflictions. He was seventy-two years of age, and his fate excited the pity even of those who condemned him. But a few years before some Jesuits had been put to death in England as traitors (in Titus Oates's plot), and now the members of that order in France clamoured for an exemplary punishment on Homel. He was broken alive on the wheel, his torments being prolonged by the clumsiness of the executioner. He died October 20, 1683.

From the Vivarais the duke descended into the plain, where the excesses committed by his troops drove the Protestants, who had hitherto remained quiet, into preparation for resistance. Louvois sent down orders, October 3, "to quarter the soldiers on the malcontents throughout the province; try the culprits; raze the houses of those who were taken in arms, and of those who did not return to their homes; demolish the temples; and inflict a terrifying desolation."

St. Hippolyte, where the gathering held in pursuance of Brousson's Project had passed off so quietly, did not escape. On the arrival of the troops the old men, with the women and children, fled up the mountains, which half encircle the town, leaving behind the young and strong men to the number of six or seven hundred. These, cajoled by the promises of the royal officers, submitted; nevertheless, some of them were executed. One, to save his life, abjured; but when another, who stood by with bound arms, reproached him for his cowardice, the poor fellow was so stung that he withdrew his recantation, and he also suffered the penalty.

Many other instances of cruelty, and of endurance by the people of these provinces, have been preserved. We give only two.

The Marquis of La Tourette, having induced a man, named Romieu, to abjure under the threat of being put to death, Romieu's wife was so indignant at her husband's weakness that she refused to see him. The marquis, in revenge, shut her up in a room of his château, declaring that if she did not follow her husband's example she should rot in prison. He took from her the child at her breast, and withheld from her every kind of comfort. In despair she tore up the sheets and curtains of her bed, tied them together, and let herself down by the window. But her weight was too great for the frail cord, and she fell on the rocky ground, where she lay bruised and motionless. Seeing she was still alive, the marquis sent her back to prison.

The Marchioness Desportes, who had been a persecutor in her earlier life, had latterly behaved with more humanity; but when she saw all around her emulous of effecting conversions, she too was eager to have a share in the glorious work, which would commend her at the same time to God and the king. In her château she kept a garrison of a hundred men, under the command of a captain, named St. Hilaire, a wretch exactly fitted to execute her plans. He seized the recusant peasants and carried them to the castle, where he tried, by turns, the effect of promises, threats, insults, and ill-usage. When he could not succeed by any of these, he let them down by ropes to the bottom of an ancient roofless tower, where he kept them until they had given the desired promise, or had wearied him out. When he received from any of his prisoners a promise to go to Mass, he compelled them to sign a declaration before a notary that they had made the change of their own free will.

These and similar atrocities were prolonged through the winter, 1683-4, which was unusually severe. They long rankled in the memory of the people; and the recollection of them, twenty years afterwards, fanned the flame of the revolt which is known as the Camisard War.

At Nimes the moderate party drew up a memorial to the king; and a deputation of noblemen, ministers, and others, waited on the Duke de Noailles to present him with a copy, October 15. He received them in the most supercilious manner, ordered them to be searched, and sent them off to prison. He wrote to Louvois: "Astonished at the effrontery of these miserable creatures, I did not hesitate to send them all to the citadel of St. Esprit." The provost would have thrust them into a filthy dungeon, but they sturdily refused to enter, protesting they would rather die than that the rights of men should be so violated in their persons.

At the same time, to overawe the city of Nimes, and to get possession of certain disaffected persons, amongst whom was Brousson, the duke sent for a large detachment of dragoons. In order to take the victims by surprise, the troops entered the city before daybreak, October 28, and, with drawn swords, went from house to house. Through the vigilance of their friends, however, they all received timely notice; one, a minister, being saved by the generosity of a priest, who hid him in his house. Brousson and another received a private intimation that they would not be meddled with if they would turn informers, which of course they refused to do. Having thus missed his prey, De Noailles made a proclamation forbidding, under severe penalties, the harbouring of the proscribed persons. It is to the honour of the citizens that not a traitor was to be found. Brousson heard the proclamation as he stood near the window of a house in which he had taken refuge; and during the night, through the partition which separated his room from that of his hosts, he heard the husband and wife in earnest consultation what was to be done with him. Their first resolve was to deliver him up, but recoiling from so infamous an act they agreed to ask him to leave them as soon as possible.* The next evening, therefore, having disguised himself, he ventured into the streets, where he wandered two or three days and nights, anxiously watching for an opportunity to leave the city. Tracked, stopped, interrogated, and let go as by a miracle, he at last discovered an open sewer, near the Jesuits' college, into which he crept, and making his way through it to the city fosse outside the Porte des Carmes, succeeded in reaching the Cevennes. Travelling with all speed he arrived in Switzerland in November, and settled for a time at Lausanne. We shall meet with him again in the course of our history.

The preacher who was saved by the priest, and a colleague who also escaped, were executed in effigy.

* Another version of the story is that the husband was for betraying him, but was withheld from his purpose by his more generous wife.

Figures were dressed up to represent them, and a gibbet being erected in the market-place, they were hanged upon it by the public executioner, the magistrates and soldiers attending at the ceremony in their official costume.

XXXIII.
CAUSES OF THE FAILURE.

Brousson's Project of Passive Resistance was a noble venture, but it was doomed to failure from the first. Even if the Huguenot camp had not been divided, and there had been a universal and simultaneous action, it could not possibly have succeeded. To lay his hand on his sword when threatened was instinctive in every Frenchman, Protestant as well as Catholic. The unresisting endurance, which had given rise to the proverb of Huguenot patience, had been the result of loyalty and prudence, rather than of religious principle. There may possibly have been many who held sacred Christ's commands on this point, but history is almost silent regarding them. We have met with one such instance only previous to the Revocation. One of the most strenuous and courageous of the pastors, in his opposition to the iniquitous decrees of the government, was Jacques Fontaine, a native of Saintonge. In the fervour of his indignation at the sufferings of his brethren, he concluded that the only remedy was for the Protestants, as in times past, to take up arms in a body and fight for their liberty. This happened not long before the Act of Revocation. A special meeting of ministers and elders, to consider what course should be adopted, was held in the neighbourhood of Royan, to which, out of regard to the sufferings he had endured for conscience' sake, Fontaine, although not yet ordained, was invited. Except himself, all present, four and twenty in number, declared that the Gospel forbids violence, and does not permit, in the utmost extremity, any other alternative than flight. Fontaine energetically protested against what he described as a mistaken and timid policy, and used all the arguments he could devise to rouse the spirit of the meeting. He was met only by a sharp rebuke, and the conference separated without coming to any decision. Unhappily, many of those who had counselled non-resistance gave way in the hour of trial, and were the first to abjure. The intendant of Rochefort warned the people to save themselves by changing their religion before the dragoons arrived. A general meeting of the Church was held at Royan on the occasion, at which Fontaine again pleaded earnestly for resistance, but with so little acceptance that he was in danger of being informed against by his own people. In their reply to the intendant, the Protestants declared that whilst they would obey the king in all matters consistent with their duty to God, nothing should induce them to deny their faith. "But," says Fontaine, "when the dragoons arrived they told a different story, the chief men amongst them turning out such arrant cowards that they trod one upon another in their struggle to get first into the church to make recantation." Whether the fear of death was too strong for these poor men, or, as may have been the case, the pacific doctrine they had vaunted went no deeper than their understanding and was not based on conviction, we cannot say.

Brousson might have known that the trial to which he was exposing his people was too hard for them. He wore a sword himself;[*] he was aware how ready the mountaineers, especially, were to repel force by force. When the temple at Montauban was threatened with demolition,

[*] In 1676, in Languedoc, the travellers whom Locke met (mostly clad in purple cloaks) were all provided with pistols, even such as rode to their fields to overlook their labourers. 'Life,' I., 122.

ten thousand Cevenols are said to have offered to come down to the rescue. It is true Brousson contemplated a purely passive resistance, but he did not take the necessary means to secure it; not a word of admonition to the people to come unarmed to the meetings is contained in the Project. Could it be that Brousson had heard of the success with which the peaceable resistance of the Quakers in England, twenty years before, had been crowned, and that he looked for a similar result? Charles II.'s Conventicle Acts pressed heavily upon that people, especially in London, where their meetings were broken up, and fines, stripes, and the prison put in requisition. When locked out of their meeting-houses they met in the street, and when the buildings were demolished they held their worship on the ruins. In vain the musketeers dragged them away and beat them, and the troopers rode them down and all but killed them; nothing could induce them either to defend themselves or to submit; and the soldiers had to confess themselves beaten. Unarmed resistance, with trust in God, must always in the end be far stronger than any force of armed resistance. But the case of the English Quakers differs so widely from that of the French Huguenots, that it is difficult to draw a parallel between them. Amongst the former there were but few men of the sword, and these few early and thoroughly accepted the peaceable teaching of George Fox. As a Church, they had no antecedents such as the Calvinists had. They were all so imbued with Christ's doctrine of the forgiveness of injuries and the ungodliness of war, that they were a whole society of peace-makers, and they needed no orders from head-quarters to abstain from resistance, nor any plan for concerted action. They were in no sense a political party. Although some, like Lilburne, may have preferred a republic, and others, like Robert Barclay, have mentally clung to James II. as their rightful sovereign, these predilections were all sunk in the absorbing work of directing men to Christ and building up His Church. Alike, under the parliament, Cromwell, Charles, James, or William, they were careful to eschew all political parties, and to approve themselves loyal subjects, obedient to every demand compatible with their duty to God. Unlike the Huguenots, too, they had lost no adherents through unfaithfulness. After "more than thirty years of suffering, not a single Quaker had been induced by it to abandon his profession." But there is another difference in the circumstances of the two Churches which must not be overlooked. The persecution of the Quakers was cruel and infamous, but it was not to be compared with that of the Huguenots. The Church of England was intolerant, but its intolerance was mild compared with that of Rome. In England, too, there was a public opinion; in France, at that time, there was none. If the same enormities had been perpetrated here, there would have been another revolution. But although the weight of persecution under which the Huguenots groaned was grinding and crushing to the last degree, it was, as we shall abundantly see in the course of this history, not so heavy but that by the grace of God, men, women, and even children, were found to bear it. If the whole Protestant Church in France had been animated with the same spirit as the Quakers, may we not believe Brousson's prediction would have been accomplished, and the king's arm been paralysed?

XXXIV.

THE PERSECUTION IN SAINTONGE, 1683-5.

The failure of Brousson's Project, and the events which followed in Languedoc and Dauphiné, rendered the condition of the Protestants in other parts of France worse if possible, than it was before. We must turn again to the maritime provinces between Nantes and Bordeaux,— Aunis (in which lay La Rochelle), Saintonge and Poitou. This territory had always been a stronghold of Calvinism: prior to the Revocation, as we have seen, it suffered more than any other part of the kingdom. The storm burst forth again in the year 1683. A commission was sent into Saintonge to complete the demolition of the temples and the suppression of public worship. At the head of the commission was Du Viguier, a penniless gambler, who had already distinguished himself in the work of persecution in the adjoining province of Perigord. Assisted by two Récollet monks whom he took with him, and by the curés and the civil authorities, he shut up the temples and threw the ministers into prison. As usual, the authorities were zealously seconded by the Catholic nobility. The Countess de Marsan, who owned the town of Pons, caused all who withstood her to be imprisoned, beaten, or otherwise maltreated. She shut up a man named Jacques Pascalet in her château, in a cell where no air came but through a hole at which the servants burnt damp hay and straw. Unable by this means to break his spirit, the servants whirled him round a table until he fell to the ground insensible; when to bring him to himself they struck him on the elbows. This was repeated until death released him. The countess laid her hands especially on the children, some of whom resisted her manfully. Petitions against her and Du Viguier were sent up to the king, and although no answer was received, the court, considering that matters had gone too far, sent secret orders to relax the persecution.

Notwithstanding the many thousand conversions of which the government boasted in these three maritime provinces, this part of France was foremost both in constancy and zeal. The proportion of those who abjured was smaller than in any other province; and the faithful were distinguished by the sacrifices they made to attend public worship. Some travelled fifty or sixty leagues to hear a minister. The ministers, on their part, spared no labour in feeding the flock, holding themselves ready night and day to preach, teach, baptize, and administer the bread and wine. Their fidelity brought upon them a double portion of suffering.

XXXV.
THE BELL OF LA ROCHELLE.

Before the hurricane had spent itself, La Rochelle had once more to endure the blast. Finding the priestly converters could effect nothing, the intendant marched the troops into the city, 200 dragoons and 800 fusileers, and packed the four pastors off to the Bastille. To show their abhorrence of the Protestant worship, a farce was enacted by the Catholic population. When the temple was demolished they passed judgment on the bell, as a principal offender. It was first flogged, then buried; after which, a *sage-femme* and a *nourrice* being provided, it was disinterred, declared to be new-born, and made to promise never again to do service for the heretics; it was then baptized and sold to the parish of St. Bartholomew. But when the governor demanded payment of the parish, he was told that the bell had formerly been a Huguenot, but that it was now a New Convert, and that, in accordance with the law in favour of New Converts, it was entitled to three years' credit in the payment of its debts.

XXXVI.
THE IMPRISONMENT OF JACQUES FONTAINE.

The state of affairs in these maritime provinces during the time of which we have been speaking, will be best understood from the personal narration of one of the sufferers. Of the multitude of such narratives to which this eventful epoch gave birth, one of the earliest is that of Jacques Fontaine, the intrepid and martial preacher spoken of in a former section.*

He was the son of one of those dignified and eloquent ministers who adorned the Protestant Church in the middle of the seventeenth century, and was born at Jenouille, in 1658. Jacques inherited his father's talents, and distinguished himself at school and at the college of Bordeaux, where he studied sixteen hours a day, Before he was old enough to enter the ministry the hand of persecution was busy in Saintonge.

In 1684, at the age of twenty-six, he took up his residence at the village of Vaux, where the temple had been levelled to the ground. Compassionating the forlorn condition of his neighbours, he invited them to join him in his family devotions. These meetings were of course conducted in secret, and many were the shifts employed to elude observation. They were not interfered with until Palm Sunday. Fontaine was absent at the time, having gone to keep the festival with some friends at a distance. His neighbours came to his house as usual. Finding he was not there they retired to a wood, where one of them, a mason, conducted the service. On the Thursday they assembled again to the number of seven or eight hundred, and on Easter Sunday as many as a thousand were present. They were betrayed by an attorney, a renegade

* See *ante*, p. 95.

Protestant: the mason was arrested and dragged to Saintes, a distance of fifteen miles, at a horse's tail. The poor fellow was so plied by the soldiers with threats and arguments that he recanted; but presently afterwards, recovering himself, he was overcome with remorse and fell into despair. Fontaine, who had returned home, so prayed with, exhorted and comforted him, that in the end he abjured his abjuration. His example saved many others from a like fall.

The next step on the part of the authorities was to get possession of Fontaine. Being informed that the provost and his archers were on the road to Vaux, Fontaine sent round to warn the people in order that they might hide in the woods: he himself refused to flee, saying that if he were to do so he should be like the hireling who fled at the sight of the wolf. Preparing a bundle of clothing and other necessaries to take with him to the prison, he knelt down and prayed fervently for grace and strength; he then went to bed, and slept soundly until he was awoke at daybreak by the provost and the archers knocking at the door. Hearing his servants tell the soldiers that he was not in the house, he opened the window and called out that he should soon be ready to go with them. With him the soldiers carried off a ploughman. The party entered Saintes in the afternoon, where a crowd presently assembled, some leaping for joy, and crying out: "Hang them! hang them!" whilst others stood aloof and wept. Fontaine and the ploughman, who was in a state of terror, were taken to the prison.

Fontaine turned his imprisonment into an occasion of spreading the truth and glorifying God. "After supper," he says, "I accosted the jailer in a polite manner: 'Sir, I am subject to a great infirmity, in regard to which I hope you will deal kindly with me. I am so accustomed night and morning to pray aloud to God in my family and wherever I am, that if I ever omit imploring divine help, I am all the day as peevish as a hermit; in all other respects you will find me the most agreeable and most jovial guest you ever had. I wish, however, to show you all possible respect, and will not annoy you by praying in the common room, but shall be well contented with this little corner for my chapel.' The jailer replied: ' You will not find me so black a devil as I am said to be; but all your cant will not make me drop the keys out of my hand.' ' Very well,' said I, ' I am delighted that we agree so well; I leave you the keys of the gaol whilst I go and seek those of eternal happiness.' Thus saying, I fell on my knees in my corner, without calling any one to join me, but had not uttered three words before my companion, the ploughman, ran up and knelt beside me, and another Protestant prisoner was very glad to join us, The next morning I did the same, and so continued ten or twelve days, by which time the ploughman was so strengthened by my prayers, that the promises and threats by which he was tempted could make no impression on him. The jailer and his wife, who were accustomed to a very different kind of lodgers, were astonished to find that there were people in the world who counted it an honour to be prisoners, and could only suppose we were disordered in our intellects."

When Fontaine had been in prison about ten days, the provost and his archers set out again on their round to apprehend those who had been at the meetings. The more timid fled as before; but Fontaine's example had so emboldened many, that more than 150 came to meet the provost, and presented themselves as ready to answer for their conduct. There was no room in the prison for so large a number, and the provost declared he would take only twenty, and that the rest might go their way. Hereupon there arose a generous strife as to who should be of the number. The archers were amazed, and did their utmost to intimidate them, but their arguments and menaces were only like bellows to a flame; the more violent their language, the more eager did the people show themselves to be taken like sheep for sacrifice. At length the provost decided to leave behind the most zealous, and to choose his twenty from those who kept in the background. But he gained nothing by this refinement of cruelty; all were equally determined to suffer and to suffer manfully. The chosen twenty were leashed in couples like hunting dogs, and tied to the tails of the soldiers' horses. Everyone bade adieu to his wife and children in a firm voice; the wives, too, saw their husbands led away without a tear.

In the prison, at Saintes, they were visited by the Protestants of the town, who brought them bedding and food in abundance. When in the evening Fontaine went to prayer, they all knelt round him. Seeing that the bishop and his chaplain and attendants were indefatigable in their attempts at conversion, he introduced their arguments into his prayers, with a refutation of the same, so that the priests made no way with the prisoners. Foreseeing also that he himself would soon be removed as the obstacle to their conversion, he provided that when he was taken away, one of them should occupy his place, and so on so long as two should be left together.

Being brought before the court, he was examined on the charges on which he had been put in prison, and also on having in the prison given offence to the Roman Catholics and prevented the conversion of the Protestants. France has always had a name for the impartial conduct of judicial trials, with a large liberty of speech to the accused; and although the president of the court (the seneschal) used every effort to frustrate justice, he could not prevent Fontaine, who defended himself with singular coolness, firmness and skill, from confounding the witnesses one after another. Even the king's advocate, who had vehemently accused him, was moved by the words with which the prisoner concluded his defence: "I am ashamed to have to plead before Christians as the Christians formerly pleaded before pagans. Consult, I pray you, your own heart; if God should send you some affliction, what would you think of a religion or of a man who should impute it to you as a crime to have cried to God out of the depth of your tribulation, and yet should urge you to embrace his religion?"

In spite of this appeal, and of law and justice, the seneschal ordered him to be taken to the Tower of Pons, to a filthy dungeon already occupied by a murderer. When he heard the sentence, Fontaine replied: "It is in vain that you send me to a dungeon, to hinder me from praying to your Creator and mine, for if you could send me to hell I should expel the demons by my importunate communion with God. The greater my affliction, the more earnest would be my supplications, and I should also pray for your soul, as Jesus Christ prayed for those who crucified him, for I believe you would need it, because you, being my judge, are convinced of my innocence, and yet are more hostile than the king's advocate, who is my legal prosecutor." The seneschal replied coldly: "I thank you, but I desire none of your sermons."

The next morning Fontaine was put into the tower. How long he might have remained there is uncertain, but owing to the importunity of a lady of rank, well acquainted with the seneschal, who represented to him the infamy of his conduct, Fontaine was released the same evening, and removed to the bell-tower of the town hall. Here he lay three months, the seneschal detaining him, as Felix did Paul, in the hope of extorting money from him. His legal adviser would often say, taking gold and silver coins from his pocket: "See; here is the key of your prison." "I know it," replied Fontaine; "but it is a key I will never make use of." His Protestant friends likewise begged him to let them arrange the matter with the seneschal, saying it should not cost him a penny. His answer was that if they did so, he should look upon them as his greatest enemies.

In August, Fontaine was brought up again for trial. Amongst other questions he was asked if he was not aware that the king had issued a declaration forbidding conventicles. Hoping to protect, not himself only but his fellow-Protestants who were to be tried after him, he answered: "I have read and re-read the Declaration of his majesty forbidding all unlawful assemblies, and can find nothing which forbids meetings to worship God. It would be to cast an atrocious and indelible reproach on our very Christian king to suppose that he calls such meetings unlawful assemblies. I hope you have too much respect for the king, and are yourselves too much of good Christians, to call those assemblies unlawful to which no arms but the Old and New Testament are taken, at which nothing is debated but the salvation of souls, and no word uttered but in accordance with the Holy Scriptures; where prayer is made for the kingdom, the king and the royal family, and even for the conversion of those who persecute Christ's Church." Being urged on by the judges, who hoped to entrap him in some imprudent expressions, he proceeded to contrast the religious meetings of the Reformed with the revels of the villagers on the green, and the balls and convivial parties of the rich in the city, accusing his judges of flagrant injustice in condemning the one, whilst they permitted and indulged in the other, and warning them of the day of retribution at the hands of the Sovereign Judge. This denunciation irritated the seneschal, who, to give the counsellors some idea of what he called the prisoner's obstinacy, proceeded to put a question to him out of curiosity: "Do you believe that a private person, an artizan, for example, can understand Holy Scripture better than all the doctors and councils together?" "Sir," replied Fontaine, "supposing this simple artizan should be endued with the Holy Spirit, and that all the doctors and councils should not be so endued (which I believe to be possible), then he will better understand the meaning of Scripture than they, because it is only the Spirit by whom the Scriptures were dictated who can give a true understanding of them. Our Lord Jesus Christ and his poor fishermen found themselves opposed to the whole body of the Scribes and Pharisees in Jerusalem, and according to your principles you would have been as forward to condemn Him as was Pilate. The same thing happened in the time of Calvin and Luther, who certainly better understood Holy Scripture than all the popes, cardinals, and councils." At these words the seneschal and council rose up, crying, "Jesu, Maria, what perversity!"

Fontaine was taken back to prison and condemned to pay a fine of 100 livres, and forbidden to exercise his ministry. The peasants were sentenced to do public penance, to be banished for six months, and to pay fines amounting to 3000 livres, besides 100 crowns to the judges. These fines were made both individual and collective, because Fontaine was the only person who was known to be in a condition to pay them. He laid down the 100 livres, and demanded his liberty; but the seneschal refused to set him free. He appealed to the parliament of Guienne; and thanks to the president's integrity, the sentence of the senechal was reversed; Fontaine was set at liberty; he even recovered the 100 livres; but it required all his indomitable perseverance to make the officers of the court put the righteous sentence into execution. They hated the Huguenots, and had opened their mouths wide for a share of the spoil, so that the deputy-registrar, when at length he gave Fontaine the document which was to release him and his countrymen from prison, and Fontaine asked if he was satisfied, growled out: "No, nor ever shall be, until I see you with a halter round your neck."

This brings us to the fatal year 1685, of which Fontaine says: "There was now no longer preserved any semblance of justice; it was the action of a victorious and lawless army taking possession of an enemy's country. Every dragoon was at once irresponsible judge and executioner."

Fontaine afterwards escaped to England, where he married and lived many years.

On the 6th of February, this year, our Charles II. died. He professed the Protestant religion, but at heart he was a papist. He entered the Romish Church, in Paris, during his exile; and on his death-bed he sent for a Romish priest, who gave him absolution, the wafer, and extreme unction. Charles was dependent on the King of France; the annual pension he received from Louis enabled him to reign for several years without a parliament. He was succeeded by his brother, James II., who openly professed the religion of Rome, and did all in his power to bring England again under the papal yoke. A few months after James's accession, the Duke of Monmouth made his unsuccessful attempt to gain possession of the throne. He was defeated at Sedge Moor, near Bridgewater. He himself was executed on Tower Hill, and his adherents were butchered and mutilated with a barbarity equal to that which was being exercised on the Huguenots in France.

XXXVII.
THE DRAGOONS IN BÉARN, 1685.

The persecution which has just been related was not effected through the Dragonnades. Hitherto, with some occasional exceptions, that final and most convincing argument had been employed only in Poitou, *viz.*, in 1681. Now, March, 1685, Louvois decided to apply it universally.

There were at this time hostile relations between France and Spain, and a French army had been marched into Béarn, where it awaited, or professed to await, an ultimatum from Madrid. Foucault, intendant of Béarn, was a man of learning, and in one of his circuits discovered in the abbey of Moissac, near Montauban, the lost manuscript of one of the early Christian authors, De Mortibus Persecutorum ('Concerning the Deaths of the Persecutors'), attributed to Lactantius, and till then known only through Jerome's quotations. But the warning voice which speaks so loudly from that treatise could not reach the heart of the intendant. In his zeal for the extinction of heresy he rivalled Louvois and the Jesuits, and he declared he would not rest until all the king's subjects were of one religion. To enable him to accomplish this pious enterprise, 5000 volumes of Bossuet's controversial writings were sent down to him, and the army destined for Spain was placed at his disposal.

By a recent Declaration the temples in the principality had been reduced to five, and these the parliament had rendered useless by the imprisonment or interdiction of their ministers. All at once the soldiers were let loose upon every town and village of the province to carry on their accustomed game in the houses upon which they were quartered, and by tricks and violence compel the people to attend Mass. The Protestant historian fills several pages with the excesses they committed, and the cruelties practised by the intendant and priests; but the reader will weary of the continual repetition of these harrowing details. To Foucault belongs the unenviable reputation of bringing methods of torture to perfection. It was a study of the times to discover torments which should inflict the most exquisite suffering without being mortal.

Meanwhile the reports which were sent up by the intendant to Versailles speak of neither dragonnades nor violence. The conversions are represented as the fruit of divine grace. The success of Foucault's measures and the praises showered on him excited the emulation of his brother intendants; they applied for the use in their respective provinces of the army of Béarn. On July 31, Louvois wrote to the commander-in-chief, the Marquis de Boufflers, directing him to employ his troops during the rest of the year in reducing the number of the Protestants in the generalities of Bordeaux and Montauban.* They were to be billeted wholly on the Huguenots, and not to be removed until the mass of the inhabitants had abjured; and when the work was accomplished in one place, they were to be withdrawn and quartered elsewhere. Louvois estimated the number of Protestants in the generality of Bordeaux at 150,000; and his instructions to the marshal were to reduce this number until the Catholics should everywhere be twice or thrice as numerous as the Protestants; "So that," wrote Louvois, referring to the Revocation already resolved upon, "when his majesty shall no longer permit the exercise of this religion in his kingdom, there may be nothing to fear from the few who remain."

* The generalities were fiscal divisions of the country.

Accordingly the troops moved forward through Guienne and Perigord to Bordeaux, in a kind of triumphal progress. The pretended conversions took place with a rapidity which astonished even the court itself. Some made a feigned abjuration to secure time for flight; others seem scarcely to have understood that they were abandoning their faith; others, again, had no sooner taken the fatal step, than, tormented in their conscience, they returned back to their own faith, and with so much the greater fervency as having to expiate the crime of denying it.

XXXVIII.
THE DRAGOONS IN LANGUEDOC, 1685.

From Bordeaux the intoxicated soldiery marched up the valley of the Garonne, and ascended its affluents, the Dordogne, the Lot and the Tarn, as well as along the course of the grand canal, which had been constructed by D'Aguesseau four years before. Wherever they came, the authorities, civil and ecclesiastical, assembled the Protestants in the public square, and declared to them the king's unalterable will that they should become Catholics. Too many, alas! terrified and stunned at the appearance of the "booted missionaries" in their splendid uniforms, whose doings elsewhere had already filled them with dismay, hastened to declare themselves converted. A short formula was presented for their signature: "I firmly believe all that the Catholic, Apostolic and Roman Church believes and professes. I most sincerely condemn and reject all the heresies that the said Church has condemned and rejected. So help me God and his holy gospels." Those who could not write made the sign of the cross. Even this was not always required; the words, "I join the Church," or "Ave Maria," being in many cases deemed sufficient. Conversion offices were opened: when the proper forms ran short, the certificate which exempted the New Converts from the billet, written on the back of a playing card, was deemed sufficient, a token which the Protestants called the mark of the Beast.

In reading the account of this wholesale apostacy, we are forcibly reminded of what took place at Carthage in the Decian persecution. "Many," says Cyprian, "were conquered before the battle, prostrated before the attack. They did not even leave it to be said for them that they sacrificed unwillingly; they ran to the market-place of their own accord." The parallel between the two events runs indeed very close. The names differ, but the object and the means are the same. The torments which the Huguenots sought to escape were as barbarous as those inflicted by the heathen. Louis is the emperor Decius; Louvois and the ministry are the Roman senate; La Chaise and the Jesuits are the pagan priesthood.

The victory, however, was not always won so easily. The small town of Bergerac, already illustrious for constancy in persecution, made an heroic resistance. Two troops of horse and thirty-two companies of foot being brought in, Marshall Boufflers, the intendant, and the Bishops of Agen and Perigueaux, came together, and sending for 200 of the chief citizens, ordered them in the king's name to attend Mass. They replied that they were ready to obey the king in all things except in matters of conscience, but that in these they acknowledged no sovereign but God. Hereupon thirty-two additional companies of horse and foot were quartered upon them, with orders to reduce them to reason. After a short interval they were sent for again to the town-hall, and again commanded to abjure. They replied, as before, humbly and with tears, that what was required of them was the only thing they could not do; upon which the number of companies was made up to a hundred, and the work of coercion prosecuted with redoubled rigour. " Seeing no other way of keeping soul and body together, or of being delivered from intolerable torments, the whole town, except a few who saved themselves by flight, at length gave way, and were driven to Mass."

The same scenes were enacted in Montauban and many other towns.

Early in September, Louvois sent word to his father, the chancellor Le Tellier, then aged and sick : " Sixty thousand conversions have been made in the generality of Bordeaux, and 20,000 in that of Montauban. By the end of the month, there will not remain in the former 10,000 Protestants." The same day he wrote to Boufflers: "The king has learnt with the greatest joy the surprising success which has attended the execution of his orders. His majesty trusts to you to send into Saintonge as many infantry, calvary and dragoons as you may deem necessary to accomplish the same work there. If the noblemen of the religion continue to stand out, you must quarter troops on such of them as are not at present serving in the army, but not on those of the highest rank, whom, however, you will warn that they in their turn will receive the soldiers, if they do not take advice and quit a religion which is displeasing to his majesty. If this is not sufficient, you will serve them with *lettres de cachet*, a number of which the king has directed M. de Châteauneuf to send you in blank ; but this resource is to be used only with great discretion," To render the work of the dragoons more effective, Louvois again closed the frontiers. Every door of exit, whether by sea or land, being thus barred, the Protestants were in the condition of the wild animals of an Indian jungle, hemmed in on every side for a murderous and exterminating battue.

By the end of September, the dragoons had arrived at

Montpellier, a city of 30,000 inhabitants, 8000 of whom were Protestants. The reports of the atrocities by which the march of the troops was accompanied, and of the conversion of city after city, had struck terror into all hearts; and as soon as it was known that the dragoons were at the gates, a mass meeting was called to decide what was to be done. After some deliberation, it was resolved that the whole community should at once abjure. Accordingly the crowd rushed to the churches, presenting themselves in such numbers that priests could not be found sufficient to give them absolution. The news flew to Versailles: "Montpellier has abjured *en masse*."*

An instance occurred in this city which is illustrative of the French character. M. de Fourques, a Protestant nobleman, went to the bishop's house and asked to speak with him. The bishop, who had company, sent word to him to come another day. But the nobleman returning for answer that he had come on a business of the king which would not suffer delay, the bishop came out, supposing that the nobleman had brought a command from his majesty. "I am come," said the nobleman, in a serious but ironical tone, "to tell you from the king that you have to receive my abjuration. Perhaps it would have been better if I had been instructed in your faith before professing it, but the king is quite willing to dispense with this." The bishop, who knew M. de Fourques as a man of good sense, and who understood the reproach which this raillery covered, replied with courtesy, but with some degree of confusion, that since he confessed he had need of instruction there was no haste, and he might take time to receive it. "That is not the king's will," replied the nobleman." "How," answered

---

* On the fly-leaf of an old Bible this entry has been found: "Sept. 29, the whole city of Montpellier turns Catholic."

the bishop, "do you wish that I should receive you into our communion, at the very time when you affect to be ignorant of our doctrines? It is not permitted to me to do such a thing." "Nevertheless it is what the king wills," replied the nobleman, "and you know that in this as in everything else, you are bound to obey his majesty." In vain the bishop strove to excuse himself, the nobleman continued to press his demand, and in the end the bishop was obliged to receive his abjuration without more ado.

Troops had already been sent forward to Nîmes, the chief Protestant city of the South. The Marquis de Montenègre, the king's lieutenant in Languedoc, followed on the 22nd of September. The next day he closed the temple. The last sermon was preached by Cheiron, one of the city pastors. He was a vehement and pathetic orator, and on this occasion is said to have surpassed himself. He exhorted the congregation to amendment of life and to perseverance in their resistance to popery. It was, he reminded them, the last time that he should ever address them. His sympathetic audience responded with tears and sobs. And when he asked what account they would have him render to God of their souls which had been committed to him, and whether they were resolved to remain faithful, he was interrupted by confused sounds of grief mingled by loud protestations that nothing should ever shake them in their allegiance to their Heavenly King. When, however, a few days afterwards, the soldiers were let loose upon the city, nearly the whole church gave way, and Cheiron among the first. The wretched man did more; to prove the sincerity of his conversion, which was rewarded by honours and a civic office, he not only attended Mass, but even pursued the remnant of his flock which had not given in, with as much severity as any Old Catholic. He had a colleague named Paulham, who also abjured and was rewarded. Both were suspected of having maintained intelligence with the court at an earlier stage of the troubles.

The Duke de Noailles arrived in Nimes early in October, "The day after my arrival," he wrote to Louvois, "the chief notabilities of the city came to the church to make abjuration. There was afterwards some falling off, but matters have taken a good turn through the billetings I made upon the most obstinate." To such, indeed, no mercy was shown. The duke himself tells us that in two instances 100 soldiers were quartered on a single family; and one who escaped, says: "The wives and daughters of such as stood out were sent to nunneries; and on one day 300 of the men were marched off in chains to the galleys at Marseilles."

A few days later we find the duke at Florac, in the heart of the Cevennes, from whence he wrote: "Already more than a third part of the Gevaudan (a small province comprising the western side of the mountains) is converted; and if the king will have the benevolence to grant the converts some remission of the poll-tax, it will expedite the work." He adds: "In undertaking that the whole of these provinces shall be converted by the 25th of November, I have named too distant a date. I believe the work will be accomplished by the end of this month."

At Alais there was an aged minister named Bouton, who had one of his sons for a colleague. Although he was nearly eighty he was still full of ardour, and preached his last sermon, on Hebrews x. 35-39, with extraordinary power, the people often interrupting him with cries and tears. Raising his hand towards heaven, he protested that he would persevere until death, and the people, like the congregation of Nimes under the preaching of Cheiron, caught the enthusiasm, and all did the same. The Duke de Noailles, believing these scenes to be concerted, sent dragoons to arrest Bouton. When the soldiers appeared at the door and demanded the pastor, his son, with filial self-sacrifice, presented himself in his stead, and was conducted to Montpellier. Here the mistake was discovered, but not until the father had had time to flee, and, traversing the Cevennes and Auvergne, to find a safe refuge in Switerland. The son was released on condition of producing his father, or of again delivering himself up; but when he found the old man was safe, he broke his parole, which ought to have been to him more sacred than life, made his escape and joined him. It was in the midst of these scenes, and whilst the dragoons were spread over the provinces of the south pursuing their merciless task, that the Edict of Nantes was revoked.

XXXIX.
THE MIDNIGHT HOUR.

We have watched the shadows gradually deepen, and now the hour of midnight darkness has come. The Edict of Nantes had been, year by year, clipped and torn away until nothing remained but the seal and signature of its author, Henry IV. Now these were to be dishonoured and trampled upon.

The clergy in their customary orations magnified the royal wisdom and zeal by which the Church was being restored to her pristine glory. The Bishop of Valence and the Coadjutor of Rouen, both of them sons of the great Colbert, designated the means the king had made use of as the gentlest and most worthy of the Gospel that had ever been employed. The former, a noted persecutor, declared that the king without violence had brought the pretended reformed religion to be abandoned by all reasonable persons. The coadjutor soared still higher, maintaining that it was by gaining the hearts of the heretics the king had vanquished their obstinacy, for they would scarcely have returned to the bosom of the Church unless the path had been "strewn with flowers."

But whilst the incense of flattery kept the royal conscience in a state of torpor, the warning voice of truth once more reached the king's ear. The Marquis de Ruvigny was deputy-general of the Reformed Churches at the court of Versailles. In a conversation with our Bishop Burnet, he told him that knowing the king's bigotry and his gross ignorance of all matters pertaining to his Protestant subjects, and seeing that extreme measures were being precipitated, he begged an audience. It lasted several hours. The deputy-general gave the king an account of the numbers, industry, and wealth of the Protestants, and told him that if he supposed they would all turn Catholics he was greatly deceived. Many, he said, would leave the kingdom, and carry their wealth and industry abroad; many would suffer; others would be precipitated into desperate courses, and much blood would be shed. Louis appeared to listen attentively, but the marquis perceived that what he said made no real impression on the royal mind, for the king asked for no particulars or explanation, but let him go on to the end. In his reply Louis told him he took his freedom in good part, since it flowed from zeal for his service; and he believed that what he was about to do might be to the material prejudice of his kingdom, although he did not think it would go to the shedding of blood. But whether it did so or not, he considered himself so absolutely bound to the conversion of all his subjects and the extirpation of heresy, that if the accomplishment of this object should require him with one hand to cut off the other, he would do it.

Louvois had intended to defer the Act of Revocation awhile longer, but the news of the rapid and wholesale conversion of the Protestants intoxicated the court, and he was forced to go forward. At a select council of conscience, to which two juris-consults and two theologians (supposed to be Harlay, Archbishop of Paris, and Bossuet) were summoned, it was decided:—First, that the king on every possible ground possessed the power to revoke the Edict of Nantes; and, secondly, that if his majesty possessed the legal power, it was his duty to exercise it for the sake of religion and for the good of his people. The dauphin, who was present, interposed, saying that the Huguenots had already taken alarm, and that, if such an Act should be passed, they might possibly fly to arms, and in any case a large number would emigrate, which would give a blow to commerce and agriculture, and cripple the State. The king replied that he had for a long time past foreseen and provided for all this, that nothing in the world would grieve him more than to shed a single drop of the blood of his subjects, but that he had armies and able generals, whom, if necessary, he would employ against rebels bent on their own destruction. As for motives of interest, he judged them unworthy of consideration compared with the advantages of a work which would restore splendour to religion, tranquillity to the State, and authority to the laws. It was unanimously concluded that the edict should be at once revoked.

Accordingly, on the 17th of October, 1685, at Fontainebleau, the king put his hand to the Act of Revocation, by which the Edict of Nantes, and also the Edict of Grace of 1629, were declared null and void;* and the next day the great seal was affixed to the instrument by the Chancellor Le Tellier. According to law it required registration by the parliament of Paris, which body, however, being then

* A representation of the event forms the frontispiece to this volume. The original plate is contained in the Dutch translation of Benoit's 'Histoire de l'Edit de Nantes,' which appeared at Amsterdam in 1696.

in vacation, could not legally act. But no impediment was suffered to delay for a moment the launching of the thunderbolt. All that was considered necessary was to insert in the clause of the edict, by which registration was ordered, the words, "even in vacation." The precipitancy with which the act was accomplished owed something to the impatience of the chancellor, who was near his end, and panted to see the work completed. When he had placed the great seal under the king's signature, he broke forth in triumph in the words of the *Nunc dimittis:* "Now lettest thou thy servant depart in peace, for mine eyes have seen thy salvation." He died twelve days afterwards. A mausoleum of black marble was erected to his memory, blazoned with his crest, singularly appropriate to the occasion, a dragon devouring a star.

By the edict it was enacted:—

That all the remaining temples of the R. P. R. should be forthwith demolished; *

That all ministers who refused to embrace the Catholic faith should depart the realm within two weeks, under pain of the galleys;

Rewards were offered to converted ministers;

All Reformed schools were to be closed;

All children of Protestant parents thenceforth to be born were to be baptized by the priest, and brought up in the Catholic religion;

All Protestants, other than the ministers, were forbidden to leave the country, under penalty of the gallows for men, of imprisonment and confiscation of goods for women.†

---

* In 1660 the Protestants possessed 813 temples; between 1660 and 1685, 570 of these had been demolished or closed; in 1685, 243 more were demolished.

† The original document is in the Palais Soubise, Museum of the National Archives. It is engrossed on "eight pages of parchment, about 13 inches by 9, now ivory-stained and slightly wrinkled."

The Church is crowning the king, who has his foot on a globe; his left hand holds a rudder, beneath which heresy, signified by the head of a Medusa, is being crushed. The legend runs: OB · VICIES CENTENA · MILL · CALVINIAN · AD · ECCLES · REVOCATA· D.C.LXXXV. For having brought back to the Church two millions of Calvinists. 1685.

The Church, a cross in her right hand and an open book in her left, is trampling on heresy, signified by a man lying with his face downwards, in his hand an extinguished torch, and under it some torn books of the heretics. HÆRESIS EXTINCTA. EDICTUM OCTOBRIS · M.D.C.LXXXV. Heresy extinguished. Edict of October, 1685.

On the first steps of an altar on which the Host is elevated, the Church, under the figure of a woman in a robe adorned with fleurs-de-lis, is kneeling before the king, who holds out his sceptre to her. The legend is: SACR · ROMANA · RESTITUTA. The Sacraments of the Roman Church restored. This medal was struck at Rome.

Medals were struck in honour of Louis, to commemorate the supposed extinction of heresy; and a bronze statue set up, inscribed to "Louis the Great, always victorious, Defender of the Majesty of the Church and of Kings." On the pedestal was carved a bat, covering with its broad wings the writings of John Huss and Calvin.*

The exultation of Le Tellier was echoed by the whole of Catholic France, but there was no response from Rome. The news of St. Bartholomew, more than a century before, had been celebrated in the Eternal City with a carnival of joy; the Edict of Nantes had raised a yell of indignation; but the pope was too deeply offended with Bossuet and the Gallican Church now to make any response, and the tidings of the Revocation were received in silence. In France it was not only the court and the clergy who raised the *Te Deum*, but all classes,—the academy, the coteries of wit and fashion, the devotees, the Jansenists. A prize was offered for a poem on the auspicious occurrence; it was carried off by Fontenelle.

In his funeral oration over Le Tellier, Bossuet (the "Eagle of Meaux)" stooped to glorify the act and the monarch: "Ye who compose the annals of the Church, take your sacred pens, facile instruments of a ready writer and a diligent hand, and hasten to place Louis beside Constantine and Theodosius. Let us pour out our hearts over his piety. Let us raise to heaven our acclamations and say to this new Constantine, this new Theodosius, this new Marcion, this new Charlemagne, the same that six hundred and thirty Fathers said at the council of Chalcedon formerly, 'You have established the faith; you have exterminated the heretics: this is the great work of your reign, it is its distinctive character. King of heaven, preserve the king of the earth: this is the prayer of the Churches; it is the prayer of the Bishops.'"

* In 1793 the statue was melted and cast into cannon.

Madame de Sévigné, one of the most brilliant ornaments of Louis's reign, wrote to the Count Bussy-Rabutin, ten days after the signing of the act: "Father Bourdaloue is going, by command of the king, to preach at Montpellier and in those provinces where so many people have been converted without knowing why. He will teach it to them, and will make them good Catholics. The dragoons have been excellent missionaries hitherto; the preachers who are now being sent will complete the work. You will no doubt have seen the edict by which the king has revoked that of Nantes. Nothing could be finer, and no king has ever done, or ever will do, anything more memorable." The count replied: "I admire the measures taken by the king to crush the Huguenots. The wars formerly waged against them, and the Saint Bartholomews, only multiplied and strengthened that sect. His majesty has now sapped it little by little, and the edict he has just issued, supported by the dragoons and the Boardaloues, is the *coup de grâce*." Even the good Arnauld, the leader of the Jansensists, so well known in connection with Pascal and Port Royal, though he found the edict "a little violent," thought it "not at all unjust." Colbert, who died two years before the Revocation, was unhappily one of those who could say with the Roman poet: "I see the better course and approve it; but I follow the worse."* Seeing that Bossuet and Fénelon were employing their eloquence to the prejudice of the Huguenots, he said: "Gentlemen, this belongs to your Sorbonne conscience; you have another conscience; let that be heard, and you will speak a different language." Nevertheless Colbert took part in the measures which led to the Revocation.

Two men of note stood aloof from the herd, and condemned the act, Boisguillebert, whose trenchant

---

* Video meliora proboque, deteriora sequor.

description of the national decay we quoted awhile back, and Vauban, the great military engineer of the age, who applied his genius to girdling France with impregnable fortresses. Vauban, in 1688, dared to propose the repeal of all the edicts of the previous nine years, the rebuilding of the temples, an amnesty for the fugitives, even for such as had taken arms against France in foreign regiments, and the release of the prisoners for conscience' sake from the jails and galleys. In a memorial which he presented to Louvois, he deplored the loss by emigration of 60,000 Frenchmen; the ruin of commerce; hostile navies recruited by 9000 of the best sailors in France; and hostile armies by 600 officers and 12,000 veteran troops. "Persecution," he wrote, "is the seed-bed of sects. After the massacre of St. Bartholomew, a fresh census of the Huguenots proved that their number had increased by 110,000. Compulsory conversion inspires a general horror of the clergy and the profanation of the sacrament. If you follow it out, the converts must either be exterminated or thrust out as madmen. Execrable alternative! at variance with every principle, civil, moral, or Christian; fatal to religion itself! There is only one course open, at once charitable, expedient, politic, viz., to leave them unmolested; and the prudence which knows when to withdraw and yield to events is a prime element in the art of governing."

At first the Cardinal de Noailles was honest enough to raise his voice on behalf of the oppressed, but he afterwards joined the persecutors in order to cause it to be forgotten that he was a Jansenist.

A claim has been put in for another man of genius, the poet Racine. It is founded on two lines in his *Esther*:—

> "On peut des plus grands rois surprendre la justice,
> Et le roi trop crédule a signé cet édit."

It is said that under the character of Haman he painted Louvois, and that in condemning the decree of Ahasuerus, he aimed his shaft at the Edict of Revocation. But it is not probable that Racine would thus incur the risk of mortally offending the king, to say nothing of the minister. The drama was written at the express request of Louis and Madame de Maintenon, and was first acted (1689) by the ladies of St. Cyr, a celebrated house of education founded by the marchioness for daughters of the nobility.

To the above may be added, but on a different ground, the intendant Lamoignon de Bâville, styled King of Languedoc, who for so many years ruled that province with a rod of iron. He cared little for the religious question; he was devoted to the authority of the king and the law. "I have," he said, "always condemned the Revocation; it was a gross blunder, and it has thrown the kingdom into a dangerous crisis; but to return now on one's steps would be to plunge still lower into the abyss. We have no choice but to march on, finish up the conversions, close our hearts to pity and our lips to humanity, and save the State. Such is the supreme law." He could, however, give utterance to more enlightened sentiments: "I have always looked upon it as a mistake to press them on the sacraments. We must approach their hearts; it is there religion dwells. They require preachers, not Masses and ceremonies. Sermons, hymns and prayer; these are their worship."

PART III.

FROM THE REVOCATION, 1685, TO THE END OF THE 17TH CENTURY.

FROM THE REVOCATION, 1685, TO THE END OF THE 17TH CENTURY.

I.
HOW TO CONVERT THE NEW CONVERTS.

The Act of Revocation was at once followed by a crowd of consequences. We begin with the instruction of the New Converts.

As the natural result of the violent means which had been made use of, a very large proportion of the New Converts were utterly ignorant of the doctrines and practices of the Church which they had joined. It could not be otherwise. The priests were obnoxious to them, and they despised their teaching. As a class, indeed, the curés were notoriously illiterate and immoral. The Duke de Noailles, no friend to the Protestants, wrote, that when the pastors challenged the priests to public disputation, none were found learned enough to enter the lists. In the Cevennes, especially, that stronghold of Calvinism, he describes the clergy as leading vicious lives, hating the Huguenots, incompetent and indolent; and says: "A cathedral, colleges, curés, communities, can barely furnish for the Catholics themselves one sermon in the month, whilst the Calvinists, with only two or three preachers, enjoy one a day." D'Aguesseau gave a similar report of Poitou and Languedoc; and Foucault, in Béarn, deplored the scandalous lives of the clergy. The missionaries, moreover, who had been sent out to instruct the New Converts, had shown themselves altogether unfit for the work.

But it was not only ignorance of their doctrines on the part of the New Converts that grieved the thoughtful and devout amongst the Roman Catholics. Having been gained over in profession only, not in heart, they partook hypocritically of the Church mysteries. They came to the altar and received the wafer into their mouths; but they had no faith in the change which the Romanists believe to be wrought by the offering of the priest. This was regarded by good Catholics as a profanation of all that was most sacred, and the protestations against it are couched in the strongest language. The Bishop of Saint-Pons wrote to the commandant of the troops in his diocese: "You have, sir, too much intelligence not to know that you cannot with a safe conscience contribute in any degree to hasty confessions and communions. These are so many acts of sacrilege, fit to make one's hair stand on end, and enough to make one wish for the poor wretches who commit them, and the ministers who are the instruments of this abomination, that they should be cast headlong into the sea, as the Scripture says, 'with a millstone about their neck.' This universal disorder has obliged me to give instruction on the Eucharist, in order that there may be at least one witness in France that these impieties have not been the universal practice of our Church. Nevertheless, sir, I am aware it is your business to employ the royal troops to bring every one to the 'table,' without distinction. But what is the consequence? In some cases the impious who spit out the Eucharist and trample it under foot are put to death. Is not Jesus Christ more outraged when it is forced into the body of a notorious unbeliever or a miscreant, such as are many of those whom your soldiers bring up to communion? This is the 'abomination of desolation,' and it is time that all good people should weep and prostrate themselves before the Divine Majesty, who is outraged by these infinite profanations."

But these sentiments were by no means general. The opposite opinion is expressed by Godet, Bishop of Chartres, spiritual director of Madame de Maintenon: "People are afraid of making themselves accomplices in the sacrilegious acts of the Huguenots. Why did they not fear being accomplices in the lie which is uttered to the Holy Spirit when the Huguenots feign conversion? They have very wisely risen above this fear; for whilst requiring righteous acts from them, they have not held themselves responsible for the impious manner in which these were done. May we not now, for the same reason, cast aside all our scruples about compelling these people to frequent the sacraments?" With Godet agreed the Jesuits, who declared that since every vestige of Calvinism must be effaced from the land, it was necessary to put up with hypocrisy and sacrilege in a whole generation, in the hope that the next, having never had before its eyes any but the true worship, would lose the remembrance of the false.

Various means were proposed to remedy this state of things. The Assembly of the Clergy, which separated a few weeks before the Revocation, provided funds for fresh troops of missionaries to go through the country and instruct the converts; and at the same time a large number of schools were opened. In 1686 the Bishop of Saintes stated the number of New Catholics in his vast diocese at 80,000, and claimed from the State 8800 livres for six months' maintenance of forty-eight missionaries whom he employed to complete their conversion. But it was felt that this was not enough, and it was resolved, as we have already learnt from Madame de Sévigné, to send down into the provinces some of the most learned and eloquent preachers of the capital. Bourdaloue and Fléchier were dispatched into Languedoc, and Fénelon into Saintonge.

We have not much to say regarding the labours of the two former. Fléchier wrote, October 28, 1685: "I have been more than two months on the road on account of the matters of religion with which I have been occupied, all the nobility in the provinces through which I have passed desiring to be converted under my hands, and to confer with me, so that I have received on my journey more than 900 abjurations." He was rewarded for his services by the bishopric of Lavaur, and the next year by that of Nimes.

On the only occasion on which we are able to follow Bourdaloue, he had no reason to boast of his success. "I had the curiosity," says a Protestant, "to hear him, and I remember his words to the New Converts: 'How wonderful to see you united again to the children of the true Church. How glorious for our invincible monarch to have subjected you to the faith. He has gained battles, and conquered cities and provinces; but nothing sheds so much lustre on his reign as the victory over your souls.' "Indeed," adds his hearer, "he had good reason to compare these pretended conversions to the king's military triumphs, for they were gained by the self-same means. He had the impudence," he continues, "to propose to confer with the newly converted on their doubts, an audacity which cost him many mortifications, for our people being better instructed than he supposed, he often found himself embroiled in a dispute without knowing how to disengage himself. A certain coppersmith, in particular, no scholar, but practised in controversy, handled the great preacher with wonderful dexterity, catching him in his own words, and confounding him before the whole assembly. Bourdaloue angrily demanded the man's name and abode, and would have shut him up in prison if he had not made his escape. A papist nobleman, who was present, said the New Catholics were not to be blamed, since they had only used the liberty Bourdaloue had offered them. 'I do not complain,' replied the Jesuit, 'that they come to me to get information, but I will not suffer them to send me their ministers in disguise to trip me up.' His discomfiture so preyed upon him that it caused a violent spitting of blood, which gave him a pretext for breaking off the conferences."

II.

FÉNELON, MISSIONARY IN SAINTONGE, 1685-6.

Some of Fénelon's letters from Saintonge have been preserved. They depict in strong colours the attitude and agitation of the Protestant mind, and the insuperable difficulties of his undertaking.

Before we accompany him, it may be well to revive our recollection of the condition in which this province was left prior to the Revocation.* We may remember that the temples had been all closed. The last was that of Marennes; it was shut up one Saturday night. The next morning the Protestants from many miles round, having no other place of worship to go to, assembled there in great numbers; it was computed that there were nearly ten thousand round the doors. There were several marriages to be solemnized, and twenty-three infants to be baptized; but as the house was locked the vast assembly were obliged to disperse, dejected and sorrowful. "Nothing was heard," says the historian, "but sighs and groans; they embraced one another with tears, clasping their hands and raising their eyes to heaven." The infants

* See page 99.

had to be carried seven leagues further to be baptized; and, from the severity of the weather, several died on the way.

The minister, Louvois, who had estates in Saintonge, wrote in September to the Marquis de Boufflers:—" I want you to finish the work and clear the country of Protestants, especially my domain." But this was more easily said than done. In November the minister was informed that there remained in four parishes of the diocese of La Rochelle 600 unconverted, who had left their homes and betaken themselves to the woods; and in December the Bishop of La Rochelle reported 803 Huguenots as still remaining in twenty-eight of his parishes, and prayed Louvois to use means which should compel them to abjure. His request was granted; the houses of such as had fled were razed to the ground; and Louvois wrote:—" There is no better method of convincing the Huguenots that the king will not have them in France than to make an example of those on my domain." Such was the condition of Saintonge and La Rochelle when Fénelon undertook to bring back the wanderers to the fold.

Before entering on his mission, Fénelon, at the king's desire, was admitted to an audience. " It is well known," says his biographer, Bausset, " that the only request which he made was that all the troops and every appearance of military coercion should be removed from the places to which he was to be sent on this ministry of peace and charity. The king, although he expressed some fear for Fénelon's personal safety from the turbulent character of the Protestants, at once promised to grant his request." But the conditions were not observed on the part of the king, the troops not being withdrawn until two months after Fénelon's arrival. Nor, according to our ideas, did the missionary act in accordance with the principles on which he set out. It was the case of the House of the New Catholics in Paris over again. Fénelon undertook the office of instructor and reconciler, in the honest belief that the Calvinists were in danger of eternal perdition; but he had to give in his account not to God only, but to the king, and was thus in the condition of those who would, at the same time, serve two masters. The Romish missionaries in France looked on themselves as a part of the administration, bound to watch over and protect the interests of the State, and Fénelon, whilst he professed to have sheathed the sword, held it uplifted ready to smite at a moment's notice. Moreover, he found the Protestants in a state of agitation, for which he was unprepared. He took with him five abbés of note, and a staff of Jesuits. They came to Saintonge about the end of the year (1685).

On his arrival, Fénelon made such concessions as he could. He suppressed, in the public worship, the Ave-Marias and other prayers especially offensive to the Protestants, an indulgence which seems to have given umbrage to the court, for he found it necessary to explain and defend himself.

The following passages are from his letters:—

"La Tremblade, February 7, 1686. To the Marquis de Seignelay, secretary of state. Sir,—I hasten to report to you the evil disposition in which I have found the inhabitants of this place. Letters, written to them from Holland, promise an advantageous settlement in that country, and exemption from taxes for at least seven years.* I take the liberty to represent to you that in my opinion the guard along the coast, where they might embark, should be increased; also that the royal authority must not be relaxed in anything; for our arrival in this

---

* From England, also, letters were circulated holding out great advantages to such as should wish to settle in Carolina.

country, combined with rumours of war which come continually from Holland, make these people believe that we fear them, and are humouring them. They persuade themselves that there will soon be a great change, and that the war-like preparations of the Dutch are destined for their deliverance. But whilst authority must be maintained inflexible to curb these spirits, whom the least slackness makes insolent, it is important to make their life in France as easy as possible, so as to lessen the desire to leave the country. The Protestants confess we have proved that, according to the Scriptures, they ought to submit to the Church; and they offer to the Catholic doctrines no objections which we have not shown to be unfounded. When we left Marennes they were evidently more deeply impressed than they dared to acknowledge. They were so afflicted that I could not refuse to leave with them some of our gentlemen, and to promise we would all return. If these good beginnings are sustained by our preachers, they will soon become sound Catholics. The Jesuit fathers are the only persons capable of doing this work, for they are respected both for their knowledge and their virtue."

February 26. To the same. "Before leaving the three fathers of Marennes, I tried to persuade them that they ought to act as intercessors and advisers of the people in all things relating to the royal authority. It is this which will most effectually eradicate heresy. With this object, I have taken care to let many small favours which we obtained for the inhabitants pass through their hands, making the people suppose they owed them to their solicitation. The people are in a violent agitation; they perceive a force in our religion and a weakness in their own which strikes them with dismay. Their conscience is turned quite upside down, and the most reasonable see plainly whither all this is tending; but party prejudices, false shame, habit, and the letters from Holland, hold them in suspense, and, as it were, render them beside themselves. They are poor; the trade in salt, their only resource, is almost annihilated. If the religious question is aggravated by famine, no barrier will be able to keep them here. The corn you have sent from the royal bounty seems to have touched their hearts. It would be easy to make them all confess and communicate; but of what service would it be to make those confess who do not yet acknowledge the true Church or her power to remit sins; or how can we give Christ to those who do not believe they receive Him? Where there are both missionaries and troops, the New Converts flock to the communion. I forgot to tell you, sir, that a plentiful supply of books will be necessary, especially of the New Testament and translations of the Mass with explanations."

The foregoing are from Fénelon's official correspondence. In a letter to one of his lady friends he speaks more freely of the resident Jesuits:—" To Madame de Beauvilliers. The Huguenots seem to be affected by our instructions even to tears. They say: 'We would willingly listen to you, but you are here only for a while. When you are gone we shall be at the mercy of the monks, who preach to us only of indulgences and brotherhoods.' Here (continues Fénelon), there are only three sorts of priests: the secular, the Jesuits, and the Récollets. The Récollets are despised and hated, especially by the Huguenots, whom they have taken every opportunity to inform against. The Jesuits of Marennes are four mules, who when they speak to the New Converts, speak, as to this world, only of fines and the prison, and, as to the other, only of the devil and hell. We have had infinite difficulty to hinder these good fathers from breaking out against our gentleness, because by it their harshness was made more odious. After all, however, they are the best of the lot. As for the curés, they have no talent for speaking, which brings great reproach on the Church, for the Huguenots have been accustomed to ministers, who have comforted and exhorted them with the affecting words of Holy Scripture." In the same letter Fénelon tells us how he himself imparted religious instruction, an art in which he had no equal: " We try in our sermons to avoid anything which may stir up controversy. We bring forward proofs in the form of simple explanations, and in a manner likely to touch the heart. We manage to introduce all that is necessary to make true Catholics, whilst appearing to aim only at making good Christians. Nevertheless we have great difficulty in attracting the terrified creatures. Everywhere we meet with an incredible attachment to heresy. The more impression any one of our preachers makes upon them, the less inclination do they show to hear him again. Their pet proverb is: 'Fly from the voice of the enchanter.'"

March 8, Fénelon wrote again to De Seignelay: "The hard and unteachable nature of the Huguenots requires a rigorous and ever watchful authority. We need not harm them, but they must see a hand always uplifted ready to strike if they resist. Good schools for both sexes must be opened as soon as possible; and all parents must be compelled to send their children to them. The New Testament must be spread broadcast, printed in large characters, for they cannot read the small type. If we take away their own translation without giving them ours they will say (as their ministers have told them) that we keep the Bible from them for fear they should find in it a condemnation of our superstitions and idolatries. Lastly, sir, if to these helps there is joined an unslumbering vigilance to prevent emigration, and rigour in punishing it, nothing further will be needful but to let the people find as much comfort in remaining in the country as peril in leaving it."

It may be recollected that Madame de Maintenon had set her mind on the conversion of her relative, M. de St. Hermine and his family, who resided at Rochefort, in the neighbourhood of Fénelon's mission. To please the great lady, as his admiring biographer tells us, Fénelon took up the matter. He writes: "I have had seven or eight long conversations with M. de Sainte-Hermine at Rochefort, where I went to visit him. He understands well what is said to him; he has nothing to answer; but he makes no move. The Abbé de Langeron and I have acted a vigorous controversy in his presence, I playing the part of Protestant, and making use of the most specious arguments of the ministers. M. de Sainte-Hermine thoroughly perceived the weakness of my reasons, whatever turn I gave to them; those of the abbé, on the contrary, seemed to him conclusive; sometimes he himself even offered apposite objections; but he is not shaken, at least not outwardly. I suspect he is clinging to his religion from secret family motives."

The same day Fénelon wrote to Bossuet: "Our converts are going on a little better, but the progress is very slow; it is no small matter to change the opinions of a whole people. What difficulties the apostles must have found in changing the face of the world. The ill-converted Huguenots are attached to their religion to a horrible extreme of stubbornness, but as soon as the severity of the penalty comes in, all their strength forsakes them. Instead of being, like the martyrs, humble, docile, intrepid and incapable of dissimulation, these people are cowardly in the presence of force, stubborn against the truth, and ready for all kinds of hypocrisy. If one wished to make them abjure Christianity and embrace the Koran, one would only have to show them the dragoons. If they can ut keep their nightly meetings and hold out against nstruction, they think they have done enough."

Fénelon had good reason to complain of the nightly assemblies. The exiled pastors wrote to their congregations in France in terms of strong rebuke and admonition; and their letters, which were read at the meetings held under cover of darkness, for exhortation, prayer, and communion, produced a powerful effect. It was like Penelope's web; what was wrought by Fénelon and his staff in the day was unravelled at night. We have only room for a few sentences from these letters:—

"To our brethren who groan in the Captivity in Babylon, for whom we desire peace and mercy from God. We are grieved to hear of your weakness, in yielding to temptation. Consider what account you will give to Him who has commanded us to confess Him before men. Cherish a righteous horror of popery. None but the devil could use such tools to build his house. Vigilantly guard your books of piety, devotion and controversy, and carefully read them; save them by hiding them from the search of the persecutors, especially your Bibles, enduring all things rather than let those be snatched from you. You must seek for the means of deliverance at the earliest possible time. If you escape destitute and naked, you will yet be happy if only you bring away with you your souls for a prey."

Fénelon did not remain long in Saintonge; he was impatient to get back to his New Catholics in Paris. Bausset tells us that in the report he made to the king, "he praised the zeal of his coadjutors, spoke of the present and future of the great undertaking, and observed profound silence with regard to himself." Another of his biographers adds, that "he recommended the Huguenots to the royal consideration, and praised their peaceable disposition."

Fourteen years after Fénelon's mission, viz., in 1700, the intendant of Saintonge complained that there were still in the diocese of Saintes more than 60,000 heretics, and he warned the secretary of state that if there were not regular fixed penalties for neglecting to bring the children to the catechism, all the care that had been bestowed would be in vain."

III.
THE SHEPHERDS DRIVEN AWAY, 1685.

Whilst Fénelon was labouring to make good Catholics of the New Converts of Saintonge, events in other parts of France did not stand still. The country, in fact, resembled a seething caldron. We will begin with the pastors.

The Edict of Revocation enacted that whilst the flocks were close penned the shepherds were to be driven away. The banishment of the ministers was no new measure, however; a considerable number had already been sent away or had fled. Now, all who remained, perhaps seven or eight hundred, were cast forth to find an asylum in Switzerland, Germany, Denmark, Holland and England.* By the terms of the edict fourteen days were allowed them to depart in, but in many cases even this grace was denied. The pastors of Charenton were required to quit the kingdom in forty-eight hours; and Jean Claude, who had in 1678 so ably measured weapons with Bossuet, within twenty-four hours. They could not cross the frontier without passports, which were often vexatiously withheld. Three pastors of Upper Languedoc were refused this indispensable paper by La Reynie, who sent

---

* At the great Revolution, 1793, 7000 Catholic priests found refuge in England alone.

them to Versailles. Châteauneuf, the secretary of state, after amusing them several days, ordered them back to their province, which they did not reach till after the fortnight had expired. On their arrival at Montpellier, Bâville shut them up in the citadel and was near condemning them to the galleys. They were placed under a guard of soldiers, whom they had to fee heavily to conduct them out of the kingdom,

At first the pastors were permitted to take with them their families and their books; soon their wives only were allowed to accompany them. Before leaving the country they were obliged to sign a certificate, declaring that they carried with them nothing belonging to the consistories. The certificate tendered by Henri Latané being pronounced irregular in this respect, he was immured in the Château Trompette at Bordeaux, a castle which enjoyed an evil distinction amongst the many chambers of horror and living tombs bequeathed to France by the Middle Ages. By the time a clear certificate was prepared the day of grace had expired. In vain his son and himself memorialized the court against the flagrant injustice of his detention; the Marquis de Boufflers, intendant of the province, declared that seeing he was a man of ability and highly esteemed by his flock, it would be of more service to the king to let him lie in prison than to send him abroad.

It is needless to say that many of those who were thus thrust out endured severe hardships. Some died on the journey, or on reaching the land of liberty. The case of two pastors at Metz may be noticed. This is a part of the country of which we have not yet spoken. Whether it was that in the northern provinces the Protestants were less numerous and of a nature less impulsive than in the south and west, or that the rule of the intendants there was less severe, it is certain that they were exempt from the extremes of persecution which their brethren in other parts had to endure. Their worship had been interdicted, their temples demolished, their schools shut up, their civil rights forfeited, their Bibles publicly burned; but the troops had not been let loose upon them, and there had not been the same examples of wanton barbarity. These Metz preachers were both of extreme age, and almost childish. The intendant of the province, touched with compassion at their condition, inquired of Louvois if they might not be allowed to remain. "If they are imbecile," replied the heartless minister, "they may die where they are; but if they have any wits left, pack them off." When the time came for them to depart, a vast crowd accompanied them weeping down to the Moselle, where they embarked for Frankfort. One of them, David Ancillon, made his way to Berlin, whither he was followed by a large number of his parishioners, and where he was graciously welcomed by the Great Elector, who appointed him his chaplain. This was the foundation of the French Church in Berlin.

Most of the pastors stood their ground, and patiently submitted to their lot, leaving all that was dear to them on earth,—goods, family, and flock. Alas! however, a considerable number not being prepared to give these up for their Lord's sake, made their abjuration. Antoine Court made out a list of between fifty and sixty, who in this way denied Christ; and M. Douen thinks that if we had all the data before us the number would have to be doubled. Saurin, the noted preacher, in a sermon on "Buying and Selling the Truth," in allusion to the unfaithfulness of so many, thus apostrophises Rome:—
"O thou, who never ceasest to insult and defy us, do not pretend to confound us by pointing to those galleys, which thou art filling with our confessors. If thou should desire to cover us with confusion, show us the souls thou hast

robbed us of. Instead of boasting that thou hast extirpated heresy, let thy triumph be that thou hast caused religion to be denied; instead of boasting that thou hast made martyrs, exult that thou hast made apostates. This is our real tender point; it is here that there is no sorrow like unto our sorrow," It is cause of rejoicing to add that twenty-six of the faint-hearted almost immediately repented, abjured their abjuration, and, at great peril, succeeded in making their way across the frontier.

IV.
THE REIGN OF TERROR.

No sooner were the shepherds driven away than their flocks attempted to follow them. Before, however, we accompany the terrified sheep in their perilous wanderings, we must inquire what changes were produced at home by the Act of Revocation.

The edict removed the last impediment to the universal and unbridled licence of the soldiery. Whilst the troops proceeded with their grim work of conversion in Languedoc, the Cevennes and Dauphiné, fresh regiments were despatched into the northern provinces, and from thence spread over the rest of the kingdom, so that in less than four months the Protestants in every town and village of France were driven to the Mass at the point of the bayonet. The bishops, indeed, denied that such was the case. Bossuet, in a pastoral letter to the New Catholics of his diocese, dated from Claye, March 24, 1686, says: "Not one of you has suffered violence, either in person or estate; I hear it is the same in the other bishoprics. You are come back to us in peace, and you know it." But a letter from one of the sufferers to Jurien, written from Meaux, December 15, 1685, tells a very different tale : "We are overwhelmed ; the dragoons are come to Meaux after having converted Claye. Nothing can resist them. See to what a pitiful state our sins have brought us!" And in another letter, January 3, 1686: " It is with tears of blood I tell you that the dragoons have forced everybody to change their religion in the circuits of Meaux and Soissons."

A ray of hope having been kindled by some words in the last clause of the Act, which declared that the Huguenots were not to be molested in the private exercise of their religion, an agitation took place in several of the provinces. The Duke De Noailles wrote to Louvois from Languedoc that this remnant of tolerance would ruin everything. Louvois replied, Nov. 5, 1685 : " A few billetings, a little heavy pressure on those of the nobility and the third estate who still stand out, will soon undeceive them regarding the edict. The king desires that you will explain yourself very severely toward those who would wish to remain the last in a religion which is displeasing to his majesty."

The deadly strife between the oppressors and the oppressed was intensified by an edict issued in December, by which it was made lawful to take from their parents infants of five years old. " So terrible a blow," says Michelet, "swallowed up fear in the hearts of the parents. To quell their spirit, and especially that of the mother, the soldiers had recourse to every kind of torment. Their victims were pinched, larded, suffocated, singed with lighted straw like a fowl, their hair and nails plucked out, hung up over burning coals "; with other atrocities still more revolting. Where irresponsible power is placed in the hands of brutal natures there is no limit to the excesses which may be committed.

But the torment which told most in the end was the deprivation of sleep. The poor fellow on whom it was tried, if possessed of money, willingly paid ten, twenty, thirty crowns an hour to be left in peace; but as soon as the brief interval was over, the drum beat and the torture recommenced. An aged man at Nimes, thus tormented for a long season, at length yielded and signed his abjuration. The bishop who received it said: "Now, sir, you may rest." "Alas! my lord," replied the poor fellow, "I look for no rest till I get to heaven; and I pray God that for what I have just done He may not shut its gates against me." "The woman bore this deprivation better than the man. Often he would give in while she remained firm, and her words of admonition would re-inspire him. Then they drove him away and kept him out of his home, and the struggle was continued between the wife and a score of soldiers. But no humiliation could quell her spirit; she rose again by prayer, by the fixity of her faith."

The case of the little children carried off to the nunnery was equally pitiful with that of the mother. "Taken from home at so tender an age, everything was lost at once. The little bed so soft over which the mother bent, the garden, the great chimney-corner where the little girl had her chair; nothing left of all this. Alone with strangers in a vast frigid dormitory, with long stone corridors, and icy courts to be crossed in the snow to reach the chapel on a winter's morning; the kneeling during the long prayers in an unknown tongue, the frame chilled with the motionless posture; the meagre, indigestible diet; the endless classes and catechisms; the humours of teachers and mistresses without sympathy and incapable of teaching; the whip at hand for every offence. It seems to have been thought that these tender minds would soon forget the little they had learnt, and would yield a ready obedience; but it was not so; they often showed a singular tenacity, both of belief and purpose."

The soldiers revelled most when they were quartered in

the houses of the nobility and of the wealthy merchants. They locked the owner up in his chamber; they threw the costly furniture into the street, and stabled their horses in the splendid drawing-rooms, giving them buckets of milk and wine, and for litter, fabrics of wool, cotton and silk and the finest Dutch linen.

We have the testimony of a well-known English divine and historian to the fierceness of the persecution. Bishop Burnet passed through the southern provinces (and it is to these that the foregoing description especially applies), at the very time of the Revocation. "I went over France," he says, in the History of his own Time, from Marseilles to Montpellier, and from thence to Lyons and so to Geneva, whilst it was in its hottest rage. I saw and knew so many instances of injustice and violence, that it exceeded even what could have been well imagined; for all men set their thoughts on work to invent new methods of cruelty. Men and women of all ages who would not yield, were not only stripped of all they had, but kept long from sleep, driven about from place to place, and hunted out of their retirements. The women were carried into nunneries, in many of which they were almost starved, whipped, and barbarously treated. In all the towns through which I passed I heard the most dismal accounts of these things, but chiefly at Valence, where one D'Herapine seemed to exceed even the fury of inquisitors. In the streets one could have known the New Converts by a cloudy dejection which appeared in their looks and deportment. Such as endeavoured to make their escape and were seized (for guards and secret agents were spread along the whole roads and frontier of France), were, if men, condemned to the galleys, if women, to monasteries. To complete this cruelty, orders were given that such of the New Converts as did not at their death receive the sacrament, should be denied burial, and that their bodies should be left where other dead carcases were cast out, to be devoured by wolves or dogs. This was executed in several places with the utmost barbarity; and it gave all people so much horror that, finding the ill effect of it, it was let fall. It hurt no one, but struck all that saw it with more horror than those sufferings that were more felt. The fury that appeared on this occasion did spread itself with a sort of contagion, for the intendants and other officers, who had been mild and gentle in the former parts of their lives, seemed now to have laid aside the compassion of Christians, the breeding of gentlemen, and the common impressions of humanity." And he adds in a letter: "I do not think that in any age there ever was such a violation of all that is sacred either with relation to God or man."

The gloom of these dark years was occasionally relieved by a struggling ray of light. We have already met with humane and sympathizing Catholics, good Samaritans to their Protestant neighbours. Benoit has preserved a few other examples. An officer, after tormenting a woman who was sick of a fever, without being able to shake her resolution, was touched by the sight of so great courage with so little strength, and instead of taking her to prison as he was ordered, set her at liberty. Some dragoons watched by turns to prevent from sleeping a man named Beauregard, of Dauphiné; two of them compassionated him, and when it came to their turn, suffered him to sleep in quiet. A woman named Poupain, having borne many outrages, some of her tormentors relented, and remonstrated with the rest, so that in the end they all left her in peace. The jailer of the General Hospital in Paris, who at first treated with harshness a Protestant woman committed to his charge, by degrees became softened and did all in his power to make her imprisonment tolerable. A Catholic nobleman of Vendôme was so indignant at the murder of a Protestant widow of Epineaux being suffered to go unpunished, that he himself instituted a legal process against the murderer. Another instance of a jailer being won by the good conversation of a prisoner for conscience' sake appears in the following narrative.

V.
JEAN TIREL.

Jean Tirel, a pastor of Normandy, was arrested some months before the Revocation, for the crime of having made a trip to Jersey without the royal permission. The judge at Coutances, after keeping him a long time in a dungeon, condemned him to the galleys. Tirel appealed against this sentence to the parliament of Rouen, but his appeal was in vain. He was sent to the prison set apart for the forçats, to wait for the chain to be made up. Here he was obliged to share the bed of a miserable priest under sentence of death for magic, who attempted to strangle him, and would have effected his purpose had it not been for the opportune arrival of the jailer. The priest was soon afterwards taken away to be burned alive.

The jailer found himself attracted towards his new prisoner. He gave him a better lodging in an upper chamber, and by degrees permitted him, not only to receive visits from his brethren in the town and engage in religious exercises with them, but to extend his pastoral care to the other Protestant prisoners who also were waiting for the chain. One of these, an old man of seventy, died in Tirel's arms, giving glory to God. In the end the jailer allowed him to go outside the gate and take the air on the adjoining ramparts. This indulgence, however, cost Tirel his life. Seeing one day some garments on the path, he took them up; they were infected clothes spread out to air. Tirel caught the fever and died in a few days.

His three infant children had been placed, the daughters in a convent, and the son in a seminary. Endeavours were used to convert the boy, but the impressions he had received from his Protestant parents were too strong; he made a determined resistance and was released. On his way to England he saw his father in the prison at Rouen and received his blessing. The daughters, when told of their father's death, shed tears, for which offence they were obliged to do penance. Tirel's elder son escaped to Holland in 1624, and being introduced to the synod of Gouda as the son of a pastor and confessor who had never abjured, but had remained faithful unto death, the synod voted him a pension for life.

Doubtless many other acts of humanity might have been recorded. Their number would have been tenfold, but that, like Nebuchadnezzar, the king's commands were urgent, and Louis's officers, civil and military, were as obsequious as the servants of the Babylonian despot.]

VI.

AËRIAL PSALMODY.

Protracted and relentless persecution, mental and bodily suffering, with the reproaches of conscience, produced in the southern provinces a state of supernatural excitement. No act of their religious exercises was dearer to these simple people than psalmody; but this source of delight and consolation had long been forbidden under severe penalties. Grief and desire at length so wrought on their minds, that they began to hear in the air the divine songs they had loved so dearly. "In divers places," says Jurieu, "where temples had stood, voices were heard in the air so perfectly like the singing of Psalms that they could not be taken for anything else." Vivens, one of the Desert preachers, who had himself heard them, produced at one time thirty or forty witnesses of these aërial chants.

The marvel first showed itself in Béarn, in October, 1685, a month after the dragoons had left that province, when the mourning church at Orthes was ravished and consoled by these supernatural concerts. Suddenly one man hears the melody; he calls others and they too hear it; they all fall on their knees; they weep for joy; some hear the tune only, others distinguish the words. When they retire to converse on the wonder, it breaks forth afresh. The phenomenon mostly happened between eight and nine in the evening. The peasants flocked into the towns to listen to the celestial music and did not return home till the night was far spent, publishing everywhere the tidings of the happy miracle.

The poor people fondly believed that it was the angels who sang, and that they came to announce approaching deliverance. The persecutors saw in it the work of Satan: an order was made, forbidding anyone to listen to these heavenly songs or to speak of having heard them, under a penalty of 500 livres fine, afterwards raised to 2000. One night a numerous assembly saw a great torch in the heavens, and all cried out: "Behold our happy deliverance!" The torch was held by a beautiful girl in white whom no one recognized, and who invited to repentance several persons who had apostatized for money. The meeting was discovered, and many were put to death.

The hallucination spread to the Cevennes, where the music was heard for some weeks, from December, 1685, to the end of January, 1686. But the Cevenols, so much more ready to fly to arms than the Béarnese, heard other sounds besides songs of consolation and praise. Their ears were filled with the roll of drums and the sounding of trumpets for the battle.

The celestial psalmody soon passed away, but it was succeeded by another psychical phenomenon, more widespread and more enduring, of which we shall speak by-and-bye.

VII.
THE FUGITIVES.

The fourth section of the Act of Revocation swept off the pastors. By the tenth section it was sought to hinder the sheep from following them, to enclose them all in an iron fence where the wolves might worry and devour them. This ordinance, as we have had occasion to see, had already been more than once put in operation; now it was made absolute and permanent. But the government had miscalculated on this as on every other measure of its blind and bigoted policy. "The flock hungering after food turned eagerly to those hands by which it had been accustomed to be fed. No vigilance could be sufficiently alert, no cordon of jailers sufficiently numerous to close every outlet of so extensive a frontier as that which bounded France; and notwithstanding the fearful penalties annexed to detection, a very numerous emigration of the people succeeded the expulsion of their ministers." The tide of exile had in fact been flowing for twenty years; it was now increased tenfold. Men, women and children quitted by stealth the paternal hearth and their native town, and took their way, one by one or in small companies, disguised as muleteers, colporteurs, beggars, sporstmen with dog and gun. Noblemen might be seen wheeling barrows, leading an ass, or driving pigs. Not a few passed as pilgrims, their beard long, a staff and rosary in their hand, and a scallop-shell on their breast, and furnished with a certificate by some humane priest who was privy to the deception. Such a stream of pilgrims to Notre Dame de Liesse in Picardy, or to our Lady of Loretto, or St. James of Compostella, had not been seen for many a year.

The movement commenced in the south; whole parishes in Lower Languedoc were deserted, and it is said that not fewer than 800 persons at once retreated from a village in Dauphiné. The fears of the government were excited by this perilous and rapid depopulation, and force and artifice were alike employed in order to prevent its continuance. Armed peasants scoured the roads and guarded the most obvious passes; and in remoter districts, gold was lavishly scattered to corrupt the fidelity of the guides to whom the fugitives intrusted themselves.

April 23, 1686, there set out from three villages of Dauphiné two companies, numbering together 240 persons (of whom only three were men), and twenty-eight mules carrying their clothes and the little children, under the conduct of six guides who had come over from Switzerland, doubtless themselves emigrants. Their progress was exceedingly slow, for they had proceeded no further than St. Jean de Maurienne when they were arrested, June 22, and taken back to Grenoble. Three of the guides were beheaded, and their heads set on poles; the three men fugitives were condemned to the galleys for life; seventy-three of the women had their heads shaven by the executioner, and were imprisoned for life; twenty-four girls were sent to spend two years in convents; and forty-six were released on paying the expenses of their trial. Lyons and the frontier towns towards Switzerland were full of prisoners.

It was the same in the north. At Valenciennes, St. Omer, Lisle, Tournay, and as far back as Paris, the jails were bursting with men, women, and children, stopped in their flight. At the beginning of 1686, the jaileress of Tournay stated that since the Revocation she had lodged more than 700 Protestants flying from the kingdom. She added that the guards sometimes pursued the fugitives a considerable distance beyond the frontier. The guides were not always either honest or faithful; many were vagabonds from justice; and amongst the dangers of flight must be reckoned their treachery and brutality, which did not stick at attempting the honour and life of women and girls with whom they were concealed whole days in the woods, and whom at the inns they passed off as their wives and daughters.

It was by sea, however, that the most frequent, and probably the most successful, attempts at escape were made. Scarcely a vessel quitted any part of France without some contraband lading of emigrants. When other places of concealment failed, the miserable exiles secreted themselves under bales of merchandize, in empty casks, or amid heaps of stores; and if securer means of transport were not at hand, an open boat or the skiff of a fisherman was eagerly coveted for the performance of some hazardous voyage. The Count de Marancé and his lady, personages of distinction in Lower Normandy, formed part of a crew of forty souls, among whom were several women with children at the breast, who entered a vessel of seven tons burden in the depth of winter, wholly without provisions, and exposed to a stormy sea. Their sole refreshment during a long passage to the English coast was a little melted snow, with which, from time to time, they moistened their fevered lips; until, after sufferings which appeared to debar hope, this piteous company gained the shore, and found a hospitable reception.

One of the pastors, who escaped by sea, was hidden at the bottom of the hold under some bales of merchandize. A soldier, who was sent to search the vessel, using his sword as a probe, thrust it into his body. The minister had the presence of mind not only to receive the thrust without uttering a sound, but to wipe the blood from the blade as it was drawn out.

Many suffered shipwreck; the fate of others was wholly unknown. Some, from the more western provinces, were made prizes by Corsairs, and endured years of slavery in Africa. Some were thrown upon the coast of Spain, and did but exchange persecution at home for an equal measure of severity from the Inquisition. Some captains, after receiving an enormous sum for carrying the fugitives, set them ashore far from the port of their destination, or left them destitute on some solitary coast, or even put them to death. A scoundrel was hanged at Caen for having, on divers occasions, drowned Huguenot fugitives instead of conducting them to England. "The greater number, however, by daring courage, by the sacrifice of their little remaining property in order to bribe those appointed to hem them in, or by the adoption of some skilful disguise, effected their retreat: and there was scarcely any labour too heavy, any service too menial, any privation too acute, to which even women of condition refused to submit, in order to escape the yet more hateful spiritual bondage and degradation which awaited them if they remained in France."

To disencumber the galleys, stocked with condemned Huguenots, Louvois sent cargoes of the prisoners to America in crazy vessels, some of which foundered at sea. Such of the prisoners as escaped drowning and gained the shore were hospitably received by the Indians, especially when they understood that they had been driven out of their native country for adoring the Great Spirit; they opened their cabins to them, and shared with them their maize and cassava.

At length, when Louvois had filled the prisons, the

galleys, and the colonies, he reopened the barriers, relying, says Peyrat, on the well-known character of the French people, who covet the apple only so long as it is forbidden. If he really thought so, however, he was mistaken in this, as in all his former calculations. The tide of emigration rose immediately, and the king, enraged, gave orders again to close the ports.

As already observed, whilst the persecution cost France a great loss of population, the Protestant countries were peopled at her expense. The emigrants spread themselves over Switzerland, Germany, Holland, England and Denmark; England, alone, is said to have received 50,000. The generosity of the Swiss towards the refugees, their brethren in the doctrines of Calvin, was unbounded. But the loss to France is not to be measured merely by the drain of population. The refugees were excellent agriculturists, and the first gardeners in Europe. Many of them possessed commercial secrets of great value, hitherto unknown in other countries. The North of Germany, in return for its liberality, received a busy swarm, who brought with them the art of dyeing all varieties of colours, and improved methods of manufacturing cloths, serges, crapes, druggets, hats, galloons, and stockings. Berlin obtained goldsmiths, jewellers, watchmakers, and carvers. In London, the then suburbs of Soho and St. Giles, were largely augmented; and Spitalfields became the home of a new manufacture in a numerous and intelligent colony of silk-weavers. The mystery of glass-working, in which the French stood nearly alone, was not only transferred elsewhere by the removal of most of the artizans engaged in it, but became deteriorated at home. The nobles, trained to arms, engaged in foreign service; many were enrolled in Savoy, Holland, and Germany; and under William III. the regiments of Huguenot volunteers, who formed part of his army in Ireland, contributed in no small degree to the victory at the Boyne, by which his throne was secured. So short-sighted is the policy of bigoted and despotic rulers.

We cannot do better than follow some of those who sacrificed all they had and braved every peril that they might worship God according to their conscience.

VIII.

THE PERILS OF JEAN MIGAULT (*concluded*).

We begin with our old friend, Jean Migault, the reader of Moullé, whom we left in comparative quiet and prosperity in the little town of Mauzé. This state of ease was of short duration.

In little more than a year his devoted, heroic wife died of fever, a profound grief to him, and an irreparable loss. Close upon this event there followed the law, of which we read a while ago, prohibiting Protestant schoolmasters from taking in boarders; and not many months afterwards the troops were sent again into Poitou to complete the ruin of the Protestant families. For a while the Church at Mauzé was shielded from the storm through the influence of the Duchess of Lüneburg, whose brother, M. D'Olbreuze, resided in the neighbourhood. Thus favoured, Mauzé became a centre of attraction to the Protestants of Poitou, who flocked thither in order to enjoy that public worship which was denied to them elsewhere; every Saturday evening the town was crowded. But this state of things was not permitted to last. It was the year 1685, and the Revocation was at hand. Migault, foreseeing the storm, dismissed his pupils and sent away his children, so that when, on September 23, the cavalry entered Mauzé he was alone. On the approach of the soldiers he and a neighbour crept down into the dry moat which surrounded the town, and took the road to Amilly, passing on their way terrified women and helpless children, who, like themselves, were seeking safety in flight. They found a temporary refuge in several châteaux, but were unable to remain long in any, because the government had begun to station soldiers wherever the gentry were suspected of harbouring fugitives.

Providing as well as he was able for his children, Migault was now obliged to wander up and down the province, hiding in the daytime, and seldom remaining more than forty-eight hours in one place. The cavalry were spread over the whole country, and the hospitable and tender-hearted among the Catholics who were thought likely to shelter their proscribed neighbours were daily subjected to domiciliary visits. "For three months," writes Migault, "I was hunted like a noxious animal from place to place by cavalry, priests, and lay-papists, all the while torn with anxiety about my poor children."

In this emergency most of the children proved themselves worthy of their parents, especially an elder daughter, Jane. She had been taken by a Roman Catholic friend to the house of some relations, where she continued a fortnight, and would have remained longer had not an informer denounced her to the captain of a troop of horse. Two dragoons were instantly despatched in search of her. At their approach she fled from the house and concealed herself in a wood, where she remained during the night; but when day dawned, fancying her hiding-place insecure, she stole back and hid in the court-yard under a heap of straw. The soldiers, who had ransacked the house and maltreated the owners, renewing their search in the morning, discovered her, and dragged her before the Catholic priest. She firmly withstood all the arguments and threats which were employed to make her deny her faith. The form of abjuration was placed before her, and violence was used to force her to sign it, but in vain ; and when the priest, who was resolved to make it appear that he had converted her, wrote underneath that she did not sign because she was unable to write, she protested against the falsehood. How she obtained her release is not known; but two days afterwards a benevolent man conducted her to her father at the house of M. D'Olbreuze.

This good man's mansion was now the head-quarters of Jean Migault and his family ; and not theirs only, but of all who sought refuge in it. Not only the château, but the corn-lofts, barns, and outhouses were filled with persons of all ranks from Saintonge, Aunis, and Poitou, who were generously supplied with every necessary. Another Protestant mansion, that of Monsieur and Madame de L'Aleigne, enjoyed the same distinguished honour. Both were threatened with visits from the military, but for a while their rank and the relation they stood in to the Duchess of Lüneburg protected them. Of all the residences of the Protestant nobility in the three provinces, these two houses alone remained unpillaged. At length they, too, were marked for destruction. Monsieur de L'Aleigne was consigned by a *lettre de cachet* to the castle of Loches, and M. D'Olbreuze was summoned to Paris to attend at court until further orders.

Still Migault and three of his children were suffered to remain a little while with Madame D'Olbreuze, where they passed for her domestics. But now the order was issued forbidding Protestants to have any but Roman Catholic servants, and Jean Migault again found himself adrift. At this fresh trial he seems to have lost his former confidence in divine help. Thinking he saw the means of sending two of his sons out of the country, he ventured into La Rochelle. Here he was arrested, taken before the governor, and, after a severe examination, was induced to put his hand to a paper, declaring himself a Catholic.

What arts were employed to break down his resolution is not known. At this part of his autobiography four pages of the manuscript are torn out. He was set at liberty as to his body, but his spirit was in chains. "On leaving the prison," he says, "I was conducted to the convent of the Oratory, where I basely put my hand to a paper which they presented for my signature; but no sooner had my guards disappeared and I regained my liberty than I despised the sophistry by which I had been inveigled, and my sin rose up before me in all its blackness and deformity. A friend whom I met, observing my distraction, persuaded me to go home with him. To soothe my agitation he directed me to passages of Scripture from which I might derive comfort. I left him the same afternoon, and walking throughout the night arrived at Mauzé the next morning. I can but faintly describe the shame and sorrow I endured. I strove to pray, but it pleased God to hide the light of his countenance, and abandon me to my own reflections, which almost drove me to despair. The congratulations of my friends on my release from prison only increased the poignancy of my remorse; their kind words were so many stabs in my heart; it seemed to me no criminal was ever tormented by so many accusers." It was long before he could summon resolution to call on Madame D'Olbreuze. On entering the room he found her surrounded by several Protestant ladies who had sought her protection. "For a while," he says, "I remained motionless, my heart beat violently; I was, happily, relieved by a flood of tears. Nothing could be kinder than the language of this little company of Christians. They dilated, indeed, on the enormity of my sin, but encouraged me, by the example of Peter and the disciples who abandoned their Saviour, to hope in God, saying my repentance appeared to be as deep, and they doubted not my forgiveness was as complete."

Four of Jean's children succeeded in escaping to

Holland; and in December, 1687, after many disappointments, Jean found means to engage a passage for himself and the rest in a vessel about to sail with a company of emigrants from La Rochelle. He was at Grand Breuil, at the house of a charitable lady; the difficulty was to transport his family to La Rochelle without being observed. He hired a carriage, for which he paid a high price in advance, but the driver never made his appearance. With much trouble he engaged another, in which, travelling through two nights of intense cold, they made their way to the rendezvous, a small house on the seashore, near the château of Pampin, and a league from La Rochelle. In consequence of her advanced age, Jean's mother was left behind. It was here the captain had agreed to take the fugitives on board, so soon as night set in. A few lost their way; the rest, to the number of seventy-five, assembled and waited in trembling impatience for the moment of departure. The arrangements had been made by a generous-hearted man who came himself to superintend the embarkation. As the boat from the vessel could not take the whole number at once, lots were to be drawn who should have the first turn.

Migault and his children, with some others, were in the house; the rest were on the beach, anxiously watching for the boat. Suddenly, cries were heard as of soldiers in pursuit, and the name of the gentleman mentioned above was repeatedly vociferated. Running to the house he exclaimed: "The guards are on the beach! save yourselves!" and then fled, followed by some of the emigrants. It was happily a false alarm, an idle frolic played off, strange as it may appear, by some who were waiting to embark. In about a quarter of an hour the arrival of the boat was announced, and the superintendent not being present to regulate the embarkation, the greatest confusion prevailed. Migault and his family missed their way, and did not arrive at the spot until the boat was putting off, overladen with its burden of thirty-five souls. Hours passed before it returned from the ship; hours of cold, weariness and suspense; and when it came, instead of touching at the same point as before, it ran up a creek a hundred and fifty yards off. The moment the voices of the sailors were heard, everyone rushed to the spot. The most active and least encumbered arrived first, and when twenty-five had entered the boat, the sailors pushed off, saying they had been nearly swamped with the first load, and could take no more, but that they would return a third time for the remainder. Jean Migault's party were amongst those who were left behind.

Day dawned; but instead of the desired boat, which indeed could not then have reached the ship, the daylight revealed two guard-boats belonging to La Rochelle, whose business it was to look out for fugitives. "Our situation," says Migault, "was awful. We saw guards at sea; and we might expect to meet guards on land. Terror seized the whole party; we knew the unbending severity of the governor and fancied ourselves already in his power." Jean's situation was worse than any; he had six children with him, three of them too young to walk, besides a young lady entrusted to his care. Yet he could say: "At no time of my life was my faith more active. Many precious promises presented themselves; one, 'The angel of the Lord encampeth round about them that fear Him and delivereth them,' wonderfully supported me." He succeeded in returning undiscovered, with all his children, to his former hiding-place. The next day he went to La Rochelle, where he passed the evening with several others who had been disappointed of their passage. "We spent a delightful evening; every one," he says, "talked of his own adventures; I may safely assert that there was not a happier fireside in France; certainly it could not have been found in the king's palace, or in the houses of those who were accessory to this horrible persecution. The remembrance of the dangers we had incurred and the suffering we had endured, only increased our gratitude to our Almighty Deliverer. The evening was spent in serious conversation and fervent prayer."

Another attempt to leave the country, which Migault made the next April, was successful. With a portion of his children, he embarked on Easter Monday, 1688, and after a tempestuous passage of nineteen days, arrived at Brill, in Holland. The next Sunday they all attended worship at the French Church, where they listened to a sermon by Jurieu; and a few days afterwards Jean Migault made public confession of his sin in having signed the act of abjuration.

Note.—The original manuscript of Migault's narrative was discovered in the earlier part of this century, in the possession of a poor inhabitant of Spitalfields, a lineal descendant of the writer.

IX.

ESCAPE OF DANIEL BROUSSON AND FAMILY.

We have seen with shame how the wealthy city of Montpellier turned Catholic in a single day. Amongst the weak and terrified multitude, however, there were a few who deserve honourable mention.

Daniel Brousson was the younger brother of Claude Brousson. He was treasurer of the church, and was one of the deputation who, in October, 1683, presented the Duke de Noailles with a copy of the petition to the king and were in consequence put under arrest.* He was respected alike by Catholics and Protestants; but already

* See *ante*, p. 83.

some designing men, with the aid of the judges, had, under various pretences, dispossessed him of the greater part of his property.

When the dragoons entered the province, September 22nd, a week before they reached Montpellier, Daniel Brousson quitted his house, and leaving his wife behind, took with him his eldest daughter and fled to his mother's farm in the country. We derive the story of his escape from his son Claude, then thirteen years of age, who, with a narrative of his own adventures, has interwoven those of other members of the family.

"I was," writes Claude, "at Codognan (a village between Nimes and Montpellier) when I received a note from my father, directing me to join him at the farm. I arrived there at midnight, and found him in great trouble. My grandmother, who had come there to her vintage, had determined to leave her grapes and accompany us. We set out and took the road to Provence. Before arriving at Luc, whilst travelling one dark night, the mules of the litter in which the two ladies rode, stood still in the middle of a bridge and refused to proceed. The muleteer going forward, found that one of the arches of the bridge was broken away, and that if we had gone two steps further we should have been precipitated into the stream. We made a circuit to the inn where we were to lodge, and the next day proceeded to Luc.

"Arriving here my father went into the stable to attend to his horse. A moment afterwards he came to us to say that some gentlemen just arrived had been observing him intently, and that he feared he should be arrested. They were councillors of the parliament of Aix, come to Luc to demolish the temple. They immediately asked my father whence he came and his religion, and what was the object of his journey. My father avowed himself a

Protestant and said he was going to Nice on business. They arrested him. My grandmother presented one of the councillors with a pearl necklace belonging to my sister; it was politely accepted, but it did nothing for us. They made us three retrace our steps to Aix, whither they brought my father the next day. On the way we met my uncle Jean's eldest son in a litter with his tutor; they also were attempting to escape; on hearing our report, however, they turned back and went home.

"At Aix we took a lodging; and as my father, by a rare piece of favour, had liberty to go anywhere within the city, he made calls on the chief men of the parliament, who received him courteously. Several days passed in this way, but hearing that he was to be sent to Montpellier, and that there he would be obliged to submit to the royal decree, he saw that no time was to be lost. Secretly leaving the city therefore, he went to Marseilles, in the hope that my uncles would assist him to go on board a vessel. But this was impracticable, no one being suffered to leave without a passport.

"On his return, he judged it needful for us to separate. He sent me to Marseilles under the care of a cousin, and himself set out the next day, October 10, for Orange, whilst my grandmother and sister took the road for Merindol." Young Claude remarks here on the superstition of the people of Aix, where little chapels were erected at the corners of the streets, with images of the Virgin and saints. The figures were clad in the richest stuffs, and the dresses were often changed; the finest fruits of the season were offered to them and little lamps burnt before them, all the children kneeling around, singing hymns and litanies. "No such practice," he says, "prevailed amongst the Catholics in our city of Montpellier."

"At Orange," he continues, "my father engaged a guide, who, for a large sum, promised to conduct him beyond the frontier. Before setting out he put off his linen and lace and made himself as mean-looking as he could; also, I believe, smearing his face and hands with earth. After great fatigue and many dangers in traversing Dauphiné, he crossed the frontier at Guillestre, and passing through Piedmont and Savoy, arrived at Geneva, November 1. At Lausanne he met my uncle Claude, with whom he remained a few days, after which he made his way to Amsterdam, December 23.

"Whilst my father was preparing to set out for Orange, I went to Marseilles, to the house of my uncle Pierre. It was easy to see, however, that my visit was unwelcome, for a few days before, the fear of making acquaintance with a dungeon had induced him to change his religion; his brother had done the same, and as this kind of conversion was suspicious, they had reason to suppose that a sharp watch was kept over their conduct. He told me I must not expect him to give me any assistance in escaping from France; and after five or six days, during which I was not allowed to show myself, I retraced my steps to Montpellier. On the way I called at my grandmother's house but found it deserted. Thence I took the road to Codognan, where I expected to find my uncle and aunt De Paradez. I arrived there in the evening, but found no one but a valet, a papist, who had served the family more than twenty years. With tears in his eyes the poor man told me that the fear of being compelled to become Catholics had made his master and mistress abandon their house, and he did not know whither they were gone. I asked if he had any provisions; he replied that all the poultry had been consumed or strayed away, and that he had nothing but a little bread and raisins. I supped sorrowfully on what he gave me, and passed the night in anxious thought.

"The next day I sent for a girl who had been a servant

of my uncle. She told me that my aunt had taken refuge at Bernis, with the lady of the place. The village being not far off, I resolved to go thither; and as I was setting out, a papist nobleman who said he was her relation, hearing of my intention, desired to accompany me. We went together to the lady's house, where I found my aunt, and also my aunt De Gaillard. They wondered to see me, supposing I was already out of the kingdom. They besought the nobleman to intercede for them, telling him how they would be willing to part with the greater portion of their income, if only they might be suffered to worship God in secret as they had hitherto done; and that in reality this would be no great favour, since at their age they could not long enjoy it. He replied that he could not help them, because the king made it a point of honour to have but one religion in his kingdom, in which he was strongly supported by the clergy; and he advised them, as they could not long remain concealed, at once to obey the king's commands. They did not follow his advice, but my aunt De Paradez remained in concealment until her husband obtained a passport for himself and his wife, and made his way to Lausanne. My aunt De Gaillard returned to Nimes and died without having abjured.

"After two or three days at Bernis I went back to Codognan, where my old schoolmaster told me with sobs that the whole village, which I had known in past time as Protestant, had been compelled a month after I had left to turn papist. The same day I went on to Montpellier, where also a great change had taken place. The soldiers had been brought into the city, and notice given to the Reformed that they must declare for the Romish religion or have men billeted upon them. This so terrified the people that they ran in crowds to the popish churches to abjure. The concourse was so great that it was impossible to examine the motives of the new proselytes; there was not time even to give them certificates of their infidelity, without which the soldiers would not quit their houses; sealed cards were given instead."

Claude now takes up his mother's adventures. She had, we may remember, been left behind at Montpellier. " Hearing that the soldiers were approaching the city, my mother was in the greatest alarm. She thought to flee, but whither? Within the city no one could protect her; everyone had as much as he could do to take care of himself. Into the country? There the peril was even greater, from the vigilance of the curés and the rage of the dragoons. Whilst she hesitated the soldiers entered her house. Flight was no longer possible; she must either violate her conscience, or resolve to undergo the insolence of the dragoons. For some days she stood out bravely, but at length the pressure of present suffering and the dread of the future, the entreaties of her friends, and most of all, anxiety for her children, made her waver. To complete her trial she heard that we had been arrested. Accordingly she pretended to renounce her religion. The soldiers were withdrawn; but some days afterwards another detachment was sent, because it was remarked that my father was absent. She complained to the consul (city magistrate), explaining that my father was on a journey and would soon come back. He enquired how many soldiers she had. Twelve, she replied. " Well, then," was the brutal answer, " to-morrow you shall have fifteen." My mother now had recourse to a Catholic lady who was very friendly with our family, through whose interference all the soldiers were withdrawn."

Meanwhile young Claude had returned home, and the family were comforted by hearing of the safe escape of his father; but his sister, with her grandmother and an aunt, had run all over Provence without finding a place of exit.

As soon as the Protestants of Montpellier had become Catholics, commissioners were appointed for each quarter of the city to assemble them on Sundays and feast-days, and take them to Mass. If anyone was absent, soldiers were despatched to bring him; and if the offence was often repeated, he was imprisoned or heavily fined. After the great Church festivals the commissioners went round to inspect the priest's certificates of conversion and communion; where these were wanting, punishment followed. The children were obliged to attend the Catholic schools, and the masters had orders to take them to Mass every morning, and to flog those who were absent. The women, even, were forced to go to school to certain ignorant mistresses, sent down from Paris, who went under the grand name of "Sisters of Doctrine." The first ladies of the city had to obey this order, but they only ridiculed their ignorant teachers, who were infinitely less instructed than those they pretended to teach.

From the living, the authorities proceeded to the dead. An aged lady, of one of the best families in Montpellier, confessed her remorse for having betrayed the truth, and protested that thenceforth she would live and die in the Reformed religion. The priests did not wait for her death, but read at her bed-side the sentence by which her goods were to be confiscated, and her corpse dragged through the city and buried like a dog. Under the notion, inherited from the Catholics, that heaven is to be purchased by suffering, she replied that all they could do to her would only help to expiate her sin of abjuring. With these words she expired. The sentence was executed; and when some women brought vine-leaves to cover her body, the soldiers drove them away. "It was horrible," writes Claude, "to see the corpse dragged on a hurdle, preceded by trumpets, and followed by a procession of magistrates and soldiers. It was a sight which the better-minded papists could not look upon without horror. As for me, I was so affected by these spectacles that I resolved no longer to remain in this unhappy country.

"Setting out accordingly early in November, 1686, I left my mother, and went in the carrier's waggon to Lyons, in company with Mademoiselle Rigaud, daughter of a bookseller of our city. We stopped at a village inn, where the host's uncle took me aside after supper to say he had noticed that the carrier had for some time taken Huguenots contrary to the king's commands, and that the young lady with me must be a Huguenot, for when sitting down to table she did not make the sign of the cross." No further notice, however, seems to have been taken of the circumstance; they were not stopped, but allowed to proceed to Lyons, where Claude found nothing but trouble. His father's friend, a New Catholic, on whom he depended for shelter and money, turned his back on him; Mademoiselle Rigaud met with another lodging, and departed without leaving him her address; and his landlady informed him that the commissioners went round the city once a week to search for fugitives.

"I found myself," he says, "fifty leagues from home, destitute both of money and friends. I paid my landlady out of the little money I had left; but when I was going to take my clothes she seized them, pretending that I must pay her a crown owing by a cousin of Mademoiselle Rigaud." With some trouble he got free for the time from this woman, and Jean Servand, a gentleman of Montpellier, who also was dodging the hunters, offered to take him with him to Geneva. Claude accordingly removed to an inn, called "The Covered Well," where he found a crowd of fugitives, men, women, and children, assembled, with guides, ready to depart. In the evening came his old landlady, and again demanded the crown. She would not listen to reason, and M. Servand, hearing the altercation, ran up, and, to end the matter, threw her the piece of money she asked for. Now, however, she changed her tone, saying there were other matters to be settled, and that Claude must go with her to the commissioners to declare where Mademoiselle Rigaud was, and what was his business in Lyons.

Seeing the trap that was laid for him, Claude left the house under pretence of enquiring for Mademoiselle Rigaud's lodgings; and M. Servand at the same time slipped out by a back door. They met in the street, and agreed that it would be dangerous to remain any longer in the city, and that they must depart the same afternoon. They did so, travelling as far as the village of Varbonne, where they waited two days for the rest of their company, and then, to the number of about a dozen, proceeded together.

The journey was slow and painful, and the guide, whom they had to fee heavily, was not well acquainted with the byeways. They travelled only by night, and on foot; and it being near the end of November they suffered much from cold and rain, besides having to wade through torrents with the water up to their waists. In going down a mountain one of their company, an aged woman of Nimes, dislocated her ankle, and had to be carried. The next night she begged them to go on without her, and even obliged her daughter to leave her and follow the party. Passing through the town of Nantua they arrived at a small village, Les Voûtes, at five o'clock in the morning. We resume Claude's narrative.

"Our guide went forward and knocked at the door of a second-rate inn this side of the village. The host had soldiers lodging with him, and could not receive us till the next night. We consulted what to do. To reach our next place of refuge we should have to travel by day, and we were besides already tired out; we decided to go no farther. Climbing a hill close by we concealed ourselves, some in the bushes, and M. Servand, myself, and another under a ledge of rock. Here we passed the next day without food, exposed to the wind and rain. Our shoes and stockings were so soaked that we took them off to keep our feet the warmer. About nine on the following morning we saw the soldiers go past; still we could not move for fear of the peasants.

"In the evening the waiter from the village inn brought us bread and wine, and I do not think I ever made a better meal. At night he came again to tell us our companions had already come down to the inn. We slipped on our shoes, carrying our stockings in our hands; but when we were almost at the house we heard a voice call, 'Who goes there?' Our terror may be imagined; we stood still and held our breath, but the challenge was repeated; the speaker at the same time shouting to his comrades to come back. We heard them galloping up, and ran; they followed us hard, firing pistol-shots, and soon came up with us. They were revenue officers. They had passed without observing us, except one who was behind, who had noticed our movements in the dark, and caught sight of our white cravats. Our companion and I were seized, M. Servand escaping, as if by a miracle.

"We were taken to the inn, where the rest of the company had been drying their clothes. Hearing the pistol-shots they hid themselves. Our captors went first to the stable, where they found no one, although M. Servand was in reality concealed there. Then they took us upstairs, and seeing a large quantity of clothes round a great fire they concluded there were more of the party, and accordingly searched the house, dragging out those whom they found. They secured all but the guide. We were interrogated and searched, and our money taken away; and the next day, bound two and two together, were led to Nantua and put in the jail there. After we were gone, M. Servand came out of his hiding-place, and begged the host to sell him an old pair of shoes to finish the journey; but the man, who had not recovered from his fright, refused, and he was obliged to walk barefooted to Geneva, which caused his feet and legs so to swell that he kept his bed a fortnight. As for us we were taken from the prison at Nantua to that of Belley (near the frontier of Savoy) in very severe weather."

Here Claude and his companions found all in confusion in consequence of an attempt made two nights previously by the Huguenot prisoners to possess themselves of the jail, and escape. Most of them were retaken the next day, hounds being employed in the pursuit.

"On arriving in the prison I was placed, with five or six others, in the room next to the jailer's, where we lay on a little straw under the chimney. We were devoured by vermin. The prisoners had nothing to eat but the 'king's bread,' villainous stuff, and but little of it. The bishop, pitying their condition, induced the inhabitants to supply them with soup. A few days afterwards," continues Claude," I was taken down into the lower dungeons, built of great stones and vaulted. In each of them were fourteen prisoners, packed close, with nothing but straw to lie on, which was changed once a month, but in less than a fortnight was reduced to dust and almost rotten. There were double doors, because of the water, and when they were opened in the morning our breath, which had been shut in all night, issued like the smoke of a furnace, whilst from the roof the condensed breath trickled down the walls the whole day. Here we were locked in, in utter darkness from six in the evening until nine in the morning. We passed much of the night in singing Psalms and in prayer; and although we could hardly be heard in the court, the jailer, one night, listening at the door, came suddenly in and, after rating us, took out the woman whom he supposed was our leader because she sang the loudest, intending to make her pass the rest of the night in the open court, exposed to the cold. But she struck up the Psalm beginning—

> 'Jamais ne cesseray
> De magnifier le Seigneur,'

with such hearty good will, that, fearing the neighbours might take offence, he put her into another cell, where she lay a long time, separated from her husband, who was with us. Almost all the prisoners were sick.

"We had permission to walk in the court during the day, except when the jailer took a fancy to go into the town, in which case he locked us up until his return. In the court we diverted ourselves by running races, leaping, and other exercises, which helped to keep us in good spirits. There was amongst us a tailor of Montpellier, who bethought himself of dressing up some marionettes, and making them play from behind a sheet stretched across the court, a show which the jailer found so entertaining that he invited many persons from the town to see it."

Hitherto Claude, still but a boy, had bravely stood his ground; but now the horrors of the dungeon and the threats of the authorities, for he was frequently taken before the judges in the audience chamber, broke down his resolution. If his fellow-prisoners had remained constant it is more than probable he would have held out to the end, but many of them also gave way; and after six months of incarceration, he and they renounced the Protestant religion in the presence of the bishop. But although Claude abjured he was not yet free; he could not go abroad without a guard. One day the jailer took him and one of his companions to the cathedral to see some relics,—the hand of John the Baptist and the body of St. Elme, the ancient bishop of Belley, "both as fresh as when living."

They were disgusted with the spectacle, and the more so as they had to drop money in the silver basin which was held by the priest. Fresh prisoners arriving every day, the old prisoners, to the number of sixty, were turned out to make room for them. "Those who, like myself," says Claude, "had changed their religion, were now set at liberty, with orders, under pain of the galleys, to return home; those who had stood firm were chained hand and foot, and sent away under an escort.

"In the prison I had become acquainted with a young man of Montpellier, named Perié, and, as he was much older than I, I resolved to place myself under his guidance. Those of our brethren who had been set free and had taken the road to Geneva, instead of returning home, were most of them arrested. My friend foresaw this, and advised that we should stay a while at Belley. There was in the town a papist, who whilst we were in prison sold us wine under the rose, for the jailer supplied us very badly and at a very high price. As he appeared to be an honest man we went to his house; he received us kindly and lodged us; and when we told him we did not intend to remain in France, he offered to conduct us to Geneva. By the side of the river (the Rhône), at the place of embarkation, there is a road which leads to Savoy. It was agreed that we should take this route, and that Perić and I should start some hours before our friend, and wait for him at the first town in Savoy.

"Accordingly, one afternoon we went down to the river as though we were about to embark for Lyons. We had to pass through a large square tower, where we ran great risk of being discovered. Happily the guards were in their rooms on either side of the gateway, and had even shut the doors, so that, although we heard a great noise within, we passed unobserved. The same evening we arrived at a small town in Savoy, and began to breathe more freely, but were still in some fear, because the duke allowed the French soldiers to arrest fugitives in his territory. Here our guide joined us, and the next day we set out again, and although a Savoyard, who recognised us, predicted that we should infallibly be taken, we arrived safely at Geneva after several days' march. We rewarded our guide according to our small ability, giving him a louis-d'or apiece, with which he appeared well satisfied.

"I went on to Lausanne, where I saw two of my uncles, Claude Brousson and De Paradez, and where I made confession of my fault before M. Combes, an aged minister, who instructed me more thoroughly in the principles of our religion. As it was still summer I set out for Holland, in company with more than twenty refugees, and arrived at Amsterdam the 23rd of August. The joy with which my father received me, after a separation of nearly two years, may be imagined. He had no other son, and I was the first of his children who rejoined him."

Claude next speaks of his mother's escape. After enduring for awhile the intolerable burden of the soldiery, she signed, as we have seen, a pretended abjuration. She made several fruitless attempts to leave the country, in one of which, accompanied by five of her daughters and an Italian guide, she travelled safely as far as Pont St. Esprit, on the Rhône. Here they were betrayed by the ferryman, and as they were embarking were surrounded by soldiers, who cried, "Kill them, kill them!" They were not killed, however, but taken to Nimes, with their guide, who was hanged. The mother was carried back to Montpellier, where the intendant Bâville sternly reproached her for her perverseness, and, concluding it was poverty that made her desire to leave France, offered her a pension, which she haughtily rejected, declaring that she would attempt to escape as often as she had the chance. The intendant then told her she might do as she pleased, but as for her daughters he would put them in a place of safety. Accordingly they were sent to a convent, and paid for out of the King's Pence (derived chiefly from the confiscated goods of the Protestants). Unable to obtain their release, she left them, crossed the frontier, and succeeded in arriving at Amsterdam in August, 1688.

Whilst the mother was on her journey, her eldest daughter Jeanne, aged about fifteen, through the intervention of her Catholic relations, was released from the convent on bail. To secure her person, her surety kept her in his own house, but she contrived to escape, and hid herself in the city, her kind harbourers pretending to seek for her in places where they knew she could not be found. When the excitement had subsided they sent her to Geneva, where she arrived a few days after her mother had left, and where she passed the winter. Whilst she was in that city, she had the joy of welcoming her little sister Dauphine, six years old. This sister, who had always remained at Nimes with her grandmother, had been safely conducted by a guide, and when she reached Geneva was presented to Jeanne as an orphan just come from France, who had no relations abroad. Jeanne did not recognize her, not having seen her for two or three years, but she treated her with the tenderness due to her supposed forlorn condition. On being told it was her sister, her surprise and joy overcame her, and for a long time she could not restrain her tears. Jeanne proceeded to Holland in the spring, leaving the little Dauphine sick at Lausanne with her uncle Claude, who sent her forward some months afterwards, so that in less than a year the father, mother, son, and three daughters were re-united.

For four months efforts were made to obtain the release of the other four daughters. Bâville, weary of paying their board, and of the repeated solicitations of their friends, more than once consented to their release; but the nuns found them too profitable to part with, and contrived to procure from the intendant fresh orders for their retention. After awhile, however, the payment fell off; and the nuns, being unsuccessful in an attempt to obtain any money from Daniel Brousson, at length suffered them to depart. This was in 1692. They set out for Marseilles (the eldest was only twelve) accompanied by an aged servant, who managed to obtain a passport as a lady of rank going with her daughters to seek her husband. They were taken on board a vessel bound for Genoa, the captain of which was under obligations to the children's uncle. In consequence of a furious tempest the voyage lasted twelve days. They were hospitably entertained by some Protestants of Genoa, who kept them all the winter, and sent them on to Amsterdam, where they arrived in 1693.

X.

THE SUFFERINGS AND SHIPWRECK OF M. SERRES.

At the same time with Daniel Brousson, another citizen of Montpellier attempted to make his escape, but with a different result.

M. Serres, a collector of taxes, was born a Catholic, and was tonsured when only eleven years of age. For awhile he was zealous against the heretics; but through the influence of an aunt he became a Protestant, and applied himself to the reading of the Scriptures.

In September, 1685, when the dragoons came into Montpellier, he concealed his property, and sending away his children, fled into the country. His mother and aunt sent a messenger to let him know that all the Protestants in the city had abjured, and to entreat him to return home, otherwise twenty-four dragoons would be quartered in his house. He wrote back that he had offered to God not his goods only but his life, and that he could not return. Upon this his father-in-law brought his mother to his hiding-place, with two other friends, who all entreated him to submit, but to no purpose; he cried out: "Get thee behind me, Satan; thou shalt not move me." Not finding himself safe in his retreat, he wandered about till November, when he was informed against, and being apprehended was taken to the citadel of Montpellier. Here he heard that his children who, with an aunt, had been attempting in vain to quit the kingdom, had been arrested at Lyons.

Serres was removed to Aigues-Mortes, a strong place on the Mediterranean, famous in the annals of the Huguenot Church. Aigues-Mortes is not so much a fortified town as a vast quadrangular citadel, enclosing a miniature city within its walls. The walls are pierced with nine gates, and at the four corners, and at intervals between, are fifteen half-engaged towers, with another tower outside the north angle, of much larger proportions than the rest,—the Tour de Constance. In the middle of the south-east wall, and therefore almost at the opposite end of the town, is the Queen's Tower. The fortress was built in the thirteenth century, on the model of the Byzantine castles of Jerusalem and Damietta. We reserve a detailed description of the Tour de Constance for the Sequel to this work, where it plays a more conspicuous part.

Serres was placed in the Queen's Tower, in a solitary and filthy room, where for three days and nights he could neither eat, drink, nor sleep, for the flies and vermin. He fell ill and his mother obtained leave to visit him, but only on the condition that she should use her influence to convert him, and that their interview should be in the presence of two Capuchin monks. A change had come over her since she had visited him in his hiding-place. She kissed him and whispered that she could not help bringing the two monks with her, but that she would rather a thousand times hear of his death than of his unfaithfulness. At the instigation of one of the Capuchins, he was removed to a dungeon where the jailer brought him his rations once only in twenty-four hours, and where, although the fever was still upon him, no water was allowed him to quench his thirst. To keep him alive he was taken out of this hole and placed in a chamber with other Huguenot prisoners. Some of these being released the next day, he sent a letter by them to his mother and other friends, informing them that there were many prisoners in the Queen's Tower and the Tour de Constance in a destitute condition. One of his aunts came to Aigues-Mortes bringing relief, but after two days she was discovered and driven from the town.

XI.

THE ESCAPE OF NISSOLE, SALENDRES AND VIDAL.

Serres and his fellow-prisoners in the Queen's Tower were in a miserable case; they were half-starved and were cruelly tempted by the importunate monks, so that the more enterprising among them were always on the watch for some means to escape. Three in particular, Jean Nissole of Ganges, Salendres of La Salle, and Vidal of the Vivarais, agreed to make the attempt. Observing that the wood brought for fuel was bound up with a strong cord, Salendres saw in this the means of effecting their purpose. With the cord and a mulberry branch for a lever, by slow degrees and without noise, he succeeded in

Ramparts of Aigues-Mortes, south angle, and south side fronting the lagune (Etang de la Ville). The Tour de la Reine, the only tower on the south-east side (not seen in the plate), resembles the double tower to the left.

wrenching off the lock of their chamber door. There were four doors to be passed before they could get clear of the tower. The second and third gave way easily, but the fourth resisted all their efforts. There was, however, a hole in the wall, into which Salendres contrived to insert an iron rod used as a poker, and after much labour he removed two large stones, thus making an opening wide enough for a man to pass through. As soon as this was done he ran in a transport of joy to Serres' chamber, to ask if he would not join them. But Serres was too weak to make the attempt.

The three friends made a rope of their sheets and mattress-covers, which they let down outside the wall, making it fast to a log of wood placed across the opening. After they had joined in prayer, Vidal first descended and alighted in safety. Nissole followed, but being extremely weak from his prison life and the remains of fever, he had not gone down two yards before he lost his hold and fell to the ground, a distance of about thirty feet. Salendres slid down after him as quickly as possible and found him insensible, with his legs severely injured. Two others of the prisoners who had intended to join in the escape, seeing Nissole's accident, were terrified and drew back.

The writer visited the spot in the spring of last year. You pass from the Tour de Constance through a couple of ill-kept, silent streets, and emerge at the Queen's Gateway on to a half-cultivated down or common. We sat on the grass. Before us, as the central feature of the long line of battlemented rampart, rose the rounded twin towers, one on either side of the gateway, to the height of some seventy feet, the grand, stern mass of stone-work relieved by only three or four small windows. From Nissole's narrative it may be inferred that the descent was made from the little window of the right-hand tower, about half-way up the wall. To the north-east the road could be traced which leads to the Tour de la Carbonnière, and further on, to Marsillargues, now a station on the railway to Montpellier and Nimes.

Salendres and Vidal raised the sufferer and carried him two or three hundred paces, happily without being heard by the sentinel; then laying him down, Salendres went to seek a carriage amongst his acquaintances in the suburb of the city, but he was repulsed with a blank refusal, accompanied by reproaches and threats. In returning, the night being very dark and rainy, he ran against some object in the road. Recovering himself, he found to his admiration that it was an ass. He had much trouble to make the animal go with him to where Nissole lay, but as soon as he and Vidal had placed the injured man on its back, the creature proceeded at a brisk pace and with a gentle step.

They passed the guard-house without being observed, and crossing the bridge came to an enclosure where were some cattle guarded by a mastiff, which by his barking obliged them to turn out of their way. Coming to some farms occupied by Protestants, Salendres begged that the sufferer might be taken in for a few days. "But," says Nissole, to whom we owe this narrative, "they would not open their doors or even direct us on our way. We made," he continues, "so little progress, that although we set out an hour after midnight, we found ourselves, when the city clock struck four, not far from the walls. Taking the opposite direction to the sound of the clock, we passed through fields, vineyards, marshes, and sometimes high, thick osiers, which twisted themselves about my legs, causing exquisite pain. My heart and my strength failed, and I begged my kind conductors to lay me down at the foot of a tree and let me die there, telling them I should be the happiest man in the world, my conscience being at rest, and my peace made with God; but that if they carried me with them I should infallibly be the cause of their re-capture. They answered that they would not forsake me for all the treasures in the world, and that they did not doubt God would continue His favour to us and bring us to a safe place, where I might recover.

"At this point we arrived at the edge of a deep ditch without water, which it was impossible for the ass to cross. Vidal went forward to reconnoitre, whilst Salendres placed me on the ground and gave me some refreshment, which happily we had with us. On Vidal's return, Salendres took me on his shoulders and with much labour carried me over the ditch. At daybreak we caught sight of the Tour de la Carbonnière, where guards were stationed for the salt duty, and we were in great fear lest we should be arrested. One of the guards was at the gate combing his hair, whom we prayed to let us through. He replied that the master was upstairs dressing, and would be down directly and open the gate, which he did, lowering the drawbridge. We paid him his toll, and he let us pass, saying only that no doubt we were prisoners escaping from Aigues-Mortes, and that God would be our guide. My companions were delighted when we had passed safely through, for they were in such a state of fear that they took everybody we met for soldiers of Aigues-Mortes come to carry us back to prison. But as for me, God gave me grace to fear nothing, such an inward assurance I had of his help."

Nissole being greatly fatigued wished to stop at Saint-Laurent, a league from Aigues-Mortes; but hearing that a company of dragoons were in the place, they pushed on a league farther to Marsillargues. Here they applied for admission at several houses, but they were uniformly refused, until a young woman, observing their distress, generously offered them her house free of expense. They thanked her warmly, but requested only that she would direct them to a bone-setter. The man to whom she sent them found that both ankle-bones were dislocated; with the help of two other men he managed by main force to replace them in their sockets. Nissole remained two or three days with the bone-setter and was visited by many kind people, especially some young women, who supplied him with a good bed and other comforts.

Vidal and Salendres thought it safer to proceed, and parted from Nissole with mutual tears and blessings. After some time Nissole was able to regain his native town of Ganges, where he lay hidden many weeks and recovered his strength; and at length, through great fatigues and many dangers, succeeded in reaching Geneva, whence he removed into Germany. Vidal also escaped to a land of freedom, but their faithful companion, Salendres, was not so fortunate; he was retaken and hanged at Lédignan.

XII.

THE SUFFERINGS AND SHIPWRECK OF M. SERRES (*Continued*).

To return to Serres in the Queen's Tower.

"The effect of the escape of our companions," he writes, "was to render more cruel the condition of us who remained. I was committed for twelve days to a dungeon alone, and released only at the solicitation of a friend who had become a Roman Catholic. From this prison I was taken to the Tour de Constance, where I found many other prisoners, most of whom were sick. The place was extremely cold and damp, so that the water ran down the walls. It was December, yet we were not permitted either fire or candle, though we were willing to pay for them. We were obliged to burn the straw of our beds to dry the shirts of those who were sick and to warm our ration of cold broth, as well as occasionally to relieve the darkness.

"In this sad condition the Marquis de Vardes, the governor of Aigues-Mortes, took pity on us. He came to the town, and learning that we were nearly all ill he sent us charcoal and candles, offering us medical aid and giving us leave to buy whatever was necessary. He did not stop there; he desired to know our state from our own lips. He sent for me to his chamber, and to my surprise made me sit down beside him, kissed and embraced me. He spoke of the ills to which I was exposing myself by my refusal to become a Roman Catholic, and warned me that after New Year's Day the opportunity for conversion would cease, and we should be treated with the utmost rigour. I answered that I was acting according to my conscience, and was ready to suffer all things rather than abandon my religion, being persuaded that it was better to obey God than the king. 'How!' was his answer, 'do you think that the clergy, with all their wisdom and learning, are in error, and that you, one of the least in intelligence and knowledge, have found the truth?' 'Yes, my lord,' I replied, 'for I believe I am one of those of whom Jesus Christ said to His Father, 'I thank Thee that Thou hast hidden these things from the wise and prudent and hast revealed them to the little ones.' At this he smiled, laid his hand gently on my shoulder, and with kind words dismissed me. He had interviews with all the other prisoners, and the next day caused me to be removed from the Tour de Constance back to the Queen's Tower.

"The air of Aigues-Mortes being very unwholesome, and the prison-life very hard, even to the refusal of water when our thirst was intense, we were nearly always ill, and several died. The malice of our persecutors sometimes went so far as to deny burial; three of the dead bodies were carted away naked, and after being exposed in the town were cast to the dogs."

Before they became too weak the prisoners sang hymns with a loud voice, so as to be heard beyond the thick walls of the fortress, answering one another from their several chambers. The prisoners in the Tour de Constance did the same. This vexed the king's lieutenant, who forbade it under a severe penalty. Finding they did not desist, he sent the officers of the garrison into both towers, who beat several of them, dragging them by their hair.

In February, the prisons having become over-crowded, orders came to draft off a number of the Huguenots to America. This announcement created great consternation, for the voyage was hard and perilous. A Capuchin, who came to Serres with the tidings, told him that if he would obey the king, his friends would intercede for him and he need not despair of pardon. Serres replied that it was of no use to begin well if one did not persevere, and that his resolution was fixed to be faithful to God even to death.

"We set out," he says, "from Aigues-Mortes, seventeen in number, the day after we received the news. Our clothes were given to the jailer as his perquisite, and being bound two and two with cords, with seventy-nine others, men and women who had been brought from Montpellier and Nimes, we were huddled together in a boat. We arrived the next evening at Marseilles, and were at once transferred to the *Flûte Royale*, and better treated than we expected, having permission to buy what we needed, and our captivity consisting only in being guarded night and day. Three weeks afterwards, eighty-one other prisoners were brought from Aigues-Mortes and put on board our ship.

"Our company consisted of three classes of persons, in each of which there were women as well as men:—First, those who had never renounced the Protestant faith; secondly, those who, having abjured at the first consternation, or through the cruelty of the dragoons, had promptly acknowledged their fault, and striven to make reparation; thirdly, those who were so terrified at the prospect of the sea voyage, that they gave way and promised to do all that was required." The weakness of these last encouraged the Catholics in their efforts to convert the rest. All kinds of ecclesiastics, and especially the Jesuits, preached to them and disputed with them, and when they would not listen complained to the officers, who threatened, insulted, and ill-treated them. Some of the prisoners, one especially, the widow of a minister of Nîmes, disputed successfully with the Jesuits, who were so mortified at being confounded by a woman that they got her confined by herself in a little room at the poop, a sentinel being stationed at the door to hinder anyone from speaking to her. Many of the prisoners were sick, and were taken to the hospital at Marseilles, where some died, making a triumphant end.

Happily the ecclesiastics were not all alike. One day an abbé came to visit them. They were disquieted at the sight of his habit and countenance, but instead of adding to their affliction he greatly comforted them. He asked if they were determined to make the voyage, and being answered that such was their resolution, and that they only longed to depart, he exhorted them to be of good courage and persevere, for God would certainly help them. He told them that nothing happens by chance, that from all eternity God had foreseen that they would have to make this voyage, and had determined beforehand to succour and strengthen them.

The Jesuits promised that all who were willing to confess and communicate should be allowed to remain in

France. Some were weak enough to believe their word, but these were bitterly disappointed, for two days before the embarkation the Fathers told them they had been unable to obtain this favour, and exhorted them to be good Catholics in America as they were in France. The poor creatures, finding they had sold their consciences for nought, abandoned themselves to despair, and some of them died of grief.

On the 8th of March seventy men and thirty women were removed to the *Notre Dame de Bonne Espérance*, or rather were driven on board like cattle. The men were placed in one room and the women in another. One hundred criminal forçats from the galleys were also taken on board. The cabins were so small that the prisoners were obliged to lie one upon another. They were locked in, with only a narrow opening for air, and their chains were loosed only for a few minutes in the day. As there were many sick among them their condition was horrible. No communication was allowed between the men and the women, and when, in case of extreme illness, the entreaties of a wife prevailed, and she was permitted to see her husband for a few minutes, a corporal was sent with her to overhear what passed.

The vessel set sail, but the wind was contrary, and on the 6th of April the captain cast anchor off Almeria, on the southern coast of Spain. Some Dutch vessels had taken refuge in the same roadstead. Three Protestant gentlemen on board one of these, hearing that the *Bonne Espérance* was carrying slaves to America, suspected that they were some of their persecuted brethren of the French Church. What followed is related by one of these gentlemen.

"I asked the captain for a boat that I might see for myself. As soon as we came on board, the French captain ordered refreshments for us, but at that moment some young ladies on whose faces death was stamped, came up on deck to take the air. We enquired of them why they were being taken to America. They replied, in a firm voice, 'Because we cannot adore the Beast, or prostrate ourselves before images: this is our crime.' We asked if any of them were from the Cevennes. They replied, 'Two sisters, aged fifteen and sixteen years, from the town of St. Ambroix, one of whom is mortally sick, and her sister is nursing her.' The captain allowed me to send for the latter. As soon as she came up I saw that her face was familiar to me. 'Where do you come from, Mademoiselle?' 'From St. Ambroix,' she answered. 'What is your name?' 'Peirique.' They were my cousins-german! I wished to hear more from her before making myself known, but my tears hindered me: I went close to her and asked, 'Do you not know me?' She turned her eyes upon me, threw herself on my neck, and exclaimed, 'Is it possible, my dear cousin, that I see you again in my affliction?' All the spectators wept.

"The captain gave me leave to go below to see the other sister. There I beheld eighty women and girls lying on mattresses, unable to rise; my heart came into my mouth, and I could not speak a word. What they said was most affecting; instead of my consoling them they consoled me. 'We place our finger on our lips,' they said, 'and say that all things come from Him who is King of kings, in whom is our hope.' I tried to comfort my cousin; she replied, 'It is not death I fear; if God would take me away I should happily escape the miseries I have yet to suffer; but I am resigned to bear what it pleases Him to send.' As soon as we returned to our ship, our captain sent me back with poultry and other refreshments for the prisoners, and money. The next day we weighed anchor; but before we sailed I went again to bid them adieu. They begged me to pray for them that God would give them grace to persevere to the end that they might receive the crown of life."

The prisoners on board the *Bonne Espérance*, being so closely packed, were greatly distressed by the heat, especially in the night, when the vermin preyed upon them. The sailors and soldiers were touched with their misery, and said that rather than suffer as they did, they would turn, not papists only, but Turks and devils. Fourteen men and five women died on the voyage, finishing their course in peace. Of one of them the captain said to Serres: "Your good friend M. De Fouqué has confessed your religion with his last sigh."

On Pentecost Sunday the pilot reported to the captain that they were only forty leagues from Martinique, and that it would be necessary to cast anchor for the night. But the captain, by his calculation, concluded they were a hundred leagues distant, and that therefore they might still make sail. The next morning, two or three hours before daylight, the pilot going to the prow found the watch asleep, and looking carefully ahead discovered land. He instantly sang out to take in sail, but had no sooner given the word than the vessel struck violently on a rock. So great was the confusion that the sailors could not obey orders, and the ship dashing repeatedly against the rock the rudder broke, and all hope was gone.

The women who were locked in their room were forgotten, and when they were remembered the key could not be found, and the door had to be split open. The room was already filled with water, and many perished. Many of the men were unable to save themselves, being chained seven together, and their cries were heart-piercing. The officer did all he could to break their chains; but time passed; all wanted to be loosed at once; and after having released several, he abandoned the rest to save himself. The sailors, unable to reef the sails, cut away two of the masts, and lowered two long boats, into which they sprang, followed by such of the prisoners as were able. Some of the Protestants were of this number. The captain called to those who remained on board to keep up their courage, promising that none who stayed with him should perish; but a while afterwards fear overcame him, and throwing himself into the sea he gained one of the long boats which were hovering about.

We here take up Serres' own narrative. "The ship was soon broken up, only part of the poop remaining, to which we made our way, and spent the time in imploring divine help. We had begun to sing the fifty-first Psalm, when suddenly the hull sank and all were plunged into the waves. I had no strength to save myself, but God preserved me in a miraculous manner. The daybreak showed me that I was in the midst of the wreck, enclosed by some spars which prevented the waters from swallowing me up, but which, at the same time, so pressed me down that I could not breathe freely. I was bruised and wounded with the wood and the nails, and was often rolled over and plunged under water. At last, with the help of some of my companions, I climbed up on the main-mast, where I found the ship's chaplain. Even in this extreme hour he was true to his vocation:—' Well, M. Serres, here we are, both at death's door, and you especially, who are so sick; will you not become a Catholic, and make me at this moment the witness of your conversion?' 'How,' replied I, 'is the flame in you which burns against us not yet quenched? Can you think that I should forget God at a time when I ought to be preparing to stand before Him; that I should be willing to make a false step at the very end of the race? It is you who, in this extremity, ought not for a moment to put off embracing our religion, which is the purest in the world, and outside of which there is no salvation.' He was so troubled by my answer that he begged me not to speak to him any more."

From the mast Serres and three others made their way on to a long spar, but the waves continually broke over them, several times capsizing the spar, when two, who were more vigorous than the others, hauled their feeble companions up again. In this way the day was spent, and at nightfall they found themselves near land amongst islets. But now the wind failed them; and as the water continued to sweep over their heads, Serres concluded his end was come. At this moment some of them by the light of the moon saw a little bark coming towards them, and hailed it. It was manned by two negroes, one of whom spoke French. This man offered, for a crown, to take them on shore. He carried them to his cabin, where they found many of their friends already housed, and some of the crew, and they blessed God for their deliverance. Fifteen men and twenty-one women had been drowned. Amongst the latter were the two sisters Peirique. Neither bread nor water was to be had, and they suffered much from thirst and hunger. Serres soon discovered, also, that so far from having left persecution behind, it was even more rampant in the colony than in the mother country; and he contrasts the kindness of the savages, as he calls the negroes, with the obduracy of his countrymen. The criminal convicts insulted the Protestants, and the colonists treated them like dogs. Fever, heat, and want reduced them to the lowest condition. The governor, moreover, gave Serres no rest, and assured him that if he did not change his religion he would certainly come to the gallows.

Hoping to escape persecution, to find surgical aid, and to get bread, Serres walked to Saint Pierre, twenty-five leagues from the place of the shipwreck. But he had only passed from one furnace into another seven times hotter. Here he came within the reach of De Blennac, general of the French islands, a man " more demon-like than any he had left in his own country." Learning, when only too late, how he had strayed into the wolf's den, he tried for a while to elude notice, but in vain. Blennac had heard of his arrival, and soon discovered his hiding-place. " When I came before him," writes Serres, " I was in a state to melt the hardest heart, but I saw no pity in his eye. He would hear nothing I had to say, but poured out accusations, threats, and blasphemies; and ordered the guard who had brought me to him to break my head with his stick and take me to the dungeon. This hole, in which there were already two other Protestants, was so low that it could be entered only by stooping. There was no window, and being at the extremity of the guard-house, behind a large chimney where the soldiers cooked, it was almost as hot as a furnace. Although I had thrown off my shirt, the sweat poured down my whole body. The stench and corruption were insupportable."

This new kind of torture broke down Serres' resolution and that of his fellow-prisoners. " We saw," he continues, " that persecution tracked us everywhere, and that its violence only augmented. All one night I spent in prayer, beseeching God either to take me from the world, or to put into the hearts of my enemies to kill me outright, so that I might not be overcome by dint of protracted suffering. I felt that I could joyfully die by any manner of death, but I confess that I did not find myself strong enough to wear away my life in this horrible dungeon. In the end, our persecutor succeeded in extorting our signature to a recantation, but without obliging us to take an oath or to speak against our religion.

"Although," he continues, " this weakness was committed under constraint, and my heart had no share in it, my conscience reproached me the next moment, my heart uttered groans, and my eyes shed bitter tears. If the Fathers have said of St. Peter's sin, when he denied his Master, that he was so penetrated with shame and grief as to weep over it all the rest of his life, in like manner I may say that my fault appears to me so shameful that my grief for it will endure as long as I live. How tranquil is conscience whilst it is pure before God; how troubled it is as soon as it loses its purity."

The submission of the prisoners opened the door of their dungeon, but did not at once deliver them from the hands of their persecutors. Some days afterwards they were put on board a small vessel and taken to the island of St. Domingo, 260 leagues distant, their only rations being bad salt-beef and manioc bread, "such as," says Serres, "a hungry dog would not touch." If it had not been for the compassion of the captain they would have perished with hunger. They called at St. Christopher's, where they were brought before the governor, who put them in prison for a month, but sent his surgeon to attend on Serres, and treated them with as much kindness as he could venture to do. Although forbidden to hold any intercourse with Protestants, yet many, both French and English, found means to send them presents. Arriving at St. Domingo the governor told them that De Blennac had described them as very dangerous persons, who must be separated. Serres was sent to Leogane, and there permitted to proceed to the Isle of La Vache, a wearisome voyage, but which offered to him the hope of rescue by means of the English vessels which called there for wood.

Three weeks after his arrival an English bark from Jamaica cast anchor at the port, and the humane captain carried the wanderer to Curaçao, treating him with every attention. Thence he went to St. Thomas to make public confession of his fault in the Protestant chapel. He soon afterwards returned to Europe, arriving at Amsterdam,

June 7, 1688. He says:—"I find here a crowd of our refugees; this great city is full of them, and there is no town of the seven united provinces in which one does not see them." His concluding words are:—"After twenty months of prison, and so many perils and misfortunes, I cannot sufficiently bless God for having brought me hither, where conscience is so free and liberty so sacred."

XIII.
LE JEUNE.

In the course of his narrative, Serres refers to several of his fellow-exiles, and especially to Le Jeune, a native of the Vivarais, of whose constancy he speaks with admiration as of one who, unlike himself, had been faithful to the end.

This man, before he was apprehended, had sixty-four soldiers quartered upon him, who consumed his substance, and wreaked their rage on his person. They let him down into a well, drawing him up and plunging him down again, each time threatening to drown him if he would not abjure. Unable to shake his resolution they carried him back to his house, and hung him up by his arms at his own window, exposed to the mockery of the passers by, whilst they themselves in turn spat upon and buffeted him. Then they took him from the window, and stripped him to see if he had any magic letters or marks on him, and putting his clothes on again set him to turn a spit before a great fire. The fire not scorching him quick enough, they took off his shoes and stockings and basted his legs with the dripping from the roast meat which was on the spit. He would have died if one of the soldiers had not taken him up and thrown him on a straw mattress, where he lay a long time unconscious. When he came to himself he saw his goods and furniture sold by auction; so that from being a man in good circumstances he had nothing left but a handful of straw. The Bishop of Viviers and several priests came to visit him, but instead of compassionating his lamentable condition they only aggravated his sufferings by their importunities and threats.

Le Jeune was taken to the Tour de Constance, from whence he was conveyed to Marseilles, and put on board the *Bonne Espérance;* he was one of those who survived the shipwreck. In America he maintained his fidelity in the teeth of every hardship and temptation. "In the end," says Serres, writing in Holland, " God led him as by the hand into this happy country, to give him rest from his long labour and to heal his wounds. He is now at Groningen, and praises God in peace."

From Holland Le Jeune removed to London, where he died whilst still young, the ill-treatment he had endured having doubtless shortened his days.

Before returning to the internal condition of the afflicted provinces of France, we must find space for one other narrative, not of wanderings or escapes, but of the faithful endurance of a long and sore imprisonment.

XIV.
THE BASTILLE.—JEAN CARDEL.

Jean Cardel was a silk manufacturer, a native of Tours. To escape persecution he emigrated, in 1684, the year before the Revocation. He settled at Mannheim, where he established a silk factory, and by his activity, intelligence and probity, rose to wealth and consideration. The eyes of Louis's ministers were upon him. Going one day to the fair at Spires, he was waylaid and seized by some

French soldiers, who had crossed the frontier for the purpose. He was falsely accused of conspiring against the life of the king, and shut up in the Château of Vincennes, Nov. 25, 1685. In vain the Elector-Palatine protested against the violation of his territory, and William III., the States-General of Holland and the Emperor of Germany, interposed on his behalf; their representations, together with his mother's entreaties, were ineffectual; and, Aug. 4, 1690, he was transferred to the Bastille.

Here he lingered out twenty-five years, forgotten by the world, and the very cause of his imprisonment forgotten by the king. In the registers of the grim fortress nothing is said of the crime which was imputed to him; he is described as being immured on account of his religion. It is noted that "his mind was in a kind of wandering, which left him with only short intervals of reason"; and in 1714, the Marquis D'Argenson, lieutenant of police, after stating that both the reason and health of the prisoner were broken down, writes: "I think charity no less than justice points to letting him live and die in the castle." That both mind and body should give way is no cause for wonder, when we learn the treatment to which he was, at some period of his imprisonment, subjected.

He was lodged in the Corner Tower, where several illustrious persons had been immured, and where Le Maistre de Sacy wrote the greater part of his translation of the Bible. At the time when Cardel was imprisoned there, another Protestant writer in the same tower was occupied with a paraphrase of the penitential Psalms and the hymns of Scripture. His name was Constantin de Renneville. "I was," he writes, "in the second chamber of the Corner Tower, when I heard frightful cries from a prisoner in the chamber below me. As the sufferer, in the intervals, uttered affecting prayers and sang Psalms from the old version, I concluded he was a Protestant. To make sure, and to communicate to him some relief or consolation, even at the risk of being sent to the dungeon, I made a hole in the floor beside my bed, exactly over that of the poor man. I could not get him to tell me his name. Many a time, not without tears, have I watched the barbarity exercised upon him. The suffering was such that as soon as he heard the door open, he trembled in every limb. I have seen his attendant fall on his knees before the hard-hearted executioner, begging for salve and linen to dress the wounds, but all in vain. The prisoner had nothing but a pint of milk a-day to sustain him."

The registers record that Cardel "died suddenly, June 13, 1715." On being apprised of the event, the secretary of state, Ponichartrain, wrote: "I am sorry the prisoner died without making abjuration." He was buried at the foot of a pear-tree in the garden of the Bastille.

XV.
CHASTENED BUT NOT KILLED.

In the eye of the law there were now no more Calvinists in France; they had all become Catholics. Their preachers had been driven away; their temples levelled with the ground; their synods suppressed; their schools and colleges shut up. They were baptized and married (or supposed to be so) only by the parish priest; their children were sent to the Catholic schools; the Huguenot had become a being of the past; the Catholic, Apostolic and Roman Church might now repose and shine forth in unclouded glory. Such was the state of things according to the law, and such or something like it was the dream in which the king and the court indulged.

But the Church of Calvin in France was not dead. Overthrown, crushed, tormented, it was still full of life, that spiritual life which could say with the Psalmist, " My soul longeth, yea even fainteth for the courts of the Lord; my heart and my flesh crieth out for the living God";— words which still burned in many a heart, although the lips and the hand had belied them. The activity of this spiritual life was attested in many ways, one of them being, as in Poitou, in 1681, the remorse which took possession of the lapsed. As soon as the hurricane had passed over, they began to repent. " Night came and set them in their loneliness face to face with their cowardice. Those who had abjured the most lightly were the first to sit down in the ashes, to beat their breasts and tear their hair. Labourers whom the solitude of the fields left an easy prey to remorse, would suddenly leave their plough and falling on their face in the furrow, cry: ' Lord, grace, grace, mercy!' Others, who for a long time kept up the profession of their new faith, as soon as sickness came, were filled with horror. They cursed the monk standing at their pillow, and loudly declared they would die in no other faith than that of their fathers."

The more active and aggressive tokens of life were not wanting. Jurieu, the noted professor of Sedan, who fled to Holland when the Protestant college of that city was handed over to the Jesuits, uttered in 1682, three years before the Revocation, the following prediction: " Soon they will persuade the king that three-fourths of the Huguenots are converted, and that those who remain are unworthy of consideration. He will thus be drawn on to revoke the Edict of Nantes, by which act nearly two millions of souls will be forced to live without the practice of religion. It will be forbidden under pain of death to preach, but preaching will go on, in caverns, in woods, in cellars, under the darkness of night; and instead of preaching in a few places only, they will preach everywhere. The preachers will not fail to be discovered, and will be imprisoned, banished, hanged. Moreover, some of the excited and impatient will fly to arms, and the king will be compelled to shed in streams the blood of his subjects." We have already seen the first article of this sagacious prophecy accomplished; we are now to see the fulfilment of the second; the last, recourse to arms, although some warlike demonstrations took place in this century, belongs especially to the Sequel to the present work.

The narratives which follow will help us to realise the horrors of the Reign of Terror, and the unquenchable nature of the flame which burned in the bosom of the captive Church. Many other witnesses were raised up, of most of whom little is now known, except that they preached and taught Christ diligently and boldly, and that they sealed their testimony with their blood, or with years of affliction in the galleys or the dungeon.

XVI.
FULCRAN REY, THE FIRST MARTYR OF THE REVOCATION.

Fulcran Rey was a native of Nimes. Unable to receive consecration as a minister, because the synods had been abolished, he was still only a candidate. When the king banished the pastors, he took the noble resolution of remaining in France to confirm the faithful and raise the fallen. He went to Montauban, which he found "wholly given to idolatry"; thence to Milhau, where the condition of the Church was no better; and thence to his kinsmen at St. Affrique, whom, however, he found so overwhelmed with fear of the galleys that they not only refused to help him, but he could not even remain amongst them.

Returning to Nîmes, he held several meetings in the neighbourhood, but the frequent arrests which followed compelled him to desist. Here he wrote to his father: "When Abraham was going up to Mount Moriah to offer his son Isaac, he did not consult the flesh, but courageously ascended the mountain, crying: 'In the mount of the Lord it shall be provided.' God has not spoken to me mouth to mouth, as He spake to the patriarch, but my conscience inspires me to sacrifice myself for Him and His Church. If I am taken, do not murmur against Him. What happiness it would be if I could be of the number of those whom the Lord has reserved to declare his praises and die for His cause."

From Nimes he went up into the Cevennes, where he preached for six weeks. Coming to Anduze he was betrayed by his guide. He was lodging outside the town, and whilst he was engaged in meditation, the dragoons arrived, seized him and dragged him to the town-hall. From Anduze he was conducted to Alais, and thence to Nimes. Everywhere the magistrates and the monks made vain attempts to induce him to abjure, promising him life and pardon. At length he appeared before Baville.

"Mr. Rey, you have yet time to save yourself."

"Yes, my lord, and that time I wish to use for my salvation."

"Mr. Rey, you must change, and you shall have your life."

"Yes, my lord, I must change, but it will be the change from this land of misery to the kingdom of heaven, where a blessed life awaits me. Do not think to terrify me; if I had feared death I should not be here."

"Where have you preached?"

"Wherever I have found the brethren assembled."

"But the king has forbidden it."

"The King of Kings has commanded it; and it is right to obey God rather than man."

He was condemned to be tortured and hanged. He heard the sentence without changing countenance and said: "I am more gently dealt with than my Saviour was; I had prepared myself to be broken or burned alive."

Fearing the impression which the constancy of the young apostle might produce in a Protestant city like Nimes, Bâville sent him to Beaucaire. The gallows were set up outside the Beauregard gate. When Rey saw the crowd round the scaffold he began to sing a Psalm, but he was silenced. Although his feet were torn by the rack, he went cheerfully up the ladder, saying he was going up to heaven. He was twenty-four years old, and was executed July 8, 1686, after a ministry of no more than nine months.

XVII.
ISAAC VIDAL.

There was in the Cevennes in the vicinity of Le Vigan, a young man of twenty-three, a wool-carder, named Isaac Vidal. One night in November, 1685, he thought he heard a voice saying: "Go, comfort my people." His father made light of the matter, but the young man found that if he would keep a clear conscience he must obey the call. Accordingly he went from place to place, collecting the brethren and exhorting them with much force and lucidity. The people came in crowds to hear him.

At a meeting in January, 1686, held in a barn on a hill near St. Roman, 2500 persons were present. The preacher, who took for his text Isaiah lxv. 11, 12, dwelt so powerfully on the sin of apostacy, that the audience were melted to tears; and a merchant of St. Hippolyte, rising up and stretching his hand toward heaven, swore he would never again go to Mass, even if it cost him his life. Nearly the whole assembly repeated the vow; and the preacher, turning from the thunders of Sinai, comforted his audience with the gracious promises contained in another chapter of the same prophet, lv. 6, 7. At the conclusion of the service, faithful and active men were appointed as elders for the several quarters of the Cevennes, whose business it was to give notice of the meetings. Of these many finished their course in the galleys, and some were hanged. At the same time, there being no longer either consistory or synod, it was resolved to give the preacher then and there authority to administer the sacraments.

A few days afterwards Vidal held another meeting in a barn near La Mothe, in the neighbourhood of La Salle, at which nearly 4000 people came together. The barn being too small to contain so many, a pear-tree was hung with lamps for an out-of-doors meeting; but the cold was too severe, and as many as could find room had to withdraw again into the barn. The meeting was betrayed by an apostate, and several persons were arrested, amongst them a magistrate of Durfort, named Teissier, who was seized in his bed. Bâville hastened to La Salle, condemned Teissier and another man, Pouget, to be put to death, and caused the barn to be pulled down and the pear-tree uprooted. At the same time, whole woods of young chestnut-trees were destroyed to prevent their being used as places of meeting.

Vidal was one of the few desert preachers who escaped the gallows or the wheel. After a short ministry of six months, he died at Cézas of disease contracted by preaching in winter in the open air.

XVIII.
THE MARTYRDOM OF TEISSIER.

Pouget, one of the two men who were arrested after Vidal's meeting, abjured on the promise that his life should be spared; but the promise was not kept, and he was executed.

A missionary priest, named Philippe Aiguisier, of a noble Marseillaise family, was appointed to visit Teissier in prison, and has left an account of the interview. An English nobleman, the Marquis of Stafford, was present. "As well from horror of the penalty to which the prisoner was condemned, as from the belief that he would lose his soul, I did all in my power to convert him; but the more I entreated him the more fervently he raised his heart and eyes to heaven, crying: 'O, Eternal Father, my God, suffer me not to yield to temptation.' I embraced him and shed bitter tears, on which he said:—'Sir, God sees your zeal and sincerity, and will not leave you without a reward; you will die in our religion.' 'Yes,' interposed the marquis, addressing himself to Teissier, 'you will be like St. Stephen, you will convert St. Paul;' to which I involuntarily replied: 'Well, sir, pray to God to convert me.' When," continues Aiguisier, "Teissier heard the sound of putting up the gallows, he exclaimed: 'Courage! they are preparing the ladder by which I shall ascend to heaven.' I still did all I could to persuade him that if he died in 'the religion' he could not ascend to heaven, but must go headlong down to hell. He always replied: 'My God, my Saviour, I commend my soul to Thee.' The executioner, who in former years had often worked in Teissier's garden, said: 'Ah, sir, who could ever have told me this!' 'It is God's will,' replied Teissier; 'I have often grieved Him, yet He has shown me nothing but mercy.'

The executioner shed tears as he bound him. We left the prison," continues Aiguisier, "and crossed the square. As soon as he was come to the place he cried out: 'I die in the religion.' To drown his voice I shouted still louder, but the people had heard the words. He mounted the ladder; I went up two rounds with him, continuing to exhort him to repent; and called to him to let me hear his dying words. He repeated again very distinctly, 'My God, I commend my soul to Thee.'"

The martyr's words and conduct wrought so powerfully on the priest that he could not resist the conviction. "I was constrained, like Lot, to follow the angel who led me out of the Sodom of the world." He escaped from France, and was admitted into the Reformed Church in the city of Berne.

XIX.

EMMANUEL DALGUE.

Emmanuel Dalgue of La Salle, near St. Hippolyte, fled on the arrival of the dragoons, and passed eighteen months in the woods and caverns of the Cevennes, devoting himself to the ministry of the Cross. At a meeting held one night in March, 1686, near St. Germain de Calberte, he narrowly escaped being shot. The worshippers were betrayed by one of their own sentinels, who, running down with all speed to St. Etienne de Val Francesque where there were troops, gave the alarm. The captain, as he passed through St. Germain, took with him the judge, the priest, and a Jesuit. The soldiers, who came upon the assembly as Dalgue was administering the supper, fired upon the people, by which many were brought down, and then fell upon the rest with their swords, women as well as men. They pursued those who fled, and searched the rocks for those who hid themselves. Some attempted to save themselves by crossing the stream, but, unable in the darkness to find the ford, were drowned. The Jesuit cried to the soldiers to kill all, which, however, was not done, many being taken prisoners. The officer who carried the news of this butchery to the Marquis de la Trousse at Montpellier, excused the slaughter on the plea that the troops were excited and could not be restrained. The marquis replied, they ought to have slain them all.

Dalgue, who was one of those who escaped, prosecuted his ministry till the next year, when he was arrested. He was condemned, with another who had been taken, to be hanged. Dalgue was brought out first, June 26, 1687. The executioner was new to the work, and had to be assisted by the daughter of his predecessor, who had already performed several executions in her father's stead. Seeing Dalgue's firmness, the woman struck him twenty times on the face with her fist, without eliciting a word of rebuke from either magistrate or priests. Like his Master, the martyr suffered the insult without uttering a complaint. He mounted the ladder with a cheerful step, and died praying for those who were putting him to death, and exhorting them to be converted and no longer wage war against God.

XX.

ORANGE AND DAUPHINÉ.

On the east bank of the Rhône, between Dauphiné and Provence, lies the little principality of Orange, which, although thus embosomed within French territory, was then the hereditary possession of the prince of that name, afterwards our William III.[*] Relying on the supposed independence of this little State, many Pro-

---

[*] In 1713 it was ceded to France by the King of Prussia, as William's heir, in exchange for the town of Geldern in Germany.

testant families of the adjacent provinces, and some preachers, had fled there in the hope of a safe asylum. It was the practice also of congregations within reach of the border to resort thither on Sundays for worship and Church fellowship. But the parliament of Orange, fearful of offending the powerful government by which it was hemmed in on every side, acted a time-serving and cowardly part; and, unmindful of the rights of its lawful sovereign, expelled, even before the Revocation, all who had fled from French territory to put themselves under its protection.

After the Revocation the dragoons were marched in, just as though the principality had been one of the French provinces. Four ministers were arrested and sent from prison to prison, whilst the fifth, who had broken his thigh, was tormented in his own house, drums being beaten night and day to prevent him from sleeping. The poor man was afterwards transported to Valence, where a promise to abjure was extorted from him. Refusing, however, to fulfil his promise, he was again subjected to ill-usage, until by a feint he contrived to make his escape. Putting on the habit and style of a great lord, and attended by four valets, he crossed the frontier without suspicion, and arrived at Geneva, from whence he passed to Germany and Holland, and afterwards to England.

All the temples of the principality were thrown down, and the soldiers charged to make a complete conversion of the Huguenots. To facilitate the work the bishop promised exemption from certain Catholic duties which were especially obnoxious, such as praying to the saints and bowing to their images; promising also to grant the communion in both kinds. These artifices were only too successful, both the city and the principality becoming so entirely converted that scarcely a single Protestant remained.

We may remember how on the failure of Brousson's project of passive resistance blood was first shed in Dauphiné. Like the Cevennes and the Vivarais, this mountainous province, in which the outworks and spurs of the Alps come down to the Rhône, was peopled with a brave and excitable race. The persecution in these parts was hot; the resistance, which was favoured by the nature of the country, was obstinate. In 1689, March 16, Madame de Sévigné, who, as we have seen, extolled the Revocation as the most glorious act ever achieved by monarch, wrote to the Count de Bussy-Rabutin:—"M. de Grignan (her son-in-law) has been making a most fatiguing journey in the mountains of Dauphiné. His object was to ferret out and punish the wretched Huguenots, who came out of their holes and vanished like ghosts as soon as they found they were being tracked. The trouble which these flitting, invisible enemies give is incalculable and endless."

Even before the encounter at the village of Bourdeaux, in 1683,* the Bishop of Valence, one, it may be remembered, of the deputies of the clergy who addressed the king with obsequious flattery on the eve of the Revocation, had done a fair stroke of persecution on his own account. He was zealously seconded by the governor of the prison-hospital of Valence, of whom we have already heard more than once. This was D'Herapine, an Italian adventurer, who had ingratiated himself with the bishop, and who invented new and revolting barbarities to subdue the spirit of his victims. He threw down into their dungeons carrion and the offal of sheep and oxen for them to lie upon; compelled them to wear the clothes of patients who had died in the hospital; and in other ways used them so brutally that his name became a by-word, being changed by the people from *D'Herapine* to *La Rapine*.

* See *ante*, page 90.

XXI.
BLANCHE GAMOND.

In February, 1683, the bishop sent for six companies of soldiers, and billeted them on the Huguenots in the little town of St. Paul-Trois-Châteaux, in Dauphiné. One of the families which had to endure this burden was named Gamond. The bishop offered money to the mother to abjure, and when he could not persuade her, he sent his steward to the house. "It grieves me," said the steward, " to see the confusion the soldiers have caused, but the bishop is willing to make up your losses and to grant besides one hundred francs to each member of your family." The daughter Blanche, then eighteen years of age, answered him : " Sir, your money perish with you. When a garden or vineyard is exchanged, the owner of the less valuable property has to give money to make up the difference ; our religion, therefore, must be worth more than yours, since you offer us money to compensate our loss." Blanche's faith, understanding, and strength of will, marked her out as the most formidable antagonist with whom the bishop and the soldiers had to contend.

The news of the martyrdom of Chamier, an advocate of Montélimar, who was broken on the wheel, reached St. Paul. When Blanche heard of it, she asked herself : " Could I suffer the wheel or the fire, if God should call me to it? I stretched out my hand," she continues, towards the fire ; but as soon as my fingers began to burn I hastily drew it back, crying out : ' O God, in proportion as Thou layest affliction on thy children, Thou must increase thy grace and the power of thy Spirit to uphold them, for we are feebleness itself."

In September, 1685, guards were placed at the gates of the little town to watch all who went in or out; nevertheless, from time to time some would slip through and escape. Blanche was one of these, and she was followed by her parents. They hid themselves at a small farm, but hearing that the soldiers were abroad in quest of runaways, they fled to Orange. Here they were in great danger and were forced to return to St. Paul, from whence Blanche, her mother and her brother, again set off and made towards the Savoy frontier. "We three," she writes, "went forth to seek the spiritual manna which, because we had despised and trodden it under foot, had ceased to fall in France; we hungered and thirsted, not for bread or wine, but for the word of God."

They passed safely through Grenoble, but whilst endeavouring to conceal themselves in an island of the Isère, they were discovered by some horse-soldiers who were in quest of game, and were sent back to the city. The brother escaped on the way, which so enraged the guards that they cried out: "We must tie these two dogs to our horses' tails." They were carried before the intendant, who, finding he could make no way with them, said: "Take them off to jail; they'll change; the prison isn't comfortable."

In May they were again interrogated. When it came to Blanche's turn the commissioner asked:

"Of what religion are you?"

"The Reformed."

"Why do you call it Reformed?"

"Because it has been purged from the errors and abuses with which the wickedness of men had corrupted it."

"Whither were you going when you were arrested?"

"I was going to seek some lady to wait upon, although I have never been at service; but since the soldiers have consumed all our goods, we must try to earn our bread if it shall please the good God."

"Have you never abjured, never in your life?"

"No, thank God."

"Where have you spent the last seven or eight months?"

"In the forests and among the rocks."

"Do you not intend to recant?"

"God forbid!"

"If you will follow my advice you will be happy for the rest of your life. If not, you will be miserable, for you will rot in a dungeon."

"Let my body rot as much as you please, you have no power over my soul, and if only that is with God I am satisfied."

"Do you not see that all the great people of your religion have come over to us?"

"I know, sir, that I am of the little despised flock, but I would rather be with Noah in the ark, than with the whole world to be drowned by the flood."

The examination lasted an hour and a-half.

In June Blanche was again called up before the commissioner.

"Have you not changed your mind since I saw you, and do you not find the prison and the cell hard?"

"No, sir, I am the same as I was; and as to the prison, it is my sins which keep me there."

"Why will you not return to the Roman Church? Can you think that a wretched cobbler has more understanding than a hundred bishops who have studied all their life?"

"Sir, God has hidden these things from the wise and prudent and revealed them to little children."

"Will you not hear the Bishop of Grenoble, who preaches the Gospel so admirably?"

"No, sir; he is not my shepherd, and I do not know his voice."

P

"It is not permitted to women or girls to read the Bible."

"Pardon me, sir; is it not for women and girls to know salvation as well as men? Show me a single passage of Scripture forbidding us to read it. St. Chrysostom recommends and even enjoins the practice upon all, women, children, poor artizans and labourers; St. Jerome took the pains to translate the Bible into the language of his Dalmatians that they might all know it; Charlemagne, in his capitulary, directs that divine service shall be performed in the vernacular tongue, that it might be understood by all."

Blanche was now removed, with eight or nine other women, to the dungeon in the moat, a filthy hole beside which the river flowed. They were taken down by four men and searched from head to foot. The room reeked with moisture, the rats swarmed, and the stench was horrible. Nothing was given them to eat till the evening, and what they left the rats devoured. In the night one of them cried out that a rat as large as her shoe had fallen on her. The townspeople said in astonishment: "They have put women and girls into the dungeon in the moat." Two ladies came to see them, one of whom took Blanche aside and said: "I am grieved to see you here; they are determined to drive you to despair. You will have your head shaved by the executioner, your cheeks branded with the fleur-de-lys, and you will be whipped through the town." Blanche replied: "Mademoiselle, neither the hot iron, nor the scourge, nor the razor, so long as I have the help of the Holy Spirit, can separate me from my God." "What are you thinking of, you will have to suffer all your life; this is only the beginning." "Alas! I have deserved nothing less, for my sins have been very many, and therefore God makes use of men to punish me. But it will only be for a time; He will take me out of their hands when He shall think fit."

The next day one of the ladies came again and said: "My dear sisters, if you will only change your religion, you may come out of this place." Blanche answered for the rest: "Madam, we will not change; God will deliver us without changing, and at such a time as we least expect it." The lady replied: "If you believe in God as the apostles did, and look for the prison doors to open of themselves as in the time of holy Peter, then we will believe that your religion is good." To which Blanche rejoined: "The priests said to Christ when He was on the cross, that if He was the Son of God He should come down and they would believe on Him."

Promises were next tried. Being called up again before the commissioner, he told her there was a young man of good family who desired to marry her if she would recant. She replied: "If I were to do as you propose, it would not be because I have found my religion bad and yours good, but in order to get a husband; he would be dearly bought at the price of my soul."

Soon afterwards Blanche and one of her companions were brought up before twelve or thirteen councillors in the palace, and after the examination was over, and they had been taken back to their dungeon, the turnkey, accompanied by a secretary, came into the cell and read to them their sentence, which was that they should be imprisoned for life, their goods confiscated and their heads shaved, and that they should be sent to the hospital until the place of their prison was resolved upon. On hearing this terrible sentence, Blanche's other companions fell on her neck and kissed her, saying: "You are blessed, for your marriage contract has been read and you have espoused the prison." She answered: "God's will be done."

In the month of August Blanche fell ill with fever. She entreated the jailer and a lady who came to visit her, to let her see her mother. After three days she was told that her mother might come to her if she would recant, otherwise, never. Her reply was: "Though you prevent me from seeing my mother in this world, by God's help I shall one day see her in heaven." Her head was shaved with rusty razors, which caused her severe pain. Many persons came to visit the prisoners, not to console but to argue with them; monks, priests, bare-footed friars, and Jesuits.

In March, 1687, Blanche, with all the others who had not recanted, were told they were to be removed. They were impatient to know their destination, as they all trembled at the bare thought of being taken to the hospital at Valence. A gentleman who came to make a list of the prisoners' names, was touched with compassion and promised to let them know where they were to be sent. "A needle," he said, "will be the sign for La Rapine."

Four days afterwards Blanche's companion came to her in tears: "He has shown me the needle, we are to go to La Rapine. Once in his hands there is no escape. He starves his victims, stuns them with blows, throws them into the water, compels them to take the Host. I am ready to suffer any kind of death, but it is better to recant than expose myself to such usage, for once in his power I shall have no strength to resist." The turnkey now came in, and said: "I am come in the name of the lords of parliament to tell you that all who have not abjured will be sent to Valence." "Sir," replied Blanche, "if I have done anything amiss let me die in a public place by the hand of a public hangman, but do not send me to a secret executioner, a man possessed with the devil." She then went to her cell to pray, and to write to her father and mother to be at the prison door when she was taken out. While she was writing two of the prisoners, young ladies, came to her bathed in tears, and said:

"Pray tell us what you intend to do." She replied: "My intention is to follow the Lamb of God whithersoever He goes, and I hope God will be glorified in me, whether by life or death." On the morrow her mother brought her linen and other things; but she answered: "I have no more need of this world's goods."

On the 23rd of May the prisoners, four men and four women, arrived at the hospital of Valence. When the archers presented them to D'Herapine they handed also to him a packet of letters from the parliament at Grenoble. He caused the prisoners to stand before him, and said: "Here are letters from the parliament ordering the release of twenty-two prisoners whom they sent to me not long since. These prisoners have done their duty; if you do the same you, too, will soon be released." Finding promises useless he tried threats. Unable still to make any way, he said to one of them: "Beggar, thou shalt have one hundred blows with the stick. Let her clothes be taken from her, and give the dog some old rags." This monster having observed that the most hardened men, when set to beat women, will recoil when they see blood flow, chose women for his myrmidons, coarse wenches of the Rhône, whom the sight of blood only inflamed the more.

In the evening a bell rang. A woman coming to Blanche, said: "Come, do not you hear the bell?" Blanche asked whither she was to go. "To the chapel, to hear the prayer which Monsieur D'Herapine will offer." Blanche refusing to move, the girls dragged her by force; and the sœur Marie, the governess of the hospital, broke a stick over her. The next morning the prisoners were called to work at half-past four, although Blanche was so bruised that she could not raise her head. In the evening D'Herapine sent for those who had not yet yielded, and said to them: "You are a set of obstinate rebels against

God and the king; if you do not recant, you shall be beaten to death. Cursed race of vipers, I know my trade well enough. I can make you obey better than any man in the kingdom. You shall sweep from morning to night, and if you fail in your work you shall have a hundred blows; after which I will put you in a dungeon, where you shall die of hunger; but in order that you may languish the longer, a little bread and water shall be given you. We know all about it, for we have tried it again and again. When you are dead you shall be cast out on the dunghill; the king will be rid of a bad subject: Here lies a dead dog, miserable in this world, damned in the world to come." He then turned to the servants of the hospital: "Look well after these Huguenots; make them sweep, scrub, scour, from morning till night, from top to bottom of the hospital, and do not spare them. If they disobey, report them to me at once, otherwise you yourselves shall have a hundred blows."

Two or three days afterwards D'Herapine stationed himself, as was often his practice, at the door of the chapel, with a stick in his hand. As the Huguenots were dragged in, he said to one of them: "Dog, dost thou come to church like a snail?" and at the same time struck him a blow, which felled him to the ground. "These dogs would rather go to execution than to church. But it is the order of the bishop that all who are in the hospital should attend Mass daily, and I am here to execute his orders, and to see that they sprinkle themselves with the holy water and make the sign of the cross."

On the 9th of June, as Blanche continued intractable, D'Herapine was sent for. He came in a transport of rage, foaming at the mouth, and going into the kitchen said to the cooks: "Scourge this Huguenot without mercy; if you spare her you shall be put in her place." Blanche was carried into the kitchen, and, the doors being shut, six girls, each with a handful of osiers, stripped her, tied her to a beam, and struck her in turn with all their force, saying: "Pray to thy God." "Never in my life," she writes, "had I experienced such consolation as I then enjoyed; I had the honour of being scourged for Christ's sake, and I was filled with Christ's consolation." Finding she did not speak or shed tears they became furious, and beat her until they had broken their last switch and the blood flowed, the sufferer being constrained to cry out: "My God, my God, have mercy on me; I am grievously afflicted."

Other scenes, equally horrid, follow in the narrative. At length the public conscience of the city woke up; many of the notables remonstrated; and D'Herapine and the governess were dismissed from the hospital.

A few days after D'Herapine's departure a Jesuit came into the room where Blanche was, and addressed her and her fellow-prisoners with much civility, saying he was pained with the afflictions the Huguenots had undergone. "D'Herapine," he said, "has made you suffer much; but why will you not free yourselves from your affliction? It is ignorance keeps you here; you must be instructed." Blanche answered: "I have no wish to be instructed in a religion which I shall never profess." The Jesuit replied that he had made the tour of Europe, and consequently possessed an enlarged mind. "Believe me," he said, "receive instruction and quit your religion." Blanche, returning him an answer from Scripture, he replied: "The foolishness of men is better than the wisdom of women," and left the room in a rage.

The changes in the hospital brought little relief to the suffering Huguenots. The girls continued to beat them, and the monks and Jesuits to urge them to abjure. Sometimes, however, human nature got the better of bigotry.

A Capuchin, touched with Blanche's condition, said: "Do not grieve or weep, you shall not be compelled to go to Mass any more." He then felt her pulse, and finding she was in a high fever, made her sit down on the stairs. A priest coming up, said to her: "You cause a great disturbance and scandal in the hospital; take my advice and change your religion. I will draw up your abjuration in such a form that you will not offend God, and you will be released from this misery." "Sir," she answered, "God will deliver me in His own good time; and I will not forsake my pure and holy religion for one to which so much has been added. Take away the pictures and statues out of your churches; preach the pure Gospel of our Lord, and say no more Masses, for, as St. Paul says to the Hebrews, 'Jesus Christ offered Himself once for all,' so that there is no need of a repeated offering; moreover, no sacrifice is made without blood." The doctor was sent for, and Blanche was taken to the infirmary, where she was very roughly treated and sometimes entirely neglected.

We must here introduce three other women, also prisoners for conscience' sake, who were in the same chamber of the infirmary as Blanche, and whose history for a while is interwoven with hers. Their names were Jeanne Terrasson, Suzanne Peloux, and Anne Dumasse.

An order came down that in three days the refractory among the Huguenots were to be transported to America. This was fearful tidings, and so affected Suzanne that she persuaded her companions to join her in an attempt to escape. They prepared for the adventure by forcing open the old padlock which fastened the window grating, and cutting up some sheets into strips, which they knotted and sewed together, measuring the height of the window from the ground by a cord weighted with a stone. "Alas!" exclaimed Blanche, "we shall all be killed, it is fearful to look down."

It was on a Saturday night between twelve and one, that, creeping over to the window on their bare feet for fear of rousing the priest who slept in the room below, these brave girls made their perilous attempt. Anne Dumasse and Suzanne Peloux got down safely, but when Blanche began to let herself down her dress caught on a nail. Seizing the sheet between her teeth, she held with both hands; but her strength failed and she fell to the ground, striking violently on some blocks of hewn stone placed there for building. She cried out: "God have mercy on me; I am either dead or lamed for life!" Jeanne, who was the last, did not fare much better; her arms were so weak that she could not join her hands for a firm hold, and she too fell, receiving some severe bruises and a permanent injury in her back. Anne and Suzanne carried their helpless companions sixty or seventy paces to the gate of the faubourg, which they found shut. They climbed the wall and helped Blanche to the top; but when she looked down on the other side, she exclaimed: "Here is a precipice, I shall never get over, leave me and go on." So they let her down again, and tried Jeanne. With incredible difficulty they lifted her over the wall and landed her at the foot on the farther side, where they hid her in a cock of hay. Then they fled, saying: "We are exceedingly grieved to leave you; God preserve you from the hand of our enemies." They fell in with some good Protestants, who welcomed them as if they had been angels, and sent four or five men to bring away their companions; but it was too late, they had been recaptured. Anne and Suzanne got off safely, and found a refuge in a foreign country.

Blanche lay at the foot of the wall, faint and in agony, seeking relief in cries and prayer. A passer-by carried a message for her to a female friend who had been a Protestant, but who, when she came to her, not only excused herself from helping her for fear she should get into trouble, but was so base as to give information of her whereabouts to the priest. She was taken back to the hospital and placed again in the infirmary, where she was miserably attended to, or rather almost wholly neglected.

After some days, a Catholic gentleman named Payan, with his two daughters, came to visit her. The priest brought them to her bedside. M. Payan asked whether she had had any broth that day. She replied: "I have tasted nothing yet to-day, and I have had no broth for a fortnight." The priest, who had shown her some kindness, said: "I must go and scold the cooks, and in the meantime I will send you some of my own soup." While he was gone Blanche related her trials. The daughters kissed her, their tears falling on her face; and the father, putting his hand in his pocket, gave her all the money he had.

In October her mother came to see her, and stayed with her till four surgeons arrived, who set her broken bones; but the hospital surgeon, under whose care they left her, treated her brutally. One day, one of the governesses of the house came herself to dress her wounds. But when she lifted the plaster and saw the state it was in, she cried out: "O how blessed you are to suffer so much and so patiently! if you were of our religion, you would gain heaven by your sufferings."

The tribulations of this faithful confessor were now drawing to an end. An order came down from the king to alleviate the condition of those who had not recanted. Several of Blanche's companions were released, on payment of six pistoles each; and, November 26, Blanche herself was set free. She went to Geneva, where she arrived by slow stages, February, 1698. It was May before she was strong enough to attend public worship, which she did with inexpressible delight.

XXII.
JEANNE TERRASSON.

Before relating what happened to Jeanne Terrasson after her re-capture, we must recount her adventures before she was taken to Valence.

In September, 1685, on a Sunday, the soldiers came to the town of Die, in Dauphiné. where she resided. Ten were quartered in Jeanne's house, from which her husband, with her brother-in-law, had fled into the woods, so that she was alone with these " harpies of Satan," as she calls them. The officer coming in, said : " You must obey the king, and return to the good religion, otherwise the soldiers will consume all your substance." The soldiers pestered her day after day, saying: " If thou dost not embrace the true religion, we will throw thee into the fire ; but this will not be all, thou wilt burn for ever in hell." She answered : " If yours were a good religion, as you say it is, you would not use violence to make converts. When Jesus Christ sent his disciples to preach the gospel, He gave them no other arms than his divine word, accompanied by the power of the Holy Spirit." On this the soldiers rose up against her like wild beasts, and declared they would make her abjure in spite of herself. She says of this terrible time : " I had no repose in body or soul ; I was afflicted every way ; fightings without and fears within. Nevertheless, God who comforts the afflicted, redoubled in my heart the assurance of his grace, love, and infinite mercy."

The soldiers had drawn out the new wine from the vat, and were gone into an upper chamber to collect the furniture, which they intended to sell. Jeanne saw her opportunity of escape, and ran down stairs. But at the street door she met another soldier, who said he had a billet on the house for ten men. "We have already ten," she replied. He answered: "And if you do not recant, more still will be sent you." Then he began to bluster and curse, and said: "Whilst waiting for my comrades I want to see the cellar." Jeanne fetched a candle and showed him the door to it. He went down, threatening all the way; she waited until he had reached the bottom step, when she shut the door, which could not be opened from within. Before the other soldiers, who were on the top floor, were aware of what was going on, Jeanne had fled to a place of safety. The next day, twenty more soldiers arrived, who made a stable of the ground floor, sold the furniture, and then abandoned the house, leaving the doors open and allowing no one to shut them.

This was followed by a scouring of the country, during which Jeanne's husband and her brother-in-law were seized, and compelled by a dagger at their throat to promise recantation. Her husband, returning to his house, found it stripped and desolate. Learning where his wife was, he joined her. The first thing he asked her was if she had come off with a clear conscience, which, when he knew, he gave glory to God, bitterly reproaching himself for his own weakness, and fervently praying for grace to confess Christ more faithfully in future. His prayer, as Jeanne afterwards heard, was answered; to his dying hour the priests could never compel him to perform any act of the Romish religion.

Jeanne's husband provided for her a retreat, in which she lay hid from September, 1685, to September, 1686. To secure her from discovery, he spread a report that she had left the kingdom and had been seen at Geneva.

At length an opportunity offered of leaving her hiding-place, and with five or six other fugitives, all men, and a guide, she set off at the end of September. She was habited like a man, as the guide refused to undertake the charge of women, since their presence excited suspicion. When they had ascended three leagues above Grenoble, they were stopped by four or five men, who were lying in wait for fugitives. The men took them to a castellan, who had them searched. Jeanne begged him to give her back her woman's clothes which she had carried with her. He answered he could not restore them without an order from the parliament.

The prisoners were taken to Grenoble and examined. The men were sent to the dungeons, and Jeanne was taken to a room, where she found nineteen women from the French Waldenses,* and two or three young women of Dauphiné, with nothing but straw to lie upon, and in a corner a heap of putrid straw swarming with vermin. Two monks came to convert them, promising that if they would change their religion they should be set free. Jeanne warned her fellow prisoners against the seducers, but the flesh prevailed, and the next day they yielded. They did not, however, regain their liberty; and when they saw how they had been duped they wept bitterly, saying: "Alas! if we had believed you, how happy we should now be; for although our bodies would not be free, our consciences would be at peace. Wretches that we are! Why did we listen to the voice of the enchanter!" Jeanne did all she could to comfort them, exhorting them to repentance and to trust in the mercy of God. Those who had abjured were allowed to walk in the courtyard, but those who remained firm and who were accounted guilty of high treason were denied this indulgence; and Jeanne lay all the day in the prison, horribly disquieted by the vermin.

Being called to appear before the commissioner, he

* The Waldensian Valley of Prageler then belonged to France; it was ceded to Piedmont by the Treaty of Utrecht in 1713.

demanded if she did not know that the king had forbidden his subjects to depart from the kingdom, and why she had dressed herself in men's clothes, a thing forbidden even by the Mosaic law. She answered that she was aware of the royal prohibition, but thought it allowable to take every means to find a safe place where she might pray to God according to his word; that a whole life in prison was but a moment when measured by eternity; and that no prison can be so horrible as a troubled conscience. As to her change of clothing, she knew it was forbidden to the Israelites under the law, to avoid superstition and idolatry, but that now, being under grace, such a change was allowable when made for better concealment and convenience.

The prisoners were now taken out of their prison and put into the moat dungeon, where they found about sixty other Protestant women, who gave them a cordial welcome. Amongst them was Blanche Gamond. She had never seen Jeanne before, but was at once attracted towards her, and embraced her as though she had known her all her life. Jeanne's description of the dungeon agrees with that of Blanche; she says the Isère flowed so near that every morning the prisoners were wet with the mist which rose from the water and entered by the gratings, their only windows, so that their skin became infected with a loathsome disease. The men's prison was even more unwholesome, and the parliament, fearing that a pestilence would ensue, gave orders to remove the prisoners from Grenoble. After another examination, Jeanne was condemned to have her head shaved and to be imprisoned for life.

The prisoners were accustomed to sing Psalms, and their voices being sometimes heard in the Palais de Justice, which was close to the prison, orders were sent to forbid them. The prisoners replied that they were there to bear witness to the truth, and that if they should hold their peace the very stones would cry out. Jeanne was again called up; enticing promises were made to her, with threats that if she continued in her contumacy she should be sent to D'Herapine. She replied: "Sirs, you cannot promise me a greater boon than paradise, or threaten me with a worse punishment than hell. Jesus Christ said, 'Be thou faithful unto death, and I will give thee a crown of life.'"

A little while afterwards, by order of the so-called "Chamber of Mercy," Jeanne was transferred, with six men and twenty-one women, to the hospital of Valence. A crowd of citizens accompanied them to the boat, singing the eightieth Psalm. During the voyage their guards continually importuned them to change their religion, telling them they had better not wait till they were in D'Herapine's hands, for he would break them to pieces. What they said being confirmed by some gentlemen on board, most of the Huguenots were intimidated, and made their abjuration. Their cowardice pierced Jeanne to the heart, and she continually exhorted those who still remained faithful to persevere. One of the prisoners had a Catholic version of the New Testament, which the papists were accustomed to give to the New Converts; and Jeanne took occasion to show how in that translation the word of truth had been falsified, *e.g.*, in the Epistle to the Hebrews, xi. 21, where the text, "By faith Jacob when he was dying .... worshipped, leaning on the top of his staff," is rendered, "worshipped the top of his staff."*

Arriving at Valence the prisoners were put into chambers and dungeons, where D'Herapine visited them several times a day, accompanied by three or four men and five or six rough women. These all had sticks or rods in

---

* This maltranslation, found in the Vulgate, has been made much use of by Roman Catholic writers as an argument for image-worship.

their hands, which they used freely on the bodies of the prisoners, and when the blood flowed salt and vinegar were applied to the wounds, which caused an intolerable smart. When D'Herapine could not get his own way, he would fall into a rage and strike them on the face with his bundle of keys.

Jeanne's sufferings rivalled those of Blanche. On one occasion her companions, although themselves severely bruised, were so affected at the sight of her misery that they cried out : " We wish it were possible for us to bear part of your sufferings." Two of them, however, not long afterwards abjured. Few, indeed, were able long to resist such treatment. Out of fifty of both sexes only eight or nine, all women, remained faithful. These were compelled to do the work of those who abjured.

One day, on D'Herapine rating Jeanne for her obstinacy, she replied : " Sir, I am not obstinate, but I know that mine is the only true religion, because it teaches nothing but what is conformable to the law of God, and his law forbids to make the likeness of anything to worship." D'Herapine answered that the images are placed in the church for ornament only, and to keep alive the memory of dead saints. He then went on to say that infants who die without baptism are lost. "Oh, no, sir," answered Jeanne, " it is not being deprived of the sign which can render us guilty before God, but to despise the thing signified." This time he let her go without beating her.

She was set to sweep out the cells, in which dogs and a fierce hog were also kept, but the filth was not removed. " It was at this time," she says, " when afflictions were heaped upon me, that the Holy Spirit poured abundantly of the oil of gladness into my heart, so that I can say : ' When I passed through the valley of the shadow of death I feared no evil, for Thy rod and Thy staff comforted me.' "

She was seventeen days in this hole, with just food

The Chain on its way to the Galleys.

enough to preserve her life; according to D'Herapine's
threat when he sent her thither. At length, being kept three
days without food, she fainted, and was taken out and put
into the infirmary.

In the account of their attempted escape, we left Jeanne
hidden in a cock of hay. When the priest the next morning went in search of the fugitives, he came first to Blanche,
and a little while afterwards discovered Jeanne, whom also
he took back to the hospital.

Jeanne obtained her freedom fourteen days before
Blanche, and by the same means, *viz.*, the payment of a
ransom. After remaining some months in France she
went to Geneva, and thence to Berne, where she employed
herself in collecting money for her brethren who still
remained in the dungeons and the galleys.

XXIII.
THE CHAIN.

We are familiar with the coffle or slave-gang of Central
Africa; the inhuman and hideous procession haunts our
imagination and arouses our deepest abhorrence. In
France in the seventeenth century,—France, the boasted
centre of European civilization,—there were to be seen on
the highways, rivers, and canals, long chain-gangs of
human beings suffering almost as great hardships and
treated with almost as much cruelty as the miserable
villagers of Africa.

The prisoners wore iron collars, and were coupled by a
chain from one collar to the other. When they marched
two and two a long chain was passed through rings in the
middle of the cross-chains, the whole length of the procession, and riveted to every ring.* When they walked in

* Sometimes the prisoners were coupled by the legs instead of the
collar, the long chain passing as before through the rings in the middle.

single file each was linked to the one before and behind him, so that everyone, except the first and last, bore two chains fastened to his collar. This manner of march was more painful than the other. The procession could only move as a whole. If one prisoner stopped all must stop, and if one fell, which not unfrequently happened through weakness and weariness, the shock jarred all those who were near him. When the order was given to sit down, to lie, or to rise, it was important that the movement should be made all at once, otherwise all would be bruised. As it was, the diversity of size, age, and strength, rendered a completely harmonious movement impossible. The chain was guarded by soldiers with drawn swords, and officers who struck the prisoners when they lagged behind. The march was necessarily very slow; it sometimes occupied several months; and the halting-places for the night were mostly dark, unwholesome dungeons, more fit for torment than for repose. The chains were made up of two kinds of convicts, malefactors and Christian confessors of pure life and exemplary piety, all being bound for the same fearful destiny, viz., to row in chains in the royal galleys.

XXIV.
BEARING ANOTHER'S BURDEN.

In the year 1686 one of these processions might be seen making its melancholy way towards Marseilles. It was, as usual, a mixed company, and was made up of two smaller chains, coming, one from Dijon, the other from Paris, which had been joined together at Châlons-sur-Saone. It was during the dog-days that it traversed the sultry valley of the Rhône. One of the confessors, a feeble man, fainted under the burden of his chain and collar. With him was coupled a young man of thirty, also a confessor, and one in whom the spirit of the Good Master was strong. Taking his companion's collar in his hand he raised it above his shoulder, and essayed in this way to carry it for him, but that being too difficult he got a forked stick, with which he contrived to bear it up so that the sufferer was relieved of the entire weight. The sufferer was Philip Le Boucher; the Christian brother who bore his burden was Pierre Mauru. The names of both are cherished by the Church for the patient, faithful, holy temper with which they endured their cruel captivity; but of Le Boucher few memorials remain. Mauru had been arrested in flight just as he had reached the Swiss frontier, and being brought to Besançon was condemned to the galleys for life. "I saw," said one of his companions, "how little he cared for the money that was taken from him, and how great his joy was when he was condemned."

This caravan was rich in spiritual freight. Besides the two just named, it contained many other noble confessors, who when they were put to the oar never flinched, but continued faithful unto death. Of two of these a record has been preserved of no common value.

XXV.

LOUIS DE MAROLLES.

Louis de Marolles was of a good family in which the legal profession was hereditary; he possessed rare intellectual endowments; and when the new philosophy of Gassendi and Descartes appeared, he threw himself into the movement. He was a skilful mathematician.

The Revocation of the Edict of Nantes forced him to seek safety in flight. On December 2nd, 1685, he was arrested, together with his wife and four children, just before they reached the Rhine. They were conveyed to Strasburg, and placed in a prison of the city. Being interrogated, Marolles declared the plain truth without subterfuge, namely, that his purpose had been to leave the kingdom, and seek in a foreign land liberty to serve God according to his conscience. His wife and children were released, but Marolles himself was removed to Châlons-sur-Saone, where he lay six weeks in prison. The Bishop of Châlons compassionated the prisoner, wrote to the governor of Strasburg on his behalf, visited him in prison, and told him that if he could he would convey him away concealed under his gown.

For a short time Marolles was overcome by temptation. The tears of his wife and children, joined to those of two brothers-in-law who came to see him, induced him to listen to a proposal to petition for his liberty, under colour of being more fully instructed in the Romish doctrine. "A few days afterwards," he says, " God gave me to see my error, and afforded me also the opportunity of repairing it, which I embraced with tears of joy; and the Father of Mercies made use of my infirmity to give me fresh strength, so that when the offers were renewed I at once rejected them. This so enraged those who made them that they threw me into a dungeon, where I lay thirteen days." At the end of this time he was brought up for judgment, which was pronounced by torchlight. The sentence was that he should serve the king for ever as a slave on board the galleys, and that his personal property should be confiscated.

On the 11th of March he was manacled, placed in a cart, and conveyed to Paris, where he was taken to La Tournelle, formerly a royal palace, but then used as a temporary prison for the galerians.[*] Here he remained two months in a dungeon with seven diseased wretches,

[*] A name for those who were condemned to the galleys.

condemned, some to the galleys, some to be broken on the wheel. The place was so dark that they could not clearly see one another's faces. The governor, knowing who Marolles was, treated him at first with some consideration, but after a while was obliged to tell him the king had commanded he should wear the neck-chain. He wrote to his sister: "They have taken the chain from my foot and put one on my neck, which weighs, I believe, not less than thirty pounds. Do not, my dear sister, afflict yourself at my condition; it is happier than you think for; keep your tears for so many wretches who are not so happy as I am." The procurator-general, who came to inspect the galerians, seeing the chain on Marolles' neck, expressed his sincere pity, saying there was nothing he would not do to deliver him.

Marolles was removed to another room, "a horrid place, where there was not an honest word to be heard; nothing but filthiness and execrable blasphemies. The prisoners," he says, "make such a noise all day and the greater part of the night that I can scarcely find a quiet moment in which to lift up my heart to God. We are fifty-three in this room, which is not above thirty feet long and nine broad. On my right side lies a sick peasant with his head to my feet, and my feet to his head. I have had five fits of tertian fever, but I thank God am well recovered and ready for the journey to Marseilles. In Burgundy we are to take on some of our brethren." In a letter to a German minister, he says: "The dungeons in which I have been confined more than six months, and the chain I carry about my neck, so far from shaking the holy resolution God has put into my heart have only confirmed it. In my afflictions I have sought God in a way quite different from what I did in my worldly prosperity, and He has made Himself known to me by the sweetness of His consolations."

Whilst Marolles was in La Tournelle his wife visited him as often as she could, putting her hands through the grating to wash the sores made by his chain. It was reported in the city that he was beside himself. To prove the falsity of the charge he proposed a difficult mathematical problem, which was sent to his friend, the celebrated De Moivre, himself a victim of the Revocation, and who was then teaching mathematics in London.

On the 20th of July the chain departed from Paris, Marolles having, in the meantime, fallen sick with fever. His wife was so troubled she could not come to bid him adieu. A great concourse of people were assembled to watch the prisoners cross the quay and enter the boat, amongst whom were Marolles' children, who threw themselves on his neck. An aged Roman Catholic merchant, breaking through the crowd, embraced Marolles, and offered him his purse. This man afterwards removed with his family to London, and became a Protestant.

From Dijon Marolles wrote, July 30: "The fever has been continual, and has brought me to death's door; but the captain had compassion on me, released me from my chain, and kept me in his chamber or in his boat." On arriving at Marseilles he wrote again, August 25: "I have been twice at the point of death, in which condition I lay on planks without straw, with my hat for a pillow. On my arrival I was not examined, but sent direct to the galleys, supported by two guards. Some officers pitied me, and spoke to the major, who sent a surgeon to see me; and on his report I was unchained and removed to the hospital. It is a fine place, admirably well ordered; I live almost entirely at my own charges."

Here he became acquainted with Isaac Le Fèvre, who also had been arrested in attempting to flee the country, and who had come down to Dijon with the Burgundy chain. They were soon knit together in the closest bonds of friendship. "I am very well pleased," writes Marolles to his wife, "to be in company of M. Le Fèvre; our beds join, and we mess together. Thus, you see, dear heart, I have nothing to do but to pray to God and be joyful."

XXVI.
ISAAC LE FÈVRE.

Leaving Marolles for a little while, let us enquire into the history of his new friend. Like himself, Le Fèvre was a man of good family and cultivated mind; he was steward to a noble lady of Burgundy. Coming to Paris at the time of the Revocation, he says: "The spirit of fear and weakness reigned in the provinces; I thought surely I should have found more steadfastness in the great city; but, alas! all there were in a state of consternation, and I was obliged to leave." Returning to Burgundy he found the lady in great distress, the intendant having allowed her only a fortnight to choose between the sacrifice of her religion and the loss of her estate and liberty. Le Fèvre was also threatened; and when one of his friends interceded for him, the intendant interrupted him, saying: "Why do you complain, you have not yet resisted to blood;" words which remind us of the saying of the heathen Emperor Julian to the early Christians: "It belongs to you to suffer, for your Master foretold it." The marchioness and her family abjured, and advised Le Fèvre to do the same; but he answered that though he had no inclination for martyrdom, yet he loved truth above all things, and could not follow their example.

He determined to seek safety in flight, but before he could cross the frontier, he was seized near Pontarlier, February 4, 1686, and conveyed to Besançon. His horse and all he had were taken from him; he was ironed and thrown into a dungeon, where he endured temptation and hardship. "The air of the prison," he writes, "is infected, and my diet is such as would formerly have poisoned me, but I find sweetness and consolation unhoped for." Here he heard that his sister, whose faith equalled his own, had been sent to a convent at Moulins; the tidings made him cry out: "Holy Father, keep us in Thy Name."

From Besançon he was taken to Dijon, May 30, where he arrived bruised and weak. The officers showed him as much kindness as they were permitted. "If it had not been," he wrote, "for the comfort the Lord sent me at Auxonne, I should not have been brought here alive, but my irons were taken off and I was set on horseback." Le Fèvre had many friends of the upper class, but they were unable to obtain his release, as the government was resolved to make an example of him, in order to deter others. He refused many offers of money, accepting only so much as he actually needed, or could make use of for his companions in affliction, who were mostly of the poor of the land. When also he was advised to petition for special favour in the chain, he refused, saying it would be cowardice to ask it.

After two months' imprisonment in Dijon, he was taken with his companions to Châlons-sur-Saone, where they were joined to the chain from Paris. At first he was coupled with an officer of dragoons, a Roman Catholic, whose crime was having allowed Protestant prisoners to escape. On arriving at Marseilles, Le Fèvre writes: "It seems as if more than six months had passed since I left Dijon; the Lord has caused my flesh and my skin to grow old, and I have suffered the pains of death. The guards thought me dead and robbed me, one of one thing, one of another. After long entreaty, M. De St. Preuil permitted me to have a litter, on condition that I should fee the guard. But why all this care and expense to come to a place which may be called the abode of misery? For forty-eight hours I could not eat or drink what they gave me, or close an eye."

September 13 he writes: "M. De Marolles and myself have been for some days near to each other; our beds join, and we eat together; neither captivity nor sickness hinders us from being merry." When they were supposed to be convalescent, the two friends were separated, and placed in different galleys; Marolles, who was somewhat the stronger of the two, being excused the oar, whilst Le Fèvre, who could not stand, was loaded with chains. The officers compassionated them, and told them that if they had come there convicted of crime they might have expected all manner of kindness. Hearing that 150 invalid forçats were to be embarked for America, Marolles wrote: "It is no matter to me whether I die by sea or land, in Europe or America; I am persuaded that all kinds of death of his children are precious in the eyes of God. I believe even that my death would be more edifying and glorious if it should happen during my bonds."

September 23 he writes again: "They bring me bread and meat, for which I pay nine sous a-day. I am supplied gratis with wine and the king's bread, and am treated with civility by all on board." Still further to cheer his wife he indulges in a vein of pleasantry: "I am getting a quilt made, and am going to buy sheets so as to live in comfort. If you were to see me in my handsome galerian dress you would be delighted. I have a little red jacket, made after the fashion of the carrier's frock of the Ardennes; likewise a fine red cap, two linen shirts with threads as thick as my finger, and stockings. We have the most honest comite (the officer set over the forçats) of all the galleys."

The treatment of the two friends was capricious, alternately indulgent and harsh; the changes for the worse apparently following the unsuccessful attempts of the missionaries to convert them. On October 24 Marolles wrote to his wife: "M. Le Fèvre and I are no longer loosed from the chain, day or night, or permitted to go on shore, or to receive letters or write any which are not seen. I have changed my galley thrice in one week, and the intendant tells me I must prepare to embark for America. If this should befall me, do not let it affect thee, my dear child. Let us leave all to God, who knows how to bring light out of darkness, and who will do nothing but what will be for his own glory. That thou and I are separated is, considered in itself, the most grievous thing in the world; but is not so if we look upon it as the will of God. If we weep and mourn now, there will come a day when we shall be comforted. I have never been so well in health as I am now. There are at the prow two little cabins, one of which I occupy; I owe this favour to a young officer to whom I teach algebra." In another letter he traces the support granted to him, "to the prayers of so many good souls who pray for me in private and in public."

January 20, 1687, he again writes to his wife: "All the reports about me of which you send me word are false, except that for more than three months I have been confined to the chain day and night, so that I have been set free only to be taken to the Bishop of Marseilles. Thus far I have not been set to work. I have not so much reason to complain as you imagine, and the time slips away very quickly; the week is no sooner begun than I find myself at the end. When I rise, after making my prayer to God, I read six, seven, or eight chapters of Holy Scripture, and make such reflections on them as I am able. God Himself, with his precious balm of Gilead, tenderly anoints the wounds my sufferings may have made in my heart. Good M. Le Fèvre, my dear companion in bonds, has been removed to *La Grande Royale*, where they put on him fetters and two chains; but now his chains are taken off and he has fetters only at night." Speaking of some interviews he had with divines at the bishop's palace, he says: " I have followed Saint Peter's advice, to render with meekness and reverence my reasons for the hope that is in me. When I came down from the last conference, I asked leave to pay my respects to the bishop. He sent for me into his chamber, where I thanked him for his kindness and charity. He answered me in a very obliging manner, telling me he was sorry he could not make me a Catholic, but all they could do was to pray for me, and that he would willingly serve me if opportunity should offer. Last month," adds Marolles, " a chain arrived of 150 men; thirty-three had died on the way."

XXVII.
THE LAST DAYS OF PIERRE MAURU.

Meanwhile Mauru had fallen ill. The strong man, ready and able to succour others, had become the weakest of the party. Nevertheless, he was not excused from the exhausting labour and cruel discipline of the summer cruise which was always made by the galleys. He writes to Le Fèvre: " You ask me to tell you how many blows I have received with cudgels and hoop-sticks. This is impossible; it has been sometimes above forty a day for a week or more in succession; never fewer than twenty. What will you have me say? These blows are rather painful, but the joy of suffering for Jesus Christ lightens the pain; and when the comfort of the Holy Ghost abounds, that sacred balm heals all sores and gives perfect health to our souls. When I was put on board the captain had me searched, to take away my books and papers. He often sent also for priests to make me change my religion, forbidding all other persons to speak with me. A spy was set over me to insult me and to vex me with needless labour. But finding I did not complain, the man grew weary of plaguing me, so they changed my seat that others might abuse me; but I made friends of these also, when my place was again changed. This happened many times, until at last a sub-officer, ingenious in the arts of malice, undertook to subdue me. Sometimes he would make me supply all the benches with water; sometimes he pretended I had received a letter, or somebody had spoken to me, which he made an occasion to beat me. He made me cleanse all the quarters of the galley alone, and showed the superior officer some stains not effaced, to get me a beating. Seeing the constancy God gave me, they removed the forçats from my bench, and filled their places with the most profligate of the Turks and Moors; but these were more civil to me than my own countrymen. My morning bread was taken away and I was made to fast till one o'clock.

"One day, as we were making a tent, I broke two needles, and having no money to buy others, the boatswain beat me sorely. Just then, the captain coming on deck, asked what it was for, on which I desired the favour of speaking with him in private. He heard me, and put a stop to this cruel usage. But," continues Mauru, "although my body suffered all day, yet my heart rejoiced in my Saviour day and night. My soul fed on the hidden manna, and God made me possess a joy of which the world knows nothing."

Still new torments were inflicted on him, and when the galley put to sea, the severity of the labour and the blows brought him often to the point of death. "As soon," he says, "as the chaplain perceived that I fainted, he came to tempt me, but I would not listen, for my soul was rowing heavenward." Becoming very ill, he was taken to the hospital in the city, "where," he says, "though I could not stir, yet I felt no more pain, and the broth they gave me, such as it was, seemed better than anything I had ever tasted." When he began to recover, his friend, Philip Le Boucher, was brought into the hospital. They were both so weak that they could not embrace one another without assistance. A fortnight afterwards Mauru was carried back to the galley, to be continually beaten, which the steward called "painting Calvin's back with cudgels"; "but when," he writes, "I could get an interval for meditating on the words of eternal life, my heart was filled with joy; and when I looked on my bruised flesh I said: 'These are the marks that St. Paul rejoiced to bear in his body.'"

At last, after more than ten years of suffering, he was prostrated with a cough which hardly allowed him to breathe or speak. Even in this condition a missionary was sent to convert him, but it was to no purpose. He died, April, 1696. A fellow-prisoner writes: "M. Mauru died last night. He desired me to send you his thanks for all your kindness, and to tell you he waited with resignation for the Lord's hour." The same writer, a few days afterwards, says: "M. V. had a coffin made and laid your friend in it, but the chaplain coming down, caused it to be un-nailed, and took the body out to be carried away like a Turk." Another letter relates: "He preserved his senses sound to the last. The tempters who stood round him found that although his body was weak, his soul had put on fresh strength; so that seeing themselves baffled, they were constrained to leave his saintly spirit in the hands of the Sovereign Shepherd, who took him to his everlasting pastures." His body was thrown into the lay-stall.

Mauru's death has carried us forward; we must go back a few years.

XXVIII.
PATIENCE IN TRIBULATION.

The government having long enough played cat and mouse with Marolles and Le Fèvre, proceeded now to make an end of them by the slow process of solitary imprisonment. They were taken from the galleys and committed to separate prisons at the opposite extremities of the city (Marseilles), where the life was to be ground out of them.

Let us first see how it fared with Marolles. He writes to his wife, October 25th, 1689. For greater safety the letter purports to be from a third person. "You desire, Madam, to hear of your husband. This is what we learn of him from the reports in the city. The 12th of February he was removed from the galley to the citadel, and put into a little room which had served for a soldier's lodging, but so altered that most of the light now comes through the chimney. The major has placed a sentinel day and night at the outer door of his chamber, and another at the top of his chimney. They say he suffers his affliction very patiently. Farewell, Madam; be pleased to pardon me if I do not tell you my name; I am no less your servant."

August 31, 1691, he wrote in his own name: "M. Le Fèvre is an excellent man: he practises what he teaches; the Lord bless, preserve and strengthen him. My candle gives but little light, my eyes fail, the spectacles I use are broken; all this is not conducive to the despatch of business." In December he wrote again: "Only two hours ago, dear heart, I received thy letter, which gives me more sorrow than joy. I daily praise God for the singular favour He has granted me in joining me to a Christian wife, yet I have always been afraid thou hast not received with becoming submission the afflictions by which it pleases God to prove us." He then describes his condition and his prison. "After I had been three weeks in this room, I was so oppressed that I thought I could not survive four months, and now it will be five years next February. In October of the first year my shoulder and elbow were so affected that I could not undress myself. Concluding this disorder proceeded from the cold and damp of winter, I drank my wine unmixed; but finding my pains increase, I took the contrary course and drank only water, whereupon I grew better and have continued it ever since. My little sanctuary is twelve of my feet in length by ten in breadth. All the furniture consists of a bed from the hospital. I lie on a hospital mattress with a palliasse under it, in which respect I am better off than in the galley. This is the fourth winter I have passed almost without fire. I have had to suffer from cold, nakedness and hunger. The king has appointed five sous a day for my subsistence; and at first I was well fed by a cook, but his successor cheated me of half my provision. Then the major undertook to supply me, which at first he did well enough, but after a time neglected me. He opens my dungeon but once a day, and several times has sent my dinner at nine, ten and eleven at night. Once I received no bread for three days. Let not all this afflict thee, my dear, but consider, as I do, that this diet has been prescribed to me by the Sovereign Physician of my body and soul, to whom I have resigned myself. It is by this spare diet that God has preserved me in life and health." His clothes had become mere rags, but through the kindness of the chaplain he was provided with a complete galley suit, and likewise with a lamp which burned six or eight hours, instead of a farthing candle. His allowance of food was at the same time increased, and he enjoyed better health than for forty years past.

In a letter to Le Fèvre he says: " You speak my mind, my dear brother, when you say that we shall be the only persons who will not share the king's clemency. We have been brought on the stage in order to strike terror into the whole kingdom." March 24, 1692, he writes again to his wife, expressing his joy at the Christian manner in which she had received the account of his sufferings. He then acquaints her with another trial which he had hitherto concealed from her. " When," he says, " I was taken from the galley and brought hither, I found at first great sweetness in the change. My ears were no longer offended with the horrid language with which those places continually resounded. I had liberty to sing the praises of my God at all times, and I could prostrate myself before him as often as I pleased. I was besides relieved from the grievous chain. But the solitude and semi-darkness in which I spent my days, conjured up before me terrifying images. My mind was filled with a thousand false and vain imaginations, which often plunged me into a kind of delirium, sometimes lasting whole hours. For a while prayer was no protection against this evil; God was pleased that it should continue for some months. At length he heard me, and granted me a perfect calm after so many storms. Ever since those sad days he has filled my heart with joy; I possess my soul in patience. He makes the days of my affliction to pass swiftly." This is the last of Marolles' letters which have come to hand. He died June 17th, 1692.

A letter from a fellow-prisoner, of the 20th of the same month, says: " This is to acquaint you with the death of M. de Marolles, the famous confessor of Christ, who had been so long shut up in a cell of the great citadel. His body was buried by Turks among the Turks." Another confessor, who had incurred great danger to serve him, wrote to Madame de Marolles the same day: "He had almost lost his sight, so that although I sent him your last letters, he could neither read them nor return any answer. He caused me to be told that he recommended himself to the prayers of his good friends, and that he thought of nothing else but his departure. From the time that this dear martyr began to grow weak he was often visited by divines of the contrary religion, but he was not moved by their visits. He blessed his enemies to the end."

XXIX.
SLOW MARTYRDOM.

Le Fèvre withstood the effects of foul air, bad food, and solitary confinement much longer than his friend. His cell was in Fort St. Nicholas, at the opposite end of the city from that of Marolles. Here he remained till his death.

He thus describes his prison: "It was a vault of an irregular figure, which was formerly a stable, but had been found too damp for horses. There is still a rack and a manger; no light can come in but by the door, the upper part of which is broken; it is grated within and without. The air is infected, and the damp causes everything to rot; there are cisterns above. I have had no fire."

He lay on a narrow chest, having two straw cushions, the one at his feet, the other at his head. The dampness of the place produced rheumatism, and at last a continued fever. No one ventured to come near him, or look upon his cell, much less speak to him. "Be sensible of my misery," he writes to a beloved relation, "but be yet more sensible of the glory and happiness to which this misery tends. Death is nothing; Jesus Christ has conquered it for me; the dread of living long is greater than that of dying soon; but it is more honourable to endure the most miserable life than to desire death." He complains that the food brought to him was full of corruption and impurity, intended possibly thus to hasten his end. He was also almost destitute of clothing, but, as he expressed it, God sent him two shirts, as well as a bolster and some other comforts, regarding which he says: "I could never discover to whom I was indebted for them, but I fell immediately on my knees to thank God for such unlooked-for comforts." His friends proposed to give money to the major of the citadel, that he might take more care of him; but he refused the offer as likely to bring trouble both on them and himself.

One of his fellow-sufferers in the galleys wrote to him: "To do our Lord's will more perfectly we must constantly remember His example, and heartily forgive our enemies all the injuries they make us suffer without retaining the least resentment." To which Christian maxim Le Fèvre warmly responded, saying that he prayed incessantly to God to show mercy not only on those who suffer, but on those who inflict the suffering, and added: "He who commands us to love our enemies works in us what He commands." Nevertheless the cruel treatment which he had to endure at times severely taxed his patience. "They are always trying to weary out my patience; the money sent for me is not applied for my benefit. I agreed with an innkeeper to provide for me, but he cheated me, and the major winked at it. The major also promised that I should be provided with a mattress and counterpane, but he did not keep his word. They deny me all manner of commerce with the living; certainly they would use no villain as they serve me: but the Lord has pity on my weakness, and gives me such patience as I never dared hope for." His books were all taken away, except a copy of the Psalms.

In 1695 he wrote: "I am entering on the tenth year of my sufferings, and by God's grace have lost neither spirit, patience, nor faith, nor have I altogether lost my health. If I were but unburdened from the weight of my sins, if I could but disengage myself from worldly thoughts, I should be incomparably more happy than when I was in the world. But I have desired temporal liberty with too much ardour and fervency."

The zeal of the galeriens put to shame the indifference of many of the Protestants who were at liberty; they corresponded together on their duties, admonishing one another with brotherly affection, praying and exhorting one another to good works. Le Fèvre himself continually sent prayers, paraphrases and Christian poems to his brethren and friends. We do not find that during the long years of his incarceration he was ever let out of his dungeon. It was in vain also that he complained of the ill-treatment to which he was subjected; there was no abatement till death came to release him. For above a year before his death he was not suffered to receive or send any letters, and very little was known of him, except that he was alive, but growing weaker every day, and that he was preserved patient in the mind of Christ.

The last letter received from him bears date January 18th, 1701. It was to his pastor. There is to be observed in the Christian experience of this good man the same character that we have met with before, and shall often meet with again, viz., an apparent failure to comprehend the freeness and fulness of God's salvation. The Calvinists, like the Romish Church out of which they came, seem to have looked too intently on themselves, on their own experiences, good works and sufferings, and not enough to Christ. Christ was not to them in the same way or degree that He was to Paul, "the end of the law for righteousness to every one that believeth"; nor did they comprehend, as the writer to the Hebrews did, the full significance of the words: " The just shall live by faith." "I am," he writes, "not surprised at your saying that fifteen years of combat and perseverance against the devil and the world are an admirable preparation, and an infallible security of a glorious reward. But, alas! how frail in my case is this foundation. In what we do, good and evil are mixed together, and I have to confess that my best actions fall short of those inward motions which alone can make them valuable. It is true I am resolved to suffer to the end; it is true also that as much as lies in me I return good for evil; but though I strive to attain to the glorious liberty of the children of God, I force myself much, and make but little advance. Above all things, pray that I may be delivered from those great sins which always remain in me."

About the same time, having it on his mind to obtain some special victory over himself, he sent word to his friends in the galleys to join their prayers with his, appointing the hour of gun-fire, nine o'clock every evening, when the forçats were allowed to lie down, and all was quiet. He afterwards informed them that God had heard their prayers.

A kind lady had permission to visit him, although very rarely, and always in the presence of witnesses; she saw him two days before his death, when she found him very wasted and weak. He died June 13th, 1702. She caused his body to be wrapped in linen, and four of the brethren came to bury him. A memorial of him issued by the Protestants of Marseilles, referring to the vigilance used to prevent communication with him, tells us that in 1696 a sergeant who carried him letters was discovered and hanged. The man confessed the deed, but averred that he had done a good action, and that he knew certainly there was no treason in the letters. " The sergeant of the guard," continues the memorial, "attended by two or three musketeers, brought Le Fèvre his provision every day; and when they went their rounds, they always called to him to know what he was about. During the last month he kept his bed altogether. On the evening on which he died he took some broth, and told the soldiers that he should not live through the night. The same evening one of the soldiers brought him two letters, but he was too weak to read them, and desired him to take them back to the party who sent them, being unwilling they should be found after his death. The jailer's daughter, carrying some wine to him about eleven o'clock, found his spirit had already departed." Orders were sent to the galleys for four Turks to come to bury him; but, as already said, the brethren were permitted to perform that office. He was buried in a corner of the fort, in a ditch.

The governor, seeing the corpse carried in front of the prison, said to those who were near: "The suffering this poor man endured in that prison for sixteen years and two months is something wonderful." The same governor, as well as his predecessor, had often united with the Jesuits and missionaries in tempting him to abjure, and had as often gone away confounded by his answers, and wondering at his meekness, patience and constancy. When the brethren, after his death, enquired of the soldiers concerning him, they answered: "He was a saint."

XXX.
FUGITIVE LADIES.

Amongst the sad and weary wanderers who, under shade of night, through forests and over mountains, sought the land of liberty, were many women of rank and culture. "You might see ladies whose satin shoes had never touched the grass putting on sabots, and trudging thirty, forty, or fifty leagues, behind their guides, who rode before them on mules." An advocate of Montpellier, named Cambolive, who himself encountered many perilous adventures, relates that one day, as he was walking along the high road not far from Montpellier, he met two ladies of rank barefooted, carrying their shoes and stockings in their hand, and walking with difficulty because of the rain. They were pursued by some women of the village, and were in great terror. "I did," he says, "what I could to protect them. The women complained that the ladies, when they passed a stone cross, had tossed their heads in derision. I made a sign to these women not to come further, and at the same time spoke sharply to the ladies, telling them they ought to know better than to indulge in such offensive manners on the highway. This somewhat pacified the women, to whom I said: 'These people have but little discretion; you must pardon them.' Upon this the women turned back, and the ladies told me with tears that they came from the Baroness de Vauvert at Montpellier, and were going to join their cousin, the Baron of Crousete. I told them on no account to go to him, because he had abjured, and now persecuted the Protestants. They asked if I was intending to leave the kingdom, and when I answered, 'Yes,' they begged hard that I would take them with me. I replied it was impossible; that the way was too long; and that if I were discovered, my sentence would be the rope or the wheel. They left me in tears."

The shifts to which women, not less than the men, were compelled to have recourse were strange and ingenious. One caused herself to be packed in a bundle of iron rods, the ends of which projected. The bundle was taken to the custom-house and weighed, without the artifice being discovered, and was not unpacked until it had been carried six leagues within the Savoy frontier.

Another stratagem of a similar kind is related in the following narrative.

XXXI.
ESCAPE OF MADEMOISELLE DUBOIS.

Early in the year 1687 three Huguenot ladies of Lorraine, which then belonged to France, set out to make their way across the frontier to Germany. One of them, Mademoiselle Dubois, relates their adventures. They had not gone more than four leagues, when, on arriving at the village of Courcelles, a troop of horse-soldiers came upon them, who ill-treated them and stripped them of most of their clothes, but finally let them go.

Knowing that the frontier was everywhere rigorously watched, the ladies were put to their wits' end how to elude the guards. Meeting with a carrier they prevailed upon him, by the promise of a high reward, to take them on his waggon, hiding themselves in a cask of linen, in which there was only a small opening left for air. Here they remained in great discomfort three days and nights. When within fifteen leagues of the frontier and near the fortress of Homburg, they heard the drums of the garrison beat the *general*. The carrier, who was well aware he had undertaken his task with a halter round his neck, was appalled at the sound, and refused to go further. In vain the ladies entreated him with tears not to abandon them; he was so utterly unmanned that, detaching one of his horses, he mounted it and rode away, leaving his waggon and all it contained standing in the road. The ladies had everything to fear. One of the royal edicts had constituted the peasants guardians of the frontier, and by subsequent orders the spoil of the fugitives was promised to them, with a bounty of three pistoles for every Protestant they should capture. Creeping one after another out of the cask, the poor women made as fast as they were able for a neighbouring wood; but they had been seen; the peasants pursued them, and carried them to the governor of Homburg, who sent them to Metz, escorted by twenty-five dragoons. Here they were placed in separate prisons; and after lying two months their heads were shaved, and they were condemned to be confined in convents for life.

We here lose sight of Mademoiselle Dubois' two companions. She herself was taken to the convent of the Ursulines, where she remained six months, at the end of which time she found an opportunity to escape. One night, after commending herself in prayer to God, she rose, came out of her room, and noiselessly crossing a chamber in which lay ten nuns, all happily asleep, she gently opened the door. She had to pass through a window which looked down on the court below, and which was guarded by two iron bars. Filing through one bar and wrenching off the other, she leaped down, and alighted on the ground without injury. It was a stormy night; the rain fell and the thunder pealed. From this court she passed into another, and thence through a door into a garden, which was surrounded by a wall. On the inner side the wall was low, but on the further side it went down to the Moselle, which divides the city into two parts, and which flowed far beneath. A strip of linen cloth was bleaching on the grass; this she took, and binding one end round her waist let herself gently down to the river. Plunging into the water, which, although she was very tall, came up to her neck, she crossed the stream in safety. On the further side she met with some Protestants, who had the charity to take her in.

At daybreak her flight was discovered, and the nuns sent word to the governor. The city was in commotion; the dragoons were despatched to search every house, ten louis-d'or being promised to anyone who should discover the fugitive. By changing her hiding-place for dwellings which had already been searched, and by the help of various disguises, sometimes in man's attire, Mademoiselle Dubois eluded all attempts to discover her. The chief difficulty was to pass the city gates. This she contrived to do, dressed like a countryman in attendance on two ladies, with a wicker-basket (*hotte*) on her back, on the top of which was a barrel, and a pannier on her arm. A league beyond the city a guide was waiting for her with a horse. Travelling as master and man, they followed circuitous ways till they arrived at Marche-en-Famene in Luxemburg, where they were nearly being stopped; but Mademoiselle Dubois' knowledge of German saved them.

Halting at a village inn beyond this town they found some Luxemburg soldiers, who enquired of the host if he had not heard of a nun who had escaped from a convent in Metz, adding that other companies were gone in other directions in search of her, and that they were to have ten pistoles apiece if she was discovered. Taking Mademoiselle Dubois for what she appeared to be, they bade her lead their horses to water, promising her some pence for herself. She took the horses, and on her return told the guide they must set off at once and ride as fast as they could to Liège. They arrived in safety. On parting from the guide, she let him know that she was the nun about whom so much noise was being made. The man was thunderstruck, and replied if he had been aware of it he would not have conducted her for a thousand pistoles. From Liège she went on to Maestricht, where she met with a warm welcome from the brethren, and thence to some relations at Cassel, who returned thanks to God for her deliverance.

XXXII.
FRANÇOIS VIVENS.

We return to the Cevennes, always the focus of independence and of resistance to unjust and arbitrary law. Hitherto, since the Revocation, the oppressed Huguenots had borne their wrongs with Christian patience. Now the last of Jurieu's predictions began to be accomplished: "The excited and impatient will fly to arms, and the king will be compelled to shed the blood of his subjects like water."* In this and some subsequent sections of the present work, we see the shadow of the coming event. It was not until fourteen years afterwards that civil war actually broke out; but the restless and fanatical spirit which actuated Vivens and Astier seems, during the interval, never to have slumbered.

François Vivens, of Valleraugues near Le Vigan, in the Lower Cevennes, was the schoolmaster of the little town. He was of an ardent temper, and, though lame, active and daring. On the arrival of the dragoons he fled into the higher mountains, where he gathered many meetings, preaching with great fervency. One of these, held in a barn near St. Jean du Gard, was betrayed by an apostate. But the priest and the consuls, who hastened to the spot, arrived too late; they found no one there but a farmer's wife, who was suckling her infant. They took her, together with four men whom they came upon at the neighbouring village of Caderle, and lodged them in the château of St. Jean, where they remained a month, plied alternately with promises, threats and ill-usage, to induce them to abjure. From the château they were conducted to Montpellier. The farmer's wife gave way under examina-

---
* See *ante*, page 197.

tion, but the men remained firm, and were condemned, three to the galleys, the fourth to the Tour de Constance.

Vivens continued to hold meetings, some of them in the plain, even almost under the walls of Nimes. Nearly all were surprised, and much blood was shed. A frightful massacre attended one which was held in a wood half a league from Uséz. The dragoons invested the wood, and dismounting fired almost from the muzzle on the people, who had fallen on their knees, and then stabbed and slashed amongst them as long as they had strength. The Baron D'Aigalliers, a nobleman of the neighbourhood, states that there remained on the ground more than 600 corpses; and a traveller, who passed that way three weeks afterwards, saw the bodies of thirty women still unburied. The prisoners were treated with shocking barbarity. The soldiers put on the women's gowns over their own uniforms, and in this hideous guise entered Uséz, driving the wounded and trembling crowd before them with their bayonets. The captain, who had hanged a young man with his own hands, received Báville's thanks, the intendant only blaming him for not cutting off the noses of the women!

The ordained pastors having, as we have seen, been all removed, Báville set himself to get rid of the Desert preachers. In August, 1687, he offered Vivens a free exit, with as many of his people as should desire to accompany him. In a moment of weakness Vivens consented, and a list was made out of 300 of the Huguenots whom he was to take with him. Two parties of these, one consisting of forty-eight, amongst whom were Vivens and four other preachers, the other of twenty-two, were accordingly set off. But instead of allowing them to follow the direct and safe way through Geneva, Báville obliged them to undertake a long and perilous journey. He sent the former company by way of Spain, no doubt in the hope that, being destitute of money and provisions, and ignorant of the language, they would either die of want, or fall into the hands of the Catalonian banditti (*miquelets*), or of the Inquisition. But the energy of Vivens balked him of his prey. Some perished, indeed, but their leader with the greater part, most probably by the help of their swords, succeeded in gaining the sea-coast, and embarked on board a vessel which carried them to Holland. The party of twenty-two, in still more flagrant disregard of the compact, were shut up three weeks in the fort of Brescou, where promises, hunger, and ill-usage were employed to make them abjure. Finding them immoveable, Bâville had them taken to Cette, and put on board a vessel which landed them in a destitute condition on the Italian coast. With great difficulty they traversed the Apennines and the Alps, arriving in Switzerland in November. The 230 who remained of the 300 were in no better case than their fellows: the possession of their names served as a guide for their apprehension; and Bâville gave orders to the communes to which they belonged to bring them up for trial, threatening that if this was not done within a fortnight, the soldiers should be billeted on the communes at free quarters.

From Holland, Vivens went to Switzerland, writhing under the wrongs of his afflicted Church, and the treachery which had been practised on himself.

XXXIII.
GABRIEL ASTIER.

Of a like disposition with Vivens was Gabriel Astier, a labourer of Dauphiné, and a disciple of Du Serre, of whom we shall read presently. Pursued in his own province, he crossed the Rhône to Baix, in the Vivarais, where he began to gather followers, and from whence he set out to hold meetings in the Cevennes. The news of his coming was carried by night from village to village; and men and women, old and young, even mothers with infants, quitted their dwellings and climbed up the mountains to hear him. Often they did not return to their homes for several days, but followed the preacher from height to height, supporting themselves, as he did, on apples and walnuts. His cry was, "Repent," and under his impassioned appeals and prayers the whole multitude would fall prostrate, with their faces to the earth, crying out: "Mercy, mercy." But he was not satisfied with winning back his hearers to their old faith; he mingled the carnal with the spiritual, calling on them to take up arms and secure their freedom. He told them God would fight for them, and keep them secure from sabre and ball. He declared that the Prince of Orange, just become king of England, would invade France at the head of 100,000 troops, and that the demolished temples should be miraculously rebuilt and should shine whiter than snow, whilst the Catholic churches which had replaced them should evaporate in smoke, and a star should fall on Rome and burn up the pontifical chair. Many conflicts between the troops and the mountaineers followed these meetings, but for a whole year Bâville sought in vain to lay hands on the daring preacher. At length, descending to Montpellier, Astier ventured upon the esplanade to watch the manœuvres of some troops on their way to Spain and Italy. He was recognised by a soldier in the ranks, arrested, and, April 2nd, 1690, was broken alive at Baix, the place where he had commenced his insurrectionary attempt.

We must spare a few lines for another Desert preacher, who the same year fell a sacrifice to his enthusiasm before he had attained the age of manhood.

XXXIV.
THE YOUTH MAZEL.

He was of the hamlet of Banières, near St. Jean du Gard, and began to preach in 1688. At the commencement of 1690 he was betrayed by a criminal who had murdered his own brother, and who now purchased pardon by this act of treachery. Mazel was taken to the prison of Pompidou, near Florac, where he was examined by the Abbé Du Chaïla, so notorious, some years later, as the immediate cause of the Camisard war. Curious to discover how a mere youth who had not studied could occupy a pulpit, the abbé invited him to preach. Mazel did not require twice asking; he entered at once upon one of the questions of controversy between the Catholics and Protestants, which he handled so skilfully that the priest was amazed. Then turning to the persecution, in which Du Chaïla was playing an active part, he declared that the blood which was being shed, like the blood of Abel, cried to heaven; and raising his voice he thundered out the divine maledictions in the words of the old prophets in so awful a manner, that the abbé, almost beside himself, threatened he should be instantly shot if he did not hold his peace.

Transferred to Montpellier, Mazel maintained before Bâville the same defiant attitude which he had held before Du Chaïla; and he preserved the same unfaltering composure to the end. He was hanged on the esplanade on the 11th of February, 1690. Some days afterwards the intendant, conversing with a colonel on the execution, the latter could not conceal his convictions: "It must be confessed, my lord, that if the God whom these people worship is the same whom we worship, we run great risk of being eternally lost."

Seeing that the " Huguenot patience " was being strained to the utmost under the recent atrocities, and that the mountain population was upheaving in an ominous manner, Baville began to provide for the emergency. After the death of Gabriel Astier, and the departure of Vivens, he disarmed the Protestants of Languedoc, and enrolled 40,000 militia to assist the regular troops, placing over the detachments told off for service in the Cevennes, apostate Huguenots, more keen-scented in hunting down their brethren than the Old Catholics. He also repaired the mountain roads, cut many new ones twelve feet wide for the passage of troops, and erected cantonments and forts.

XXXV.
THE PROPHETS, 1688.

We have spoken of the aërial psalmody with which the overwrought feelings of the distracted Huguenots were soothed ; and of its being succeeded by another and more lasting phenomenon. In the notice of Gabriel Astier, we have a little anticipated this remarkable movement, which made its first appearance in Dauphiné, in 1688.

In Mont Peyrat dwelt a tribe of glass-blowers, who had been ennobled in the fourteenth century, and, two centuries later, had embraced the Reformed Faith. Their superior education and piety gave them a moral ascendancy over their neighbours, and when the pastors were expelled they became readers, catechists and preachers. One of this fraternity was Du Serre, an aged man who dwelt in the town of Dieu-le-fit. His trade took him to Geneva, where he held intercourse with the refugee pastors, and whence he brought back books and mysterious hopes. In 1686 appeared Jurieu's famous treatise on the Apocalypse under the title of the 'Accomplishment of the Prophecies, or the Approaching Deliverance of the Church.' Like many others, this speculative writer had lost himself in the interpretation of the visions seen by John in Patmos. He took the death of the two witnesses (Rev. xi.) to signify the Edict of Revocation, October, 1685, and interpreting days by years, confidently predicted that their return to life, *i.e.*, the deliverance of the Church, would come to pass in April, 1689. His treatise came into Du Serre's hands during one of his journeys; he read it with eagerness, and brooded over it in his solitary hours until it absorbed his whole being. He communicated his aspirations and his enthusiasm to the children and young people whom he employed in his trade, and they in their turn, at the harvest times of corn, wine, and oil, spread the infection through Dauphiné and Provence. Like the heavenly music, it was the natural outcome of an excessive strain on the mental and physical organs, and it ran through the country like wildfire.

The young of both sexes were the especial subjects of this state of rapture. It may be described as commencing with a sensation of heat, which suddenly took possession of the heart and impeded the respiration. The possessed fell to the earth pale and covered with sweat, their limbs violently agitated and their body swollen. Some smote their breasts, others writhed in convulsions, and even sprang from the ground with such force that it required several men to hold them down. Gradually the paroxysm spent itself, and was followed by a kind of comatose sleep, and when the patients awoke, a stream of utterances flowed from their lips, sometimes in threatenings, sometimes in consolation. It was reckoned one of the miracles of the phenomenon that peasants unable to read, and young children who spoke habitually in patois, should pronounce long exhortations in good

French; but this was easily accounted for; their oracular eloquence was only a reminiscence of what they had heard at the meetings.

Three young shepherds, aged respectively eight, fifteen and twenty years, were amongst the first to exhibit these ecstacies. The authorities were vigilant, and the juvenile apostles were speedily taken up and secured in prison. But their fate had no effect on the movement; the prophets went on increasing in number, especially amongst the children. By February, 1689, there were five or six hundred in Dauphiné and the Vivarais. Presuming on their supposed divine gift, even young persons presided at religious meetings, cited apostates before them, and performed the ceremonies of baptism and marriage.

Amongst the women, one of the foremost was Isabeau Vincent, whose father, a woolcarder of Saou, had abjured before the Revocation. She had been present at the combat of Bourdeaux,* 1683, when the outrages perpetrated by St. Ruth sank deep into her soul. Driven by indigence from the paternal cabin, she withdrew to the house of her godfather, who set her to keep his sheep and pigs. When she was about sixteen years of age, a stranger came one day to the farm and preached; and on his departure she felt herself clothed with the prophetic spirit. She did not know a letter, and had learnt only a few verses of the Psalms and a morning and evening prayer. During the seasons of trance which now began to come upon her, her body became insensible, so that she could not be awakened, even if pricked till the blood came. She preached with great success, and her fame spread everywhere. In May, 1689, an advocate of Grenoble, attracted by her fame, came to her abode. He asked for a draught of water, and whilst she was serving him, he observed her attentively.

---

* See *ante*, page 90.

He describes her as slender and low of stature, with large forehead, dark eyes, and sunburnt complexion. "Sister," he said, "I thank God He has permitted me to see you, that I may be strengthened in my faith." "You are welcome," she replied; "this very evening I am to preach at the house of a young lady in the mountains." They set out at dusk, accompanied by a score of peasants. A numerous company was waiting for her. Falling on her knees, she cried: "Loosen my tongue, if it please Thee, O God, that I may declare Thy word and console Thy afflicted people." She offered a long prayer. "I thought," said the advocate, "I was listening to an melodious voice and then preached. The sermon was so angel." After the prayer she gave out a Psalm in a pathetic, yet animated with such holy boldness and zeal, that "one could not," he goes on to say, "but believe she received superhuman help. She bewailed the sufferings of the Protestants, promised them grace and peace, and predicted the re-establishment of their Church in France. The sentences flowed from her lips impetuously, like water long kept back. Her career was of short duration. Hardly had she preached four months when she was arrested, June 8, 1688. The intendant of Dauphiné, Bouchu, came to Crest to examine her. "Here I am, my lord; you can put me to death if you will, but God will raise up others who will declare the truth better than I can." She was committed to prison, and from thence to a convent near Grenoble. Wherever she went she continued to fall into the ecstatic trance. They shaved her head, took away her clothes, exorcised her with holy water, and put her in fear of her life. Her end is unknown.

After her there appeared another Isabeau, named Redostière, native of a village near Alais. She was eighteen years of age, and was known as the Fair Isabeau. She had a comrade, named Pintarde, aged sixteen or seventeen. They travelled together from place to place, exhorting the people to repent and come out of Babylon. After a ministry of two years, Isabeau was apprehended and brought before Bâville, who interrogated her with his usual severity.

"How, forsooth; are you one of those women who preach?"

"I have exhorted my brethren to be mindful of their duty towards God, and, when the occasion presented, have sought God in prayer for them. If your lordship calls that preaching, I have been a preacher."

"But," retorted the intendant, "you know the king has forbidden it."

"Yes, my lord, I know it well; but the King of Kings, the Lord of heaven and earth, has commanded it."

"You deserve death, and must look for no better treatment than other preachers who have suffered that penalty."

"My lord, your threats do not terrify me; I am, by God's grace, ready to die in his service, and so to glorify him."

Instead of being put to death, she was sent to the Tour de Constance for the remainder of her life. She kept the faith to the end.

Pintarde was remarkable for the pertinence of her exhortations and her fervent prayers. She was arrested a little while after Isabeau; and when examined by Bâville gave her answers with the same self-possession as her companion had done. She was immured for life in the château of Sommières, where she endured great hardships, which, however, could not shake her faith.

At the same time a new kind of illusion showed itself in Lower Languedoc. At La Capelle, near Castres, a little girl, who was tending cows, saw an angelic vision. A child of her own size, in a white robe, issued from a bush, and advancing towards her, said: "My sister, I am come down from the Lord Jesus to forbid thee to go any more to Mass." The news of the vision spread; the people flocked to see the young shepherdess. The Romish churches were deserted. The priests applied to the subdelegate, who shut up the little prophetess in the tower of Caudière, examined her, and wilily proclaimed by sound of trumpet that it was quite true an angel had appeared to the child, but that so far from forbidding her to go to Mass, he had expressly enjoined her to do so.

The inspiration of the children caused great perplexity in families. To vindicate themselves and to turn away suspicion, parents informed against their own offspring, and caused them to be shut up. In one case a father would have buried his daughter alive, if he had not been prevented. A rich peasant and his wife were hanged for allowing their two sons, aged about twenty, to prophesy. One of the sons continuing to do so after his parents were put to death, was enrolled in the army; and beginning to prophesy at the head of his corps, was instantly cut to pieces.

After a while the agitation subsided; for several years little is heard of the prophets. But about the turn of the century the epidemic revived with redoubled force, and exercised a powerful influence on the character and course of the persecuted Church. We propose to examine this re-appearance of the phenomenon in the Sequel to the present work.

XXXVI.

THE RETURN OF THE SHEPHERDS.

In bidding adieu to their flocks, the exiled ministers left them their blessing: "In our absence the Spirit of the Lord will dwell among you; Jesus will be your

Shepherd, O, desolate sheep of Israel! Rather than leave you without consolation, He will speak to you by the mouth of unlettered women and little children." The more courageous and faithful amongst them, however, were not satisfied with words only; they resolved to return to France at the earliest opportunity. By the end of the century fifty had been found willing to jeopardize their lives in fulfilment of Christ's command: "Feed my sheep;" but it is remarkable that amongst these fifty there was not one theologian nor one celebrated preacher.

The court received early notice of this movement. In January, 1686, Seignelay wrote to the intendants: "The king is informed that the ministers are about to return, disguised as merchants or cavaliers, to seduce the New Converts. Take care that you omit nothing that may make their punishment exemplary." And, April 16, 1688, he wrote to La Reynie, the chief of the police: "Information arrives to the king every day that the New Converts in Paris are holding meetings, and that many of the preachers administered the Supper during the late Easter festival. His majesty directs you to mark seven or eight of the chief men of the New Converts, whom we have most reason to suspect of bad faith, and set on their track some of the most active of your people, in order to obtain exact information of all the places they frequent."

The penalty of the galleys being found insufficient to deter the pastors from returning, it was ordained that all Protestant ministers, French or foreign, who should be discovered in the kingdom, should be put to death, as well as all persons who should be taken at any religious meetings, other than those of the Catholic Church. The penalty of death, however, for the attendance of meetings was found to be impracticable, and it was rescinded. It was also ordered that all who should harbour the ministers should be sent, the men to the galleys, the women to prison or the convent.

Before we proceed to relate the trials of the ordained pastors who returned, we must speak of a "lay" preacher who was one of the first thus to venture into the wolf's den.

XXXVII.
THE ADVENTURES OF JEAN ROMAN.

Jean Roman was a thriving citizen of Dauphiné, who fled to Lausanne at the Revocation. At the end of two years, sympathy with his suffering brethren and the desire to strengthen and comfort them, drove him back to France. The better to carry on his ministry he disguised himself as a hawker, going from door to door with his pack. When he saw in the house neither crucifix nor box-plant (blessed by the priest), nor image of the Virgin, he put in a word for religion; and if this was well received, he called upon his hearers to brave expatriation, and even martyrdom, rather than continue in the false position in which they were.

The abbé du Chaïla sent troops in pursuit of him; and on February 5, 1689, ten soldiers, led by an apostate, surrounded the house where he was. Roman was taken to Vébron, where he resisted all attempts to convert him. Thence he was transferred to the fort of Alais, and thrown into a filthy dungeon, the abode of rats and toads. Here he remained about eight months. At the end of the year he was removed to the château of M. de Montvaillant, at St. Jean-du-Gard. Being brought before Bâville and the Count de Broglie, they promised him his life if he would reveal the retreat of Vivens and Brousson, who had in the meantime returned to France, and were carrying on their work with equal activity and secrecy.

"If," he replied, "there is no other means of saving my life, have me executed at once; I am as ready to die as you are to condemn me." Whereupon De Broglie seized him by the hair, and, shaking him several times, said if there were no other to do the job he himself would turn executioner. Roman was condemned to be hanged the next day, and the gallows were set up; but when the morrow came the prisoner was not to be found.

There was in the château a young woman of eighteen, daughter of a pastor, named Guichard, who, to escape persecution, had engaged herself as lady's-maid to Montvaillaint's daughters. She had often seen Roman at the desert meetings, and now determined to save his life at the risk of her own. The enterprise was difficult. Bâville and De Broglie lodged in the château; a numerous guard occupied the courtyard; and four dragoons watched at the door of Roman's dungeon. Nothing, however, could deter this heroic woman from her purpose. As soon as night arrived she commenced by plying the dragoons with drink, and when they were sunk in heavy slumber she called to the prisoner through a crack in the wall, and with much trouble, by means of a bayonet inserted through the opening, she loosened the knot by which his hands were bound. With the same instrument, which she passed to him, he himself unfastened his other bonds. Then she passed him a pair of pincers to wrench out the bars of the door. But this being beyond his strength she showed him, by tapping, the place where the bolt entered the stone. Working a hole with the bayonet, he succeeded in forcing back the bolt. But he was not yet free. To cross the courtyard where the guard were on watch and so to gain the principal gate was not to be thought of. The only alternative was to flee by the back of the château; but the window through which Roman would have to make his way stood in sight of the guard, and, moreover, was above that of Bâville's chamber. Nevertheless, as the less desperate expedient of the two, Roman chose it. Letting himself down through the window he got away without being seen, and escaped to the hills, where he hid himself in a cave.

On the morrow, when the gate was opened, Mademoiselle Guichard slipped out and betook herself to a house of safety ; but when she heard of the fury of Bâville and De Broglie, who threw the blame on M. de Montvaillant, and spoke of executing him instead of the preacher, this brave girl returned to the château, and confessed that she alone was responsible for the prisoner's escape. Unmoved by her self-sacrifice, Bâville threatened to send her to the gibbet. He contented himself, however, with having her publicly whipped, and shut up in the château of Sommières. Moreover, he banished Montvaillant to his estate in Upper Languedoc, and confiscated 40,000 francs which would have come to him from a relation.

Three days afterwards Roman came out of his hiding-place, and, as a thank-offering to God for his deliverance, held a meeting in the neighbourhood of St. Jean-du-Gard. It was not long, however, before he was exposed to fresh dangers. On the 10th of March, 1691, he was fired on by a party of soldiers, but escaped by throwing himself into a torrent, which he swam, hiding in a thicket on the other side. Some time afterwards, when again pursued, a musket-ball broke his ankle, and obliged him to remain three months in a cavern, where some friends took care of him. As soon as he could walk he resumed his work, and as he could not stand he preached sitting. In 1693 he found himself compelled to quit France, and took refuge in Geneva ; but he could not rest, and, some years afterwards, returned once more to the Cevennes. He was again arrested, and again delivered ; this time at a frightful cost of the lives and liberties of others.

On the 9th of August, 1699, as he was presiding at a meeting near Boucoiran, he was betrayed, pursued, and overtaken. Covered with blood and wounds, he was conducted to the village, to the White Cross Inn, where he was chained to the bed-post till troops should arrive. Meanwhile, forty or fifty young men from the villages round, armed with guns, swords, and axes, hastened to deliver him. They were received by a discharge from the guard, by which several of them were wounded, but rushing forward they broke open the doors and unbound the prisoner. The first use Roman made of his liberty was to prevent his deliverers from putting the soldiers to death. He himself escaped, but many of the young men, with others who had been present at the meeting, were arrested. Ninety persons were brought to trial, of whom two were broken alive, and seventeen sent to the galleys; others were immured in the ancient dungeons of the Inquisition at Toulouse, where six of them died.

Roman went into Germany and became pastor of Waldenburg, where he remained till his death.

XXXVIII.
PAUL CARDEL.—THE ISLE OF STE. MARGUERITE.

Hitherto our historical enquiries have seldom led us to Paris. The reader may remember that no temple was allowed in the great city itself, the nearest being at Charenton, two leagues distant. There were other reasons which left Paris in the background during these fearful times. Although the populace were especially hostile to the Reformed Church, the government, as already intimated, did not pursue the meetings in the northern provinces with the same severity as in the south and west. Moreover, the representatives in the capital of the Protestant churches belonged to the party of moderation, and disapproved of the bolder measures taken in the south.

One of the first of the pastors who returned was Paul Cardel of Rouen. Expelled at the Revocation, he had passed by Dieppe into England and thence to Holland. Like many others, he was stimulated by Jurieu's interpretation of the Apocalypse, and declared that he came back to await the deliverance which God was about to send to his children.

In company with another refugee minister, Paul Cardel travelled, in 1688, through the northern provinces, strengthening the weak and encouraging the faithful. On their arrival in Paris at the end of October, they found there several other pastors, whom they joined, preaching in every quarter of the city, administering the Supper, celebrating marriages, circulating Protestant books, recovering the relapsed, and even making new converts to the Reformed faith. But Cardel's ministry was of brief duration. He was betrayed by a woman, who sent for him to visit a sick person, and he was arrested, with seven or eight other Protestants who were in the house. On being examined, he frankly confessed for what object he had come. Three of his fellow-prisoners, two of them physicians, and one the wife of a locksmith, who had all abjured at the Revocation, also declared they were ready to shed their blood in their Master's cause.

If Cardel had been arrested in the south he would have been at once put to death, but being in Paris his fate depended directly on the king, who personally had much more repugnance to shed blood than the intendants. It was some time before Louis could make up his mind what was to be done with the prisoner. He decided at last on

The Island Fortress of Ste. Marguerite.

perpetual imprisonment in a state fortress. Whether, however, to bury alive is more merciful than to kill is questionable. For some reason or other the king took every precaution to conceal the fate of the preacher. Cardel had been lodged at first in the Bastille. Seignelay wrote to the governor: "The king commands me to tell you that the prisoner Cardel is to be sent forward to the place named in such a way that no one shall be able to know what is become of him." The place chosen was the famous fortress of Ste. Marguerite, on an island of the Mediterranean.

This stronghold was the prison of the Man in the Iron Mask who, in fact, occupied one of the chambers at the very time that Cardel was sent thither. It stands on the summit of a rugged cliff, which rises abruptly from the sea, and was built in the reign of Louis XIII. The little island, which, with that of St. Honorat, make up the Lerins, lies about four miles from Cannes. It is covered with a pine wood; there is no fresh water; and the summer heat is not tempered, as at Cannes, by the sea-breezes; it is the hottest place in Provence. The walls of the tower where the Iron Mask was confined are twelve feet thick, and its solitary window is guarded by three tiers of iron bars. It may be remembered that Marshal Bazaine was imprisoned in the fortress, December, 1873, and that he made his escape from it at night, August, 1874.

The governor of the island at the time of our narrative was St. Mars, a distrustful, taciturn man, devoted to the king's service so far as a selfish regard to his own interest would permit. He occupied himself with the smallest details which affected his prisoners; "everything aroused his suspicion, even the absence of anything to suspect."

The king himself wrote to St. Mars, April 18, 1689: "I send the man named Cardel, formerly minister of the

R. P. R., to be kept in confinement the rest of his life. You are to have him put in the safest place possible, carefully guarded, and debarred from communication with anyone, either by word of mouth or letter, under any pretext whatsoever." Seignelay also wrote: "I add to the king's letter that it is his majesty's will the matter should be kept profoundly secret, so that no one may know who the man is." And, May 24, Louvois wrote: "When you have anything to tell me respecting the prisoner, you may use the precaution of putting your letters in a double envelope, so that no one but myself may know what they contain." A month later he says: "If the prisoner should be in pressing need of being bled, it must be done in your presence, taking all precaution to keep the surgeon in ignorance who the patient is." January 16, 1690, the minister wrote again: "When the prisoner is not so compliant as he ought to be, you may correct him until he is so."

During the past year, two other preachers, Lestang, a native of Guienne, about whose presence in Paris the king had been much disquieted, and Pierre De Salve, had been committed to the same prison. December 20, Louvois wrote to St. Mars: "I have received your letter concerning the three ministers. When they are sick, the king is of the mind that you should cause some trustworthy ecclesiastic to see them, who may endeavour to convert them before they die."

St. Mars' zeal and greed carried him beyond his instructions; he starved the prisoners and used them like dogs; so that Pontchartrain had to administer a sharp rebuke. "His majesty commands me to write to you [May 24, 1690] that he is astonished that you have acted thus without order, and desires you will not use such harshness again. Your duty consists in guarding the prisoners and preventing them from having communication either within or without the prison; and the allowance made for each is sufficient to supply all their wants and afford them good nourishment.

What the prisoners endured from loss of liberty, solitude, and the want of occupation,—from heat, cold and damp, foul air, hunger, the cudgel, the priest, despair,—will never be known until the day when all secrets shall be revealed. Whatever it was, it was sufficient to overthrow reason; by the year 1693 all three had become insane. The next year Paul Cardel died, at the age of forty. The secret of his death was so well kept that a refugee pastor, writing about the year 1704, supposed him to be still living. "For fifteen years," he says, "he has been in this deplorable condition without being heard of. It is the same," he adds, "with MM. Mathurin,* Malzac and De Salve, three other pastors who left the United Provinces on the same mission." He remarks that the ignorance of their friends concerning what might have happened to them during so long an imprisonment, was a certain proof of their unshaken steadfastness; for if they had shown the least weakness, it could not fail to have been published.

The pastors and the prisoners of State were by no means the only persons who were confined on the island. Besides the tower, there were several other strong places, where numerous prisoners were immured, and amongst them many Huguenots who had been apprehended at the desert meetings. A letter of the minister of war, written in 1704, speaks of sixty-eight sent there from Languedoc at one time.

* The writer is mistaken as to Mathurin, who was not sent to Ste. Marguerite.

XXXIX.
MALZAC AND DE SALVE.

Matthieu Malzac and Pierre de Salve, two ministers whose names occur in the last section, were expelled from France at the Revocation, and had found an asylum in Holland. They were men of like character, and personal friends. The pastors abroad were continually solicited by their flocks to return and comfort them, sometimes with reproaches for having abandoned them. These solicitations met with a response in the consciences of the two friends. They asked counsel of Jurieu, of whom we have frequently spoken, and of Basnage, another Protestant divine of reputation, but could get no decided opinion from either.

Being together one day at l'Ecluse, near Ardembourg, where De Salve filled the office of pastor, they chanced to see the dead body of a Frenchman who had been executed on the charge of attempting to take a plan of the fortifications. They reflected that here was a man who had been willing to expose his life in the service of his king, whilst they had not the courage to do the like for the honour of God. These thoughts were strengthened in Malzac's mind by reading the history of the Christian martyrs and Plutarch's Lives of Illustrious Men, in the latter of which he saw how idolaters even had sacrificed themselves for the good of their country. They agreed to return to France together, to do the Lord's work.

Soon after their arrival in Paris Malzac wrote: "I thank God I have so much to do that I know not which way to turn. Already I have held several meetings, and have received many persons into the peace of the Church. I make them sign a little formula which I have drawn up;

but the misfortune is that we cannot meet more than twelve or fifteen together. Few or none have been really lost to us; all have received me with inexpressible joy. If our ministers knew the sweetness of this occupation they would be eager to engage in it." But the police were on his track; one of their agents rendered to the government an almost daily account of his movements. He spent six months in Paris, from January to June, 1690, when he departed southward, intending to visit La Bastide, in Languedoc, where he had been pastor. He got only as far as Lyons, travelling in the guise of a cavalier. In that city he saw all the New Converts, received back the penitents, and administered the bread and wine. Performing the same offices as he went along, he made his way back to Paris. His movements were always kept secret; when he had finished in one place, a guide took him to another, without letting him know whither they were going. When they arrived, the guide introduced him; he preached, broke the bread, and received back the wanderers. He journeyed by night and rested in the day, never venturing abroad in the daylight, except to visit the sick. He passed under two other names besides his own; letters to him being addressed sometimes in one, sometimes in another. His ministry lasted a little over two years.

In Paris he pursued his gospel work until February 11, 1692, when he fell into the hands of the police. At a house in the parish of St. Germain l'Auxerrois, the officers took cognizance of six persons whom they made out to have assembled for the celebration of the Lord's Supper. Two others arrived afterwards. The house was invested and entered, and all who were present were apprehended; Malzac, his guide, who was a surgeon, named Pierre Baril, another gentleman, and five ladies, including the mistress of the house.

They were examined; and Pontchartrain wrote to La Reynie: "I have read to the king the notes of what you have learned from the minister Malzac; and his majesty relies on your care to draw from him all the information possible regarding his conduct and designs. You will receive an order to send him to the Bastille." Malzac and Baril were in the first place committed to the custody of Desgrez, special officer of arrests, conversions, and espionage, whose "oven" enjoyed an infamous notoriety. Baril was thence removed to the Bastille, in the records of which fortress we find this testimony: "On being interrogated he said that he had always made profession of the R. P. R., although, in obedience to the king, he once abjured, knowing that if he did not the dragoons would compel him." He died August 26, 1699, without ever partaking of the sacrament, in spite of the exhortation of Father Desbordes.

One of the five ladies who were arrested with Malzac was Mme. Contandière. She had once abjured to recover her liberty, but had recanted, and had come to Paris in the hope of living unobserved in the crowded city. After her examination she was committed to the Château du Pont de l'Arche, and thence to the Castle of Angers; but being found intractable, Louis directed she should be removed to Nantes, whose governor was notorious for subduing the most incorrigible. With the prisoner Pontchartrain wrote in 1700: "She is the most stubborn Protestant we have ever had; you will have plenty of work for your talent of conversion. His majesty knows you are more able to succeed than any other man, although he will be agreeably surprised if you do." What ultimately became of this lady is unknown; three of the four others are believed to have been shut up in the Bastille.

On the 25th La Reynie again examined Malzac, and

learnt from him that since his return to France he had preached to 20,000 New Converts, and received the abjuration of several Old Catholics. March 10 he was again examined at length, immediately after which, instead of the Bastille, he was taken to the Castle of Vincennes, and was thence removed, May 15, to join Cardel, De Salve, and Lestang, in the fortress of Ste. Marguerite. The order was as follows: "The king has determined to send the minister Malzac to the island of Ste. Marguerite, where there are some already; and I enclose with this letter an order from M. Auzillon to conduct him thither, so that you may charge him to do it with the same precautions as in the case of the other." The king at the same time wrote to St. Mars, to which letter Pontchartrain added: "The minister must be carefully guarded and moreover treated with humanity, and his expenses shall be paid at the same rate as the others."

The arrival of Malzac rekindled the zeal of the other captive ministers, who hearing Psalms sung in one of the cells joined in. Another contrivance by which the prisoners communicated with one another was by means of the pewter plates on which their food was brought to them, and on which they traced minute marks, a sign, a name, or a reference to a text of Scripture, so that the plate, circulating from room to room, carried refreshment for the soul as well as food for the body. In a letter to the governor, June 29, Pontchartrain writes: "I have received your letter respecting the last minister who has been sent to you. Certainly you must not suffer these ministers to sing Psalms aloud. But if they continue to do so after you have forbidden it, instead of ill-treating them you should remove them to distant apartments of the tower, where they cannot hear one another. With regard to their writing on the plates, it is easy to remedy this by giving them nothing but earthenware. They are very obstinate fellows, who are much to be pitied and whom you must treat with as much humanity as possible."

Nearly a year and a half afterwards another letter from the secretary of state alludes to the deplorable condition into which these poor men had fallen. "I have received your letter informing me of the condition of the four ministers. You must closely guard those who are deranged, treating them, however, with kindness. As to the other, you must do what you can to make him a Catholic." This last was Malzac, who had been only eighteen months in the Tower; Cardel had been four years and a half; and De Salve and Lestang three and a half.

In spite of the strict surveillance to which he was subjected, Malzac found means to communicate with his friends, who had supposed he was dead. One of these wrote to the Dutch ambassador: "I have received a note in his handwriting, brought by one who has conversed with him several times in the island of Ste. Marguerite, from whence he himself has escaped,* and who, not venturing to enter the tower, left for him in the mouth of a cannon, paper, ink, and pens. From memorials presented to the Dutch ambassador at Versailles, in 1724–1725, we learn that Malzac was allowed neither fire nor candle, and was supplied with only one meal a day; but that he enjoyed two hours of exercise daily, an indulgence procured for him by Marshal Villars, when he was president of the council of war. Whilst his friends were thus interesting themselves on his behalf, an order came for his release; not from the king, however, or from any earthly tribunal, but from that court which no human power can gainsay. He died on the 15th February, 1725, after thirty-three years of martyrdom.

* No doubt one of the Huguenot prisoners spoken of in the last section.

XL.
GARDIEN GIVRY.

Gardien Givry was a native of Vervins in Picardy, and was ordained pastor of the church in that town, but in consequence of some irregularity of conduct he was deposed in 1678. He removed to Lausanne, where, repenting of his misconduct and believing himself called to return to his charge, he was restored to his office. Expelled from France at the Revocation, he came to England, was ordained afresh by the Bishop of Exeter, and served the French Church in Plymouth three years and a half. But still believing he was called to minister to the oppressed Churches in the desert, he left Plymouth, May 1, 1691, and passing through Holland crossed the frontier at Mons, a town which, six months before, had fallen into the hands of the French.

He directed his course towards his native town, stopping at Landouzy-La-Ville, a hamlet three leagues to the north of it, where he had family connections, and where the inhabitants were all Protestants. Here he wrote: "I was ravished to see my brethren rise from their fall and return again to the bosom of the true Church." At another village, St. Pierre, where he found that a meeting on Sundays was kept up, so many assembled to hear him that the house could not contain them; and at Lemé more than 800 came together, and eleven infants were brought to him for baptism. Proceeding to the town of St. Quentin, messengers from the neighbouring villages, where his mission had been heard of, came to invite him to visit them. They were Catholics, who had never seen a Reformed preacher, and who showed no little eagerness to hear the truth. "I went," he says, "at the time named, and had the pleasure to see 500 people assembled, all papists by birth, and all desirous to renounce the superstitions of Rome." He preached to them by torch and fire-light from nine in the evening till one the next morning. A week afterwards he again exhorted them, and found they still desired " to come out of Babylon." But seeing that many of them were weak in faith, he forbore to receive them into the Reformed communion.

Passing through Paris, he took his way, January, 1691, to Sedan, a town which at the Revocation had, like Montpellier, abjured *en masse*. Here he was received with open arms, and from hence he travelled over the northern part of Champagne as far as Bossuet's diocese of Meaux. He is eloquent in praise of one of the villages in which he laboured, Monneaux, near Château Thierry, a place inhabited wholly by Protestants, and which he describes as "more blessed temporarily and spiritually than any other in France." For several years the people had held their meetings twice a week, two brothers having been raised up to read and pray with them in place of their pastor. The quiet they enjoyed was owing to the favour of the local magistrate, and to the friendly disposition towards the Protestants of the lieutenant-general of Château Thierry. This gentleman sent for Givry, and conversed with him two or three hours on religious subjects. But the good officer did not escape the jealous vigilance of the court. October 14, 1692, Pontchartrain wrote to the intendant of the province: "The lieutenant-general's conduct deserves severe punishment, but his majesty, with his usual clemency, has ordered me to send for him that the king may know from himself what has passed, and endeavour by gentleness to bring him back to his duty, being persuaded that such a man, acting in good faith, might contribute more than anyone to the real recovery of the New Catholics. It will not be necessary, therefore, to have recourse to persecution in this district until I have conversed with this officer, when I will make known to you his majesty's resolution."

On his return to Paris, Givry found the brethren in sorrow and consternation on the betrayal of Malzac, an event which drew from himself the following aspiration: " Thou art sparing me, O my God, to continue my work; I am transported with the thought; behold me ready to do Thy will. Give me strength to glorify Thee, whether free or in prison, amongst Thy people or before Thy enemies, in life or in death." Hardly had he traced these lines than his faith was put to the test. He was arrested at a house in the Rue St. Martin, May 3, 1692, together with another devoted pastor, Elisée Giraud, who had returned to France on the same errand. They were taken to the château of Vincennes, from whence, in June, 1694, they were sent to join Malzac, De Salve, and Paul Cardel, at Ste. Marguerite.

Little is known of Giraud and Givry's history in that gloomy fortress; the few traits which have survived, however, may help us to picture the living-death in which they and their fellow-confessors passed their days. It was not easy to cure St. Mars of his avaricious practices. He received an annual sum for the prisoners' maintenance, which, it would appear, suffered a considerable defalcation before it was applied for their use. " I am surprised," wrote Pontchartrain, January 9, 1695, " to see in your report a number of expenses for the five prisoners, for which you ask reimbursement. In allowing 900 livres for each, his majesty understood this sum was for food, clothing, linen, and everything; it is, in fact, much more than the allowance to other prisoners. Pray be contented, and let them have all necessaries with kindness and charity." Pontchartrain, however, was strict enough on other points. July 21, 1694, he wrote: " You must take away from the last two ministers I sent you all their writing materials, and let me have what writings you find with them. But you may give them and the others good books to read, as already ordered." In September, 1695, St. Mars was made governor of the Bastille, and was succeeded at Ste. Marguerite by De la Motte-Guérin. In reply to a request from two of the pastors, made through the new governor, to be allowed paper, Pontchartrain wrote: "Paper must not be given to the one who wishes to make notes on Holy Scripture, for fear he should use it for some other purpose. As to the other, whose mind seems to wander, you may let him have some, and send me what he writes." February 18, 1701, the minister wrote to a commissary: "The king desires, as soon as you arrive at Toulon, you should go over to the Isle of Ste. Marguerite to see the five ministers detained there by order of his majesty. Converse with them, and see how they are affected towards religion, and send me a report of the state in which you find them, without letting anyone know that they are there, or why you go thither."

Nothing further has come down of the history of these martyrs.

XLI.

THE RETURN OF VIVENS AND CLAUDE BROUSSON.

We left Claude Brousson, in 1683, at Lausanne,* where he devoted himself to the service of his suffering brethren in France. His appeals helped to open the door for the honourable reception of the rufugees in foreign countries, and to secure for them the sympathy of Protestant Europe. For a while, indeed, the German Lutherans regarded the Calvinist emigrants with almost as much

* See *ante*, page 94.

mistrust as they would have done Roman Catholics, so that in Würtemburg they were refused admission into the inns and hospitals; and at Erlangen it is said some died of want. But the league between Louis XIV. and James II. for the destruction of the Reformed faith, caused the sister Churches to draw closer together; and this religious union again produced a political alliance. It is supposed the first idea of the Protestant coalition of 1689 was conceived by Brousson.

Brousson's labours whilst abroad were incessant. He wrote to the Catholic clergy, setting before them the real merits of the question at issue, and the fatal effects of continued persecution. He exhorted the New Converts, the great body of whom were still Protestants at heart, to quit the kingdom and suffer the loss of everything rather than remain unfaithful to their conscience. Many of the refugee ministers, when they heard of meetings in the woods held in spite of edicts and massacres, of the "intrusion of ignorant and vulgar men" into the ministry, and especially of the part played by the prophetesses, were greatly troubled. Brousson replied by calling on the pastors to leave their asylums of safety and peace, brave all dangers, and return to France to look after their scattered flocks. This appeal naturally brought upon him the retort: " Why not set us the example ?" and he began to consider whether instead of only defending the Church at a safe distance he ought not to nourish and sustain her by his personal presence. The words of Ezekiel rose continually before him : " Thy prophets are like the foxes in the deserts; ye have not gone up into the gaps, neither made up the hedge for the house of Israel to stand in the battle in the day of the Lord;" and those of Deborah : " Curse ye, Meroz, because they came not to the help of the Lord against the mighty." The mental strife thus kindled within him lasted nearly a year. In a letter, written some time afterwards to the intendant Bâville (July 10, 1693), he says: "I protest before God that it was neither by the order nor advice of any foreign power that I came back to France, but wholly by the motion of my own conscience and of the Spirit of God. This motion was so powerful that in consequence of putting off obedience to it I fell into an illness, the cause of which the doctors could not discover; and seeing plainly that God would take away my life if I longer resisted his Spirit, I set out whilst yet ill, without consulting with flesh and blood, and it pleased God to restore my health on the journey."

Whilst Brousson was in this state of agitation, Vivens arrived at Lausanne, not, like his friend, hesitating whether or not to embark on the desert mission, but eager for the fray, as ready to enter upon it in the field as in the pulpit. The perfidious treatment he had received from Bâville had in his own opinion released him from his promise not to return to France, as well as from every obligation he owed to the government. Moreover, the sanguinary deeds which had been perpetrated during his short exile, some of which we have alluded to, had further embittered his spirit and whetted his desire for vengeance. Might not he say, as Elijah said in the cave in Horeb: "They have thrown down thine altars, and slain thy prophets with the sword; and they seek my life to take it away?" The slaughter of the four hundred prophets of Baal, at the Brook Kishon, was perpetually before him.

Leaving Brousson to follow when his resolution should be taken, Vivens quitted Lausanne in the early days of 1689, and as soon as he reached the Cevennes resumed his preaching and pastoral work with his accustomed ardour, whilst at the same time he intrigued with foreign powers, and organized and armed a band of men amongst the mountain population. Having collected some three or four hundred followers, he did not wait for aid from abroad, but began to scour the country. His rash course was speedily checked. Bâville and the Duke de Broglie came upon him, unexpectedly, at the Pont de Montvert, when he was defeated, and many of his followers taken and executed. He himself escaped to the forest and hid in a cavern, where he lay concealed. One day a stranger was announced. "Let him come in," said Vivens in a subdued tone; "heaven takes pity on my misery and sends me a consoling angel." It was Brousson.

Brousson left Lausanne, July, 1689, six months after Vivens, and he too made his way direct to the Cevennes. Unlike some other preachers who returned with him, and who carefully concealed their movements from the authorities, Brousson wrote at once to Bâville, informing him of his return, and remonstrating with him on the measures of the government and the conduct of the priests, as fit only to drive the people to despair. He had not long pursued his work in the desert when he found his way to the cave where Vivens had sought shelter. During the winter this retreat was their joint asylum.

Brousson severely blamed Vivens' conduct; especially he deprecated invoking foreign interference, for he saw that "conquered provinces, if the invasion should be successful, would be a perpetual source of war." But, as we have seen, his objection to war was not grounded on Christian principle; he held that oppressed subjects, as a last resource, might lawfully rise in arms against their sovereign. He wrote to Bâville: "The State must perish if liberty of conscience be not established. No one knows the danger which is incurred in forcing two millions of people to abjure the only religion which, as they are persuaded, is conformable to the word of God. It is, we acknowledge, a strange thing for subjects to take up arms against their prince; it is never to be done except in defence of life, when they are threatened with being massacred. The patience of the most moderate is changed to fury when it is driven to extremity. The most pacific at last become weary of being devoured without cause, treated like slaves, and slaughtered like beasts. What are these miserable people to do? They are in despair at being forced to abjure their own religion, and they regard the religion they have embraced with more horror than ever. What course remains for them to take? They have tried supplication and remonstrance times without number, but always in vain. When they meet without arms to worship God they are butchered. Is it then a strange thing that they should take some precautions to avoid being slaughtered? Do you wish they should wait for foreign powers to invade the kingdom that they may throw themselves into their arms?" With these views Brousson was not in a position altogether to condemn Vivens, nor was he prepared to break off his intimacy with him.

Whilst Brousson and Vivens were in the cave they were visited by the two youthful prophetesses of whom we have spoken above, Isabeau Redostière and Pintarde, who, hearing that the two preachers were in concealment in the mountains, went up thither to partake of the bread and wine with them. Brousson was charmed with Isabeau. He describes her as "a vessel brimful of the grace of God," and her prayers, taken from the Psalms and the prophets, and offered with fervour and humility, as very affecting.* At the same time, the brethren who were with him entreated Brousson to undertake the office of pastor, and thus qualify himself to administer the Supper. He consented, looking upon this call as a sufficient ordination under the circumstances in which he was placed.

* The prophets seemed to have exercised a ministry independent of the state of trance: this ought to have been noticed earlier.

XLII.
BROUSSON'S DESERT MINISTRY.

Early in 1690 the two pastors quitted the cavern, and taking different routes, departed for their respective work in the desert. The term "desert" had by this time come to signify, not heaths and mountains only, but any place in country or town in which the meetings were held in secret.

Brousson took with him Henri Guérin (better known as Pontaut), a young man of twenty-five, well acquainted with the country. Brousson's activity was prodigious. When the nightly meeting was over he would take a few hours' repose, and where it was safe, remain a second night, preaching, instructing, and administering the Supper with untiring energy. To help him on his way, a staved cask and a mattress were sometimes placed for him in the woods, with bread for his supper. He preached with apostolic fervour, not sparing the backsliders or the lukewarm. The usual length of his sermons was three hours, but when he celebrated the Communion he spoke more than four; and his prayers were long and fervent. Mr. Quick, an English gentleman who knew him well, says: "He told me of a meeting where no fewer than 5000 persons were kneeling together on the ground before him, with sighs and groans, and the tears streaming down their cheeks, bewailing their unfaithfulness, and with uplifted eyes and hands calling God to witness that they for ever renounced Rome and her worship."

To himself, Brousson's ministry was an unfailing spring of delight. "God made me by his Spirit a partaker of unspeakable consolation, especially during the sacred meetings, and most of all when I administered the Supper." It was the same when he took up the pen.

When unable to go himself to any place, he sent letters and sermons, which Henri Pontaut, whom he taught to write, assisted him in transcribing. The woods and caves were their study; their desk was a small board which Brousson carried with him and placed on his knees, and which he called his " wilderness-table."

Brousson's sermons supplied the spiritual food of his countrymen; they were published under the title of 'Mystical Manna of the Desert.' He insists in them on a righteous life as strongly as on doctrine or faith. " If, dear brethren, we would be the sheep of Jesus Christ, we must keep His commandments. God will not suffer His people to be worldly, drunkards, unchaste, false, usurers, litigious, vindictive, profaners of the sabbath, swearers, renegades, blasphemers. He sifts His mystic wheat that the chaff may be blown away." Sometimes, however, the shepherd leads the sheep to pastures where the herbage is less wholesome. One of his favourite similes was the dove. " As the dove is a pure and clean creature, so the Church of Jesus Christ is pure from the filth of the age; but the Romish Church, sullied for many ages, is not the dove of Jesus Christ. The dove is gentle and the true Church is gentle, peaceable and meek; but the Romish Church despoils the faithful of their goods, drives them from their homes, casts them into dungeons, torments them in the galleys, tortures them to death, or massacres them wholesale. Ah! she is not the dove of Jesus Christ. The dove is faithful to her mate, but the Romish Church prostitutes herself to gods of gold, silver, wood and plaster; she cannot be the dove of Jesus Christ. The dove is a feeble creature; she has no claws or terrible feet to defend herself; but the Romish Church is strong and terrible; she is the mystic Beast to whom the dragon has given his power. She is not the dove of Jesus Christ." It is not that these eloquent words were false, or that there was any lack of provocation, or that the feelings of the writer were other than natural; but it was not wise to serve up such high-spiced condiments to spirits already heated. The sound, practical counsel contained in the 'Manna' might be forgotten; the refrain, like a popular song, would be sure to fasten itself in the memory, and rise continually to the lips. Moreover, as will appear more plainly in the next section, Brousson had only to look on Vivens and his comrades to see that his own Church was far from being altogether dove-like.

Brousson's labours bore fruit. The meetings became more and more numerous, and the people more earnest. Sometimes both preacher and hearers contrived to elude all the vigilance of the authorities; at other times the meetings were surprised or informed against, and terrible suffering ensued. In January, 1691, Brousson held a meeting in the wood of Boucoiran. Information was given by a spy that a nobleman who had renounced Calvinism to retain his estates was present and stood near the preacher during the service. The spy not being prepared with the nobleman's name, punishment fell on the innocent. Six of the chief landed proprietors of the district, ex-Protestants, who had never attended meetings since their abjuration, were apprehended; two were sent to the galleys and the rest to a prison at Lyons for life.

Amongst the dangers to which the desert preachers were exposed, not the least was that from false brethren. A former fellow-student of Brousson, named Gautier, abjured, but kept his conversion secret in order the more easily to betray the Huguenots. He caused himself to be put into prison with some of the confessors, to whom he recounted his pretended trials, and obtained in return information of Brousson's movements. Finding, however, this means insufficient, he left the prison, and began himself to hold meetings. After a time he sent a message to Brousson, requesting an interview, in order to ask his advice whether he should continue to preach or should escape out of the kingdom. Brousson's suspicions were awakened, and he refused to see him. But Gautier was not to be thus put aside. He got a young Protestant who attended his meetings and who had no suspicion of his treachery, to conduct him to Brousson's lodgings. Arrived at the house, the young man entered first to inform the pastor that Gautier had come to speak with him. Brousson at once saw the trap that was laid for him, and upbraided the young man with betraying him. The latter, comprehending the case, hastily turned back to the door and told Gautier that Brousson had left the house. Thus balked of his prey, Gautier threw off the mask, and placing himself at the head of parties of soldiers, scoured the districts in which Brousson and Vivens held their meetings, making many arrests, and receiving as his reward a liberal share of the confiscated property. But his career was brief; he was drowned in a river, whether by accident or design was not known. Bâville boasted that he had eight hundred more such men in his pay.

XLIII.
INTRIGUES WITH FOREIGN POWERS.

Bâville left no stone unturned to get possession of Vivens, putting to death several persons on the mere suspicion of having harboured him. The warlike preacher was not slow in retaliating. Several persecuting priests met their death in a mysterious manner. One was poignarded at noon-day whilst carrying the Host; four others were found dead in their houses or by the road. To the corpse of one whose offence had been that he had seized a preacher and had him sent to the galleys, was attached a note: "From the Desert, touching the fate of this Judas. Passers-by, do not wonder at his death! God allowed it, because this miscreant sold innocent blood. I appeal to your justice. This wretch would have betrayed the powers, as he has betrayed a member of our Lord. We killed him to prevent the repetition of such disorders, and we have resolved that as long as such traitors exist, we will, with God's help, seize them, even if they were enclosed in the strongest fortress in France."

Vivens and Brousson met sometimes in the course of their circuits. The project of a foreign invasion was renewed. The Count de Schömberg, who was in Savoy with an army of French refugees, sent a Cevenol soldier named François Huc to the two preachers, to arrange the terms on which the invasion was to be undertaken. The envoy arrived at a moment when Brousson was reduced almost to despair. Most of the brave men who had returned with him to France had perished on the scaffold or been sent to the galleys, whilst he himself was worn down with countless dangers and incessant fatigue, and was prepared to welcome almost any means of deliverance. Nevertheless, at first he refused to enter into the scheme, telling the messenger he was wholly occupied with his gospel ministry. The vehement solicitation of Vivens, however, acting on his own despondent feelings, prevailed; and when his exultant comrade drew up a plan of the proposed invasion, with an itinerary of the Cevennes, Brousson transcribed the document with his own hand. By the terms of the compact, 2000 troops were to enter France by the Savoy frontier and take possession of the mountains, and 8000 more were to be landed on the coast of Languedoc.

This dangerous paper was carried by Poutaut to Nimes and given to a guide named Gabriel Picq, who was about to depart for Geneva with a company of fugitives. It was addressed to Pictet, a professor of theology in that city, who was in correspondence with Schömberg. For greater security Picq sewed the paper in his waistband. Unhappily, the fugitive party were stopped by the French officer at the gates of Geneva, March 24, searched, and the document discovered, together with a letter in cypher, dated from the Desert and signed Olivier, a pseudonym of Vivens. The French resident sent the papers to Bâville, who kept them as evidence of the highest importance, and caused Picq to be hanged.

Disappointed in his attempts to possess himself of Brousson and Vivens, Bâville, in November, offered 2000 livres for each of them, dead or alive, and 200 for information of a meeting,* It was afterwards made known verbally that 10,000 livres would be given for Brousson's apprehension, and this sum in the sequel was raised still higher.

XLIV.
THE DEATH OF VIVENS.

But Vivens' career was near its close. In February, 1692, one of his companions, being apprehended and subjected to the rack, revealed the preacher's hiding-place. A party of soldiers were sent in pursuit and found him, with two companions, in a cave situated in a valley between Alais and Anduze. The soldiers arrived at dawn. A dense thicket hid the mouth of the cave, which was also protected above by a ledge of rock. Vivens' watchful ear caught the stealthy tread of the soldiers as they came on, and hastily burning his papers, and making a short prayer, he took his gun, and posting himself at the mouth of the cavern, defied the boldest to approach. The first

---

* A copy of the printed proclamation is still preserved at Junas, near Sommières.

who appeared was a sergeant; Vivens fired and the man fell dead. Two soldiers who followed him met with the same fate; and a lieutenant was wounded at the fourth discharge. But as Vivens was taking aim at the commandant, an officer of militia, a renegade, who had climbed up behind the rock, seizing the moment when Vivens put out his head, fired almost at point blank and shot him dead. His companions, who had loaded the guns and handed them to him, surrendered on promise of their lives. But the promise was not kept. They were carried in triumph to Alais, with the corpse of the preacher, whither Bâville joyfully hastened to bring them all to trial, the dead as well as the living. The lifeless body was condemned to be burnt; and the two prisoners to be hanged on gallows erected beside it. Vivens was in his thirtieth year, and had been seven years in the desert ministry. Notwithstanding his fiery and even vindictive temper, his brethren entertained the highest esteem for him. "He was," says Quick, "of spotless life and singular piety; well versed in the Scriptures, and incomparable in prayer; by his ministry the lukewarm were animated and the frozen inflamed with the love of God." Unhappily such paradoxes are to be met with in every age; they are a stumbling-block to the inquirer after truth.

XLV.

DELIVERANCES.

Vivens being dead, Bâville's one object was to get possession of Brousson, who was tracked like a wild beast. For four or five months he could travel only by night. He wandered in the woods and on the mountains, where he lay on straw or faggots, and under bushes. In winter, when the cold on the hills is extreme, he seldom dared to make a fire, for fear the smoke should betray him, or to go out into the sunshine for fear of being seen. His deliverances were many and strange. Before Vivens' death he fell ill and went to Nimes, where he hid himself in his mother's house. Bâville's spies soon discovered his retreat, and the intendant wrote to the bishop, Fléchier, to arrest him. The letter lay open on the bishop's table, and whilst he was conducting a visitor to the door, a nobleman, a New Convert, entering the room, chanced to cast his eyes upon it, and seeing what it was, in agitation went hastily out of the house to give Brousson warning. The pastor had time to change his quarters before the soldiers arrived.

Some time afterwards Bâville learnt that he had withdrawn to a wood on the hill of Bouquet, between Uzès and Alais. Warned in time, Brousson, with a trusty companion, avoided the place. It was a season of much rain, and the soldiers who were sent after him, and who were kept three nights in the woods, suffered so severely that several died. The first two nights were passed by Brousson and his companion under a bush; but the third night the violence of the rain forced them to take shelter under a rock, where they could neither stand nor lie at length. The next morning, wet through and benumbed with cold, Brousson proposed that they should go to the neighbouring village and dry themselves. Hardly had they left their retreat when they heard voices. It was a detachment of a dozen soldiers, who were only a few yards from them. The fugitives had barely time to hide in the thickets. Fresh detachments appeared; they counted 104 men, and heard the officers consulting in what direction they should continue the search. The danger was the greater, as amongst the soldiers were many countrymen who knew the district perfectly, and who had with them dogs to track the fugitives. Brousson, in anguish of spirit, fell on his knees; his prayer was heard; the weary troops separated to search the neighbouring villages, including that to which he had proposed to go.

Bâville was ready to catch at any shadow which promised possession of his victim. Whilst Brousson was in Nîmes, a priest of the cathedral called on the intendant and asked if he had found the minister, adding: "He is in the city at this moment, and if you desire to have him one of my acquaintances shall deliver him to your lordship." The intendant replying that he would give all the world to put his hand on him, the priest informed him of a magician in the service of the nuns of a certain convent who could infallibly discover Brousson's retreat. The intendant, says Brousson in relating the story, who would have had no objection to go to the devil himself to rid the earth of the preacher, despatched a messenger to bring the sorcerer to him. The man soon arrived and asked how he could serve his lordship. "Can you assist me in discovering and apprehending Brousson?" "Yes, my lord, I will do it": and he at once set about practising his secret art. All his efforts, however, were in vain. He was obliged to confess: "Brousson is hidden from me, and protected by the Most High from the power of the intendant." Bâville felt himself insulted, and vented his rage on the priest, who in his turn broke out into bitter invectives against the sorcerer. But he found his match. "As for you," retorted the magician, "you are insulting me and exposing me to the intendant's anger, while you know very well that you have learnt the art of sorcery from me, but not to much purpose; your familiar spirit is not so powerful as mine." On which the intendant drove them both from his presence.

Many motives disposed Brousson at this time to leave France. His hiding-places were all known; his *signalement* was everywhere posted up; his health was undermined;

his family required his presence; and he wished to publish his writings. He, therefore, once more took the road to exile, and arrived at Lausanne, December 17, 1693, after a perilous ministry of four years and five months.

During this period the French were at war with England, Holland, and Germany; and in 1692 the Duke of Savoy and the Count de Schömberg invaded France on the side of Dauphiné with 30,000 men, expecting the Protestants to rise and join them. But Vivens was then dead, and had left no successor; the Cevenols, held in restraint by Brousson's influence, did not move, and the Protestants of Dauphiné rose only to aid in repulsing the foreigner, under the conduct of a youthful heroine, Mademoiselle de la Tour Dupin, whose portrait and arms the king placed in St. Denis beside those of Joan of Arc.

XLVI.
CLAUDE BROUSSON'S SECOND DESERT JOURNEY, 1695-6.

On his return to Switzerland at the end of 1693, Brousson received regular ordination, and soon afterwards left for Holland. He visited England, where he met with Mr. Quick, who writes: "The exiled pastor, Mestayer of Saint Quentin, brought Dr. Brousson to my house in Bunhill Fields, where I was favoured to converse with him five good hours. The time seemed very short; not a vain or idle word dropped from his lips. He seemed an angel in a human form, who was not content to go to heaven alone, but would carry his friends, countrymen, and strangers, all with him."

Brousson was recalled from England by the Walloon Church at the Hague to become one of their pastors, and for eighteen months he occupied that important post.

CLAUDE BROUSSON.

Beloved and liberally maintained, however, as he was, his position was not entirely to his mind. "The little lawyer pastor," says Douen, "swarthy, sunburnt,* always in motion, and more zealous than all his friends, suffered from the restraints by which he was surrounded. His excessive freedom, his unmeasured denunciation of popery, his highly allegorical interpretation of Scripture, gave offence, and it may be also some lack of variety in his sermons, and even his southern accent.† Hardly could he get permission to print his books." As his health returned he began to sigh for his beloved churches in the wilderness, which were languishing for his presence; and in the month of September, 1695, he again set forth on his perilous mission. This time he entered France from the north.

Making his way through the armies encamped on the frontier (France was then at war with the allies), he threaded the unfrequented paths of the Ardennes, having for companion and guide another fugitive, Jacques Bruman. In a letter to his wife of September 20, he pours out his feelings on resuming his old vocation: "I cannot express the joy I felt when we began again to walk by night through sequestered paths; it brought back the memory of my former pilgrimages, and of the grace God used to grant me, and I felt animated again with the old spirit." In another, of the same month, he writes: "Thanks be to God, I am in perfect health. It is desirable that it should not be known in what part of the country I am. Suffice it that I am where there are many pious souls, who are left pretty much unmolested." October 25, he wrote from

---

* The portrait in the Nîmes museum represents Brousson as of a *fair* complexion, remarkably so for a southerner. It was painted in Holland, by Bronkhorst. Our plate, from a photograph, does scant justice to the original. It is a countenance you return to again and again.

† He pronounced sanctifier, santifier; and accent, assent.

Sedan: "It was not my intention to stop here, but finding seven or eight villages in which were many of our brethren hungering for the word of God, I could not pass them by. They were so eager to be received again into the peace of the Church, and so fearful of losing the opportunity, that they neglected to take the necessary precautions; so that when I ventured to hold a small meeting in the suburbs of the city it became known, and the next morning the house where we lodged was invested. I put on a bold front, and asked the chief officer: 'Sir, what do you want?' Without replying he cast his eyes upon Bruman, who had a staff in his hand as though he was setting out on a journey; and after putting several questions to him, had him arrested. Turning my back as though I was the master of the house, I passed into a small room and hid myself behind the door, which did not thoroughly conceal my person. The officers and four or five soldiers came into the room, remarking to one another that they had secured the minister, and must now find his books. They looked about; if they had turned their heads they must have seen me, but, like Elisha, I prayed to God to smite them with blindness; and they left the room without having discovered me. In an adjoining chamber one of them seeing two children of five or six years old, enquired where the minister had slept. The children, instead of at once replying, ran into the room where I was, and when they saw me ran back to the officer, crying, 'Sir, here, here!' But the officer did not understand what they meant, and left the house with the rest of the party."

> "The innocent spirit bears
> A charm against the evil power,
> And God's good angels every hour
> Watch round it unawares.
> And never yet, I ween, was ward
> Of sentinel, or portal barred,
> Like those white wings of theirs."

"As," continues Brousson, "I saw that the mistake would soon be discovered, I disguised myself as a groom with a bundle on my shoulder, and so passed through the guards." We are not told what became of Bruman.

On his way to Orleans in December, Brousson wrote: "Would to God my honoured colleagues could see the eagerness of our poor brethren to hear the Gospel. It would be impossible that they should not be moved to come over and help them."

In Normandy a numerous meeting, which he held near Falaise, led to the arrest of many of his hearers. One of them, a young wife, was flogged three consecutive market-days. She suffered with great constancy; the only thing which appeared to move her being that, in taking her out to receive her sentence, they took from her the infant at her breast, which had been born in prison. It is cordial to relate that she was visited by some Catholic ladies, who did all they could to alleviate her sufferings.

Brousson writes again: "January 5, 1696. Wherever I have been, I have found the people famishing for the word of God's grace. Scarcely one in a hundred has gone back. I have already held thirty-five communions, two of them of 400 communicants each. The people here are at present unmolested; they read the word together, and in some places sing Psalms and pray aloud. Many have been married at the Roman Catholic Church; others make a contract of marriage, and then live together. I have advised these to have their banns published by the crier in presence of two witnesses, and afterwards to present their contract to the judge, certifying the publication, and requesting him to enter it on the register. But as the court has annulled many of the marriage contracts, I fear nothing will avail. That which I most of all deplore is that the parents, in order to evade the penalties of the law, allow their children to be baptized by the priests. They everywhere promise me, however, that this shall not be repeated. Thank God I have no occasion for money; if I would let them, our poor brethren would give me their very bowels."

In the course of this journey, Brousson met with a number of zealous preachers, who had been raised up in the place of exiled or unfaithful pastors, and he desires they should be allowed to administer the sacraments. "It is true," he writes, "they have not received the imposition of hands, but the grace of God is not so bound to an external ceremony." He goes further: "Baptism and the Supper are excellent, but the grace of the Spirit is not so bound up with these visible signs that God cannot communicate it without them." Again: "It is not absolutely necessary that those who are chosen for pastors should understand the languages, seeing that Divine Providence has caused the Scriptures to be translated into a language they are conversant with. Nor is it necessary they should be philosophers; rather has philosophy been the cause of many pernicious errors. Nor that they should be eloquent orators, or adepts in history or polite literature. What is necessary is that they should be of a pure and holy life, zealous for God's glory, and apt to instruct their brethren with meekness and charity." He urged all the churches to appoint elders, who should take counsel with heads of families, that order might be maintained.

The zeal which was kindled in Brousson's heart, as he journeyed through the thirsting churches of the north, could ill brook the chilling letters he received from Holland. March 22, he writes to a friend at the Hague: "I regret you have not yet sent to the press my 'Letters to the Roman Catholics.' You remark that there is something exaggerated in them, and that they contain mystical interpretations pushed to an extreme, and quite out of season. I have no doubt my writings bear marks of infirmity; but these human considerations are not dictated by piety. We are to preach the word in season and out of season. If people only knew the disposition which prevails here to receive the truth and to come out from the communion of Antichrist, they would not thus judge. Before our dispersion we were forbidden by law to speak of idolatry, of Antichrist, of the kingdom of the devil, as such expressions hindered our people from joining the Romish Church, and made our enemies furious. An unhappy deference was shown to this prohibition, because those who threatened us were very powerful; and so, when the great persecution ensued, our people allowed themselves to be seduced by the vain argument: 'Do we not believe as you do, in God the Father, Son, and Holy Ghost? Are we not Christians, as you are? Come with us, and believe as you like.'"

By this time the rumour of Brousson's return to France had spread everywhere. Pontchartrain sent a circular, June 20, to the intendants, with the description of the preacher, received from Bâville, and with orders to track and arrest him. The effect of this activity was soon apparent. Brousson was traced to the centre of France; but being warned in time he eluded his pursuers, traversed Franche Comté, and arrived at Bâle at the beginning of September, 1696.

This year was memorable for a hurricane, which destroyed the crops. Some of the thoughtful among the Catholics regarded the calamity as a punishment on the nation for the cruelties inflicted on the Huguenots.

At the same time, the administration fell into the hands of the Cardinal de Noailles, the leader of the Jansenist party, who, as we have seen, deprecated in his heart the Act of Revocation and the persecution of the Huguenots. He exerted himself to procure a relaxation of the laws against them, and even obtained from Louis a promise to issue a remedial edict in their favour. But the court and the clergy were too powerful for him; and the peace of Ryswick, September, 1697, put an end to his hopes. For nearly ten years France had been at war with England, Holland, and Germany; at the disbanding of the armies half a million of soldiers were spread over the country, many of whom it was found convenient to employ in subduing the Protestants.

XLVII.
CLAUDE BROUSSON'S LAST JOURNEY, 1697-8.

By the end of the year we find Brousson in Holland, engaged with the other refugee leaders in pleading with the powers to obtain the insertion of a clause in the treaty of Ryswick for the protection of the Huguenots. But the Elector of Brandenburg and the king of England were too much occupied with their own interests to make any sacrifice for their suffering brethren. All that the allies did was to present a note on their behalf to Louis, after the treaty had been signed, an abortive act, which only drew from him a supercilious retort: "I do not pretend to prescribe for William rules regarding his subjects, and I expect the same freedom as to my own."

Finding nothing was to be hoped for from kings and potentates, Brousson resolved once more to revisit the Churches. His first intention was to proceed across France direct to Poitou; but what he heard of the state of Dauphiné and the Vivarais caused him to alter his plan, and he resolved first to visit those provinces. December 24, 1697, he wrote to his wife: "This part of the country seems to be entirely abandoned by the pastors; but what I have seen of the marvellous works of God would astonish the whole earth. In some parts, indeed, the people have suffered so severely that they have almost lost heart, but those who have preserved their fidelity are animated with a wonderful degree of piety." In January, 1698, he wrote again: "The persecution is redoubled; it is as hot as at the first." And in March: "The soldiers break up and carry off all they can sell, often to priests, who buy the spoil dirt-cheap. When they have consumed all, and find their victims still firm, they send the husbands to prison, and shut up the daughters in convents, dealing hardly with those who resist. If the frontiers were open, one would behold a vast multitude taking flight to other countries; this emigration would be even greater than the former."

Brousson drew up five several petitions to the king, which he put into the post at Nimes, where they were opened. With this clue to his whereabouts, the militia made a fresh and more rigorous search for him, and he had several narrow escapes. Once the house in which he had taken refuge was surrounded by troops. His host had barely time to let him down into a well, where he hid in a niche at the surface of the water, constructed possibly as a hiding-place for proscribed ministers. The soldiers, one after another, looked down into the well at least twenty times, and one, who was acquainted with the niche, was even let down, but, blinded by the darkness, or by fear or cold, he saw nothing. Brousson escaped, repassed the Rhône, and took refuge in Orange. This was in April.

By the end of the month he had returned and was on the road to Béziers, when he writes again: "The further I advance into the country the more misery do I find. The people are as it were stunned; the towns are almost ruined for want of trade; the roads are full of beggars, who follow travellers half a league at a time. I have been exposed to many dangers, but hitherto the Lord has preserved me. He enables me to be careful for nothing, but only that I may finish my course with joy and the ministry with which He has entrusted me. A price has been set on my head of six hundred louis d'or of fourteen livres each." In May he wrote: "It is not easy for me to get your letters; still less so to send mine. Almost all the papists of this province are under arms as militia. They distress us exceedingly. All groan under the bondage and cry: 'How long!'" From Toulouse he wrote, August 17: "God has everywhere re-animated his people. It is true that in some parts they are yet in the condition of Lazarus, with their hands and feet bound; but they assemble with eagerness to hear God's word and to receive the symbols of covenanted grace. I commend myself again to your fervent prayers and to those of the Church. To me it appears that the fields are white unto the harvest."

This was his last letter. Crossing Foix and Gascony he hastened into Béarn, where he had not before travelled; and arriving at Pau, September 11, he put up at the Red Cap, kept by one Bedora. The disguise in which he made this journey was that of a person of quality, in scarlet cloak, a sword by his side, and pistols (unloaded) in his holster.* Whilst at Pau he held at least one meeting. He had with him a letter of recommendation from a refugee minister at the Hague, to a Protestant nobleman, M. d'Espalangue, Baron of Aroir. One evening at supper the conversation of an abbé with a Catholic nobleman made Brousson aware that a baron of Aroir was expected that night at the hotel. Accordingly a guest arrived and was lodged in the same room with Brousson, who the next morning enquired of his companion if he was not the Baron of Aroir. The answer being in the affirmative, Brousson made himself known to him; but noticing some

* When he was arrested three wigs were found in his portmanteau, a black, a flaxen, and a *petite perruque d'abbé*

embarrassment in the gentleman's behaviour, he repeated the question: "Are you really the Sire of Espalangue, Baron of Aroir?" To which the other replied that the Sire of Espalangue was at the States at Lescar, and would not be back till evening. Brousson had made himself known to the wrong man; there were two noblemen bearing the title of Baron of Aroir, and this was an apostate.

Brousson lost no time in quitting the house and was followed by his host. He crossed the mountains to Oleron, where he arrived in the evening and put up at the hotel of the Poste. He had been already denounced; the police were on his track; and the next day but one, September 18, as he was drawing on his boots in readiness to mount his horse and ride off, the town assessor put his hand roughly upon him and asked if he was not Brousson. He replied without hesitation that he was. He was conducted to Pinon, the intendant of Béarn, who was then at Lescar, three miles from Pau. Pinon received him with expressions of regret at being compelled to be his judge. Being asked whether he was aware that in returning to France he had violated the king's command, Brousson answered that he was quite aware of it, but that he had done so in obedience to his conscience, and that his sole object was to call his brethren to repentance. The intendant ordered the money which had been taken from him to be restored; and when the informer applied for his reward, Pinon is said to have exclaimed: "Wretch, do you feel no compunction when you look on your fellow-creatures whilst you traffic on their blood? Begone! I cannot endure your presence."

Bedora was taken and hanged, and his wife was shut up in a convent, where she was still in confinement in 1712. The house was demolished.

XLVIII.
TRIAL AND MARTYRDOM OF CLAUDE BROUSSON, 1698.

Brousson was removed to Pau and placed in the donjon tower of the ancient castle, in one of whose chambers Calvin had preached before Margaret of Valois, and in another Henry IV. had first seen the light. As soon as tidings of the capture reached Bâville he wrote to Fléchier: "This to confirm the good news that Brousson is taken. I am dying of fear lest this wretch, who is so cunning, should escape. He has done much mischief, and if suffered to live would do much more; never fanatic was more dangerous." At the same time Bâville despatched three couriers in succession to Pinon, requiring the prisoner to be given up to him. Pinon, regarding this demand as irregular, wrote to the king, who directed him to comply with Bâville's request. Accordingly, after five weeks' detention in the castle of Pau, Brousson was sent to Montpellier. Previous to his departure he asked for an interview with Pinon, whose indulgent treatment he gratefully acknowledged, expressing regret that he was not to have him for his judge rather than Bâville, and adding: "My lord, during the short time which I have to live, I shall devote part of it to praying to God on your behalf." Pinon was visibly affected, and gave express orders that the prisoner should be treated well on the journey.

Whether Pinon's compassion was only simulated, or whether, as seems more probable, he was really a man of humane feelings, but pliant and time-serving, it is not easy to say; but his letters to Bâville strangely contradict his treatment of the prisoner. October 26, he wrote:

"Brousson's demeanour the last days he has been here, gives me some cause to hope that he may be shaken by torture. He told one of the guards that he did not mind dying so long as he had not to suffer beforehand, and he was often seen in tears. When a man fears torture it is a sign that he begins to waver." Again : " When you have tried this wretch, you will give me pleasure by sending me the sentence, because the New Converts hereaway are so insolent as to say that the authorities will not dare to put him to death, for if they should do so it would be avenged in England and Holland on the French Catholics."

In order that he might not be recognized, Brousson was removed from Pau in a close carriage, attended by an escort of twenty grenadier guards. He was left unfettered, having given his promise that he would not attempt to escape. At Toulouse, the Count de Broglie, who had several interviews with him, sent him forward by passage-boat on the grand canal. On the way the soldiers, one after another, all fell asleep; and when the boat stopped at Somail, Brousson had only to step ashore to regain his liberty. But he had given his word and he could not break it. Leaving the boat at Béziers, he was escorted by two companies of grenadiers within a league of Montpellier, where Bâville's own chaise met him with an escort of one hundred guards. More than four thousand persons came out from the city to see him : they were in tears; but he saluted them with a tranquil air. He was taken to the esplanade, where Bâville awaited him and had him conducted to the citadel. Here he was so closely watched that he could not communicate with anyone. Fifty men guarded the prison gate. His meals were supplied from the intendant's table, but he would taste of nothing but bread and water, and passed his time in meditation and prayer. Bâville always addressed him as "Monsieur," and would not allow either handcuffs or fetters to be put on him.

It was Thursday, the thirtieth of October, when Brousson arrived. On Friday and Saturday he was subjected to long examinations. Required to declare where he had preached and to whom he had administered the Supper, he refused to reply, saying he was no informer, nor a child of the devil, to accuse his brethren. Bâville wrote to Fléchier: "Brousson gives me much trouble, not by his skill, but by the frightful prolixity of his answers. He admits all the charges against him. He is very intelligent, but violent, presumptuous, and capable of doing much mischief." Bâville sent his chaplain, the Abbé Camarignan, to Brousson, to instruct him, but the chaplain found he had to do with a man of superior ability, and reported that no one had ever spoken better. He was also visited by a doctor of the Sorbonne, with whom he had a long dispute, bringing him to agree with him on several points, so that at the close of their conference Brousson embraced him, saying: "Sir, I perceive with great joy that you are not far from the kingdom of heaven."

On Sunday he was again interrogated, after which he asked for paper, and spent a great part of the day in writing a circumstantial letter or memorial to the king. According to his custom on that day he ate nothing till after sunset. He was refused paper to write to his wife and son, but it was promised to him that any message he might send should be communicated to them. His injunction to his son was to follow his steps and die for the holy gospel.

On Tuesday, the fourth, at seven o'clock, before it was broad day, the court met in the citadel to try him. The chief counts of the indictment were: First; that he had held meetings contrary to the king's orders. Secondly; that he had had a share in the Project of Toulouse of 1683. And, thirdly; that he had written to Schömberg, pointing out the way by which he might invade the kingdom. The first and second articles were undeniable; with respect to the last he entrenched himself behind the provisions of the Peace of Ryswick, and the royal amnesty consequent upon it.

A circumstantial report of the trial is given by De Brueys, who was present. Of the three contemporary historians, Roman Catholic, who have treated of this period, he is considered the least trustworthy, and he would seem in this instance to have drawn somewhat on his own imagination. We give his narrative entire, deferring until afterwards an examination of the contrary evidence.

"On the fourth of November M. de Bâville went to the citadel with the officers of the presidial court. Brousson was set on the stool. He was still ignorant that his judges were in possession of his project to introduce the enemy into the kingdom. He was well aware that his valet, Henri, who was the bearer of it, had been taken and punished, because this was a matter of public notoriety; but he supposed that the original draft in his handwriting had not been discovered, for M. de Bâville had kept this a profound secret. What confirmed Brousson in this belief was, that he had hitherto been treated with great leniency, and had not been placed in irons during his passage to Montpellier.

"Accordingly he at first appeared before his judges with the confidence of one who thought he could only be convicted of preaching and holding meetings, in which he was prepared to glory. But his judges were in possession of too many proofs, and M. de Bâville was minded to confound the vanity of the accused, and undeceive the Protestants, for which reason he admitted those who were curious into the chamber, so that this false apostle might be publicly unmasked. The prisoner was allowed to speak without interruption, which he did with much firmness for a quarter of an hour. He said he was a minister of the Gospel and had exercised his ministry in France. He insisted chiefly on the reputation he had acquired as a man of honour and probity at home and abroad. M. de Bâville demanded, since he boasted of being a minister of the Gospel, what business he had in the Cevennes and elsewhere. He answered that his sole object was to uphold the truth and follow the example of the apostles. M. de Bâville asked whether the apostles preached revolt and conceived projects against the powers established by God. He replied no, and that he had never done the like. Whereupon M. de Bâville produced the letter, and setting it before his eyes asked if he knew the handwriting, and whether the apostles did such things. At sight of this paper, Brousson, who until now had been firm, grew pale and changed countenance, and after some moments of hesitation made up his mind to deny his handwriting, and to declare, though with trembling, that he had had no hand in the scheme. M. de Bâville, who saw his confusion, contented himself with saying that now at least he was not imitating the apostles, who did not lie; and that there were at hand convincing proofs that he was not speaking the truth, although with uplifted hand he had sworn to do so. Brousson having acknowledged that certain papers found on him were in his own handwriting, experts were directed to compare the two. But the thing was too patent, and Brousson confessed his guilt. What took place in the citadel was made public the same day, so that all the Protestants were undeceived, and learnt with amazement that their pretended martyr, in order to save his life, had uselessly added perjury to his other great crimes."

Most Protestant historians deny De Brueys' narrative *in toto*, regarding it as a pure invention. This would seem improbable, not to say impossible; nevertheless it is difficult to reconcile his statements with the documents which recent researches have brought to light.

On several occasions before the trial took place Brousson distinctly admitted the part he had taken in the correspondence with the Count de Schömberg. Whilst at Pau he was subjected, October 19, to an examination. In his answer he first sheltered himself under the provisions of the Peace of Ryswick, by which a general indemnity was granted to all those who had served the party of the princes in the war, and which indemnity was confirmed by the royal declaration of June following, registered by the several parliaments. As to his own conduct, and referring to the hot pursuit to which he was subjected, he says: "In this state of desperation the respondent had the misfortune for a moment to lend his ear to the offers of succour made to the Protestants of the Cevennes by the late M. de Schömberg." Similar interrogations were put to him at Montpellier on the 31st of October, to which he gave similar answers. Moreover Bâville, in his letter to Fléchier, quoted above, says: "He admits all the charges against him." Lastly, we have Brousson's memorial to the king penned the day before his trial: "The petitioner confesses, sire, that François Vivens, who had already arrived in the Cevennes, and had been rigorously searched for, finding himself in danger, implored help of the king of England, and that he received the sum of one thousand livres, with which, as your petitioner has since learned, he purchased powder; but your petitioner is not aware that any city, village, or person of consideration entered into the designs of the said Vivens. It is true, sire, that in the sequel, the petitioner being continually searched for in towns and villages, and pursued night and day into woods and caverns, so that he passed three whole months without entering a house, the late M. de Schömberg, the son, sent to him and to the said Vivens, the man named Huc, to let them know that his Britannic majesty intended to send troops to procure them some repose. The petitioner, sire, informed the said Huc, that it was his purpose to apply himself solely to prayer. It is alleged (*On pretend*), however, that the petitioner, who had always death before his eyes, and who suffered hardships and afflictions such as perhaps never were since God had a Church on earth, distracted by the presence of danger, and by so many calamities, allowed himself to be worked upon by the solicitations and reproaches of the said Vivens and of M. de Schömberg, and transcribed with his own hand a note to the said M. de Schömberg, which the said Vivens had already drafted, and in which it was pointed out how troops might be sent into the Cevennes, which note was intercepted and rendered abortive."

Brousson then pleads, as he had before done, the indemnity of the Peace of Ryswick, and proceeds: "The petitioner nevertheless very humbly supplicates your majesty to consider that the fault he may have committed in the deplorable condition in which he found himself and for which he most humbly demands pardon, is without doubt worthy of the clemency and pity of a great prince. But this, sire, is not all. Soon recovering from his distraction, the petitioner entirely changed his conduct to devote himself wholly to prayer. In fact, sire, since the death of the said Vivens, there has not been seen in the province of Languedoc the least movement against your majesty's service, although during that time M. de Schömberg entered Dauphiné with an army. It is even notorious that in Languedoc, during the life of the said Vivens, not only had the petitioner no part in his acts of violence, but that when he met with Vivens in his hiding-places, he condemned his conduct and remonstrated with him in the strongest terms. On the other hand, the petitioner has gone about year after year without arms, and like a lamb in the midst of an infinite number of people who sought him day and night to take away his life. It is notorious also that he never suffered arms to be brought to the religious meetings which were gathered by his ministry. So that everyone, even the most distinguished Roman Catholics, have rendered public testimony to his moderation and prudence."

If in the above memorial the part Brousson took in the project of invasion is not explicitly avowed, it is at least fully implied, and there is no denial of any of the charges. No more explicit confession was to be looked for from a Frenchman writing to such a sovereign as Louis XIV. The reproach of perjury, therefore, cast on the martyr by De Brueys, falls to the ground.

The sentence pronounced on Brousson was that he should undergo both the ordinary and the extraordinary torture, and afterwards be broken alive upon the wheel. "He heard the words," says Quick, "without emotion, for he was borne above the love of life and the fear of death, being entirely resigned to the will of God."

Before his execution the intendant sent two learned Dominican friars to convert him. They reasoned a long time with him, but Brousson defended the truth with such strength of argument that they were put to silence. At parting they desired to embrace him, and he in return earnestly pressed them to abandon their idolatrous religion, warning one of them in particular not to put off the work, for, he said, "the coming of the Lord draws nigh, and I am persuaded you and I shall meet again in a very short time." The friar died three days after Brousson's execution, and his companion quitted his convent and fled to Amsterdam, where the next year he abjured the Romish religion.

The sentence was pronounced in the forenoon, and at two o'clock Brousson was taken into the torture chamber and examined by two councillors of the presidial court. The *procès-verbal* signed by them is still preserved in the archives of Montpellier. Omitting some repetitions, and an unimportant question, it is as follows: "We repaired to a store room of the citadel of Montpellier, whither we had caused the said Brousson to be brought, and after reading to him the sentence requiring that the ordinary and extraordinary torture should be applied to him, and putting him on oath, we interrogated him as to his name, age, quality, abode and religion, and then asked:

Who was mixed up with him in the project found in his handwriting.

Said, it was only Vivens who composed it; and that he, Brousson, wrote it out.

Asked, in what places he had preached.

Said, he could not violate the secrets of his ministry, being concerned solely with the worship of God.

Asked, whom he had visited in Languedoc.

Said, he had answered that question already.

Asked, who had given him letters of recommendation and where they resided.

Said, that as this solely concerned the worship of God, he could not say.

Asked, if he had been with all those whose names were in his note-book.

Said, there were many whom he had not seen but whose names were given him by the refugees.

Asked, if he had spoken to M. de Schömberg, received letters from him, and seen him.

Said, no.

Asked, if he was not a long time with Vivens, and if he had not received a grant from abroad.

Said, no.

Asked, if Vivens had received such a grant.

Said, he once received one thousand livres, sent by the Prince of Orange.

Asked, if he had not sent for prophets and prophetesses in the Vivarais.

Said, no; it was all given in his statement.

Asked, if he did not aim at renewing the fanaticism of the Vivarais.

Said, no.

Asked, if he had not been at Bordeaux.

Said, he had never been there.

Asked, if he had not been at Montauban.

Said, yes; and that he saw only one family, whose name he could not give.

Asked, if there were no noblemen of the province implicated in this matter.

Said, no.

Asked, if it was not he who proposed this project to M. de Schömberg.

Said, no; but that M. de Schömberg had sent Huc, who spoke to him, and he replied.

Asked, why he said that all the princes of Europe were interested in his piety.

Said, that the princes were interested in the infraction which would be made in the treaty of Ryswick by punishing him for a matter which was already condoned.

This done, we caused the said Brousson's feet to be bound, and his arms bound behind his back; and we caused the turn of the wheel of the ordinary torture to be made."

We here interrupt the dry matter-of-fact statement of the two officials, by a record derived from a more sympathetic source. When he was stretched on the rack, Brousson said: "Gentlemen, you may do what you please; but if you were to break all my bones you could not make me say more." Then, with his eyes raised towards heaven, he cried: "Lord, have mercy on thy poor creature; do not forsake me in the pitiful condition in which Thou seest me, but grant me strength and courage to support the pains Thou art about to let me suffer, to the glory of Thy holy name."

The official statement continues: "This done, we caused the turn of the extraordinary torture to be given, whereupon he declined to say anything.

The deposition being read over, he affirmed it.

(Signed, Brousson, minister of the Gospel, Loys, Jansserand, Lesellier).

This done, we had him unbound from the rack, and conducted into another room, and we read over to him this *procès-verbal* of torture and his answers, to which he declared he adhered, and had nothing to add or retract. Being read over, he affirmed it and signed. (Signatures as above)."

His clothes were brought to him to put on before going to execution. He desired that his watch should be given to the captain of De Broglie's guards; his cloak to the officer, who had always shown him kindness, and who was in tears; and his purse to be distributed to the poor.

Whilst these things were going on in the citadel, the scaffold was being erected on the Place du Peyrou. This is an elevated platform, at that time a bare tract outside the city, but now a noble promenade, reached by flights of stairs, and surrounded by balustrades. It was laid out in 1766. At four o'clock Brousson was led forth, the Abbé Camarignan walking by his side with two officers. His hands were free, and he wore his scarlet cloak, his hat and wig. A double file of soldiers lined the way from the citadel gate, about two hundred and sixty paces, to the place of execution. Three circles of troops were formed round the scaffold, but the people were so eager to get near to their beloved pastor that they broke through the cordon. More than ten thousand persons, including many of the nobility and some foreigners, had assembled to witness his last moments.

As he came out of the citadel gate he began to chant a Psalm; but the officer requested him, from the intendant, to keep silence for fear of a tumult. "There is not, sir," replied Brousson, "the least appearance of such a thing; nevertheless, I will content myself with praying in silence." At the same moment twenty drums began to beat, and did not cease till all was over. "I cannot tell you," says an eye-witness, "with what firmness he walked; he seemed to be going to a festival. His eyes were turned towards heaven, as though he saw no man; everyone was in tears as this illustrious martyr passed along. Arrived at the foot of the scaffold, he knelt and prayed, and then ascended the ladder without help. Putting off his clothes to his shirt, he gave himself up to be bound on the wheel, saying: 'It is a consolation to me that my death bears some resemblance to that of my Lord.' But he was not broken alive; an order had been received from Bâville dispensing with this most terrible part of the sentence, and directing that the condemned should be strangled before his limbs were crushed." It has been supposed that this indulgence was the result of compassion on the part of the intendant; but such was not the case. Brousson's character and position commanded Bâville's respect, and, as we have seen, he was treated with an unusual degree of consideration; but the intendant was not really touched with pity for his victim. He himself tells us that the penalty was mitigated entirely from motives of policy; he was afraid of an insurrection, and therefore made the execution as short as possible.

In consequence of the breaking of the cord, life was not at once extinguished; and the sufferer, coming to himself, was heard again to pray. Upon this the abbé went near and bade him consider that God had permitted this accident to afford him another opportunity of embracing the Catholic faith. Brousson thanked him, and said he hoped God would reward him for his charity, and that they should meet in paradise. In a few moments he was no more. His body was broken, and the instrument with its mangled burden was raised aloft on poles that all might behold it. The corpse was buried in the citadel.

Many Roman Catholics openly lamented his fate. The officials who were present at his torture said that he never even changed countenance, and that they themselves trembled more than he did. Those who attended him to the scaffold confessed the same, saying that his resignation and piety moved them to tears. The Abbé Camarignan, after the execution, shut himself up for several days, refusing to be seen. The executioner, going to purchase a silver cup at a goldsmith's shop, was asked how Brousson had died. "If I durst speak out," he answered, "I could say many things: he died a saint. Of two hundred criminals whom I have despatched no one ever made me tremble so much."

Brousson's own beloved people received the news of his martyrdom with the most poignant sorrow. In Holland his death was felt as a public calamity, and the States granted his widow a pension of 600 florins in addition to the 400 which had been paid to her husband. His friend, Peyrol, one of the two ministers who were hanged in effigy at Nimes in 1683,* was preaching in Lausanne, when a letter was handed to him containing information of Brousson's execution. He read the letter to his audience, and then, with tears, pronounced a eulogy on the martyred evangelist, concluding with severe reproaches against himself for not having followed him into France. So violent was the poor man's emotion that on returning

* See *ante*, page 94.

home he took to his bed, from which he never rose again.*

These sentiments were not shared by his persecutors. Bâville wrote to Fléchier, November 9: "The devout will weep over Brousson; but, my dear sir, he is safe; he can do no more mischief." On which cynical words, Douen has some excellent reflections. "The intendant was mistaken; even after his death, Brousson continued to mar the work of the persecutors. His story, related by the fire-side, encouraged the Protestants patiently to bear their ills, and never despair of deliverance. On the other hand, Brousson was the only man who could have prevented the Camisard insurrection. When the pastors, who preached only passive resistance, had been imprisoned, hanged, and broken, and none could be found any longer to venture into the kingdom, the government had to do with preachers of a different kind, inspired, ecstatic, prophetic, who called to arms, and whose maxim was: 'An eye for an eye, and a tooth for a tooth.' No doubt Bâville found out that the extermination of the desert pastors had been a great mistake."

---

* The 'London Gazette' thus notices the event: "Our letters from Languedoc give an account that M. Brousson, an eminent Protestant minister, was lately seized in the country of Béarn for having preached to the Protestants in several parts of France, and from thence was brought to Montpellier, where he was judged by a special commission, and sentenced to be broken on the wheel, which was executed accordingly on the 6th [4th] of this month." (No. 3446, from Thursday, Nov. 17, to Monday, Nov. 21, 1698). According to Douen (ii. 328), the 'Gazette' added this comment: "In France it is a capital crime not to be a Roman Catholic." No such words, however, are to be found there.

CONCLUSION.

The reader may ask, "To what purpose are these sad stories resuscitated? Persecution is dead; no one in this enlightened age would dream of forcing men's opinions; the Church of Rome, even if she had the power, would never return to the dungeon or the gibbet."

At the close of 1869 an Œcumenical Council was held in Rome, at which 800 of the highest dignitaries of the Church were present. What was done by this august assembly, gathered from all quarters of the globe? Here was a grand opportunity of atoning for past errors, and proclaiming to the world that the Church had entered on a new era of justice and charity. Unhappily, it was not embraced. On the contrary, the sole work of the Council was to declare the pope infallible; thus placing the seal of the Nineteenth Century on every crime and folly the Church has ever committed. In 1886 Pope Leo XII. formally approved of Henri Lasserre's translation of the New Testament, sending him, "from the bottom of his heart, his apostolic benediction." Twelve months afterwards he condemned the same translation, and placed it in the index of forbidden books!

There was a noble band of dissentients at the Council; and there are in the Church of Rome many devout men who are spending their lives in Christ's service with a single eye to his glory. But Protestants have no need to look to Rome for bright examples of piety and devotion; and it seems now to be forgotten that not only are many of her doctrines and observances directly at variance with Christ's teaching, but also that she is under the rule of a majority who, ignoring truth and justice, too often follow the maxims of expediency and worldly policy.

www.ingramcontent.com/pod-product-compliance
Lightning Source LLC
Chambersburg PA
CBHW031850220426
43663CB00006B/565